Table of Contents

Introduction

So, you've picked up this book, and perhaps you're wondering exactly what digital literacy means. Let's break that phrase down. *Digital* refers to the binary digits that computers work with (1s and 0s). When something is digital, it means that it's made up of numeric values — and it usually means that it's computerized, or at least electronic. *Literacy* means being able to communicate in a certain language. For example, someone who is English-literate can read and write the English language. Similarly, someone who is digitally literate is fluent in using digital technologies, including computers.

So you don't think you use computer technology that much? Think again. Computers are *everywhere*, including in places you might not expect or think about.

Let's assume for a moment that you're an average white-collar worker in North America.

You wake up to a digital alarm clock.

You hop in your car (with a computer-controlled engine system) and drive to your office, sliding your name badge into a slot in the door to gain access to the building.

At work you sit at a desk and use a desktop computer to plan a budget for a new project, and then you have a video conference with coworkers in another office to go over the details.

On your lunch break, you go through a fast-food restaurant, where an employee touches a computer screen on his cash register to input your order.

That afternoon you drive to meet with a client, and you use a GPS unit to help you find the address.

On the way there, you chat with your mother on your cellphone.

Then it's back home for you, where you watch a movie recorded on your DVR, send a text to your friend about the movie you just watched, and head off to bed.

Now, read that story again and count the number of computers you interacted with. Did you find all of them? And that's *just one day*. Other days you might get money from an ATM, play a game on your phone, book hotel reservations online, or send an email to your boss. It's pretty amazing when you think about how pervasive computers have become in our lives in the last few decades, in every industry.

Computers have become a central part of everyday life not only in urban and suburban areas, and not only in the Western world, but in rural areas and in every country. Internet cafes in remote villages on all continents allow people to rent computer time to explore the world of the Internet, and smart phones bring affordable Internet access to people who have traditionally not been able to afford full-featured personal computers. Farmers can use computers to plan the optimal planting times and crops and to calculate how much feed a herd of animals will need. Families in remote areas keep in touch via email with relatives in other areas. The Internet and computing has touched every part of the globe.

So, what does all that mean for you? It means that digital literacy is a must in order to keep up with our changing world. If you don't keep up with the latest digital technologies as they emerge, you'll fall further and further behind, and become more and more confused as new technologies build upon the previous ones. In other words, *you need this book!* So let's get started.

About This Book

This book is designed to help you become digitally literate — that is, fluent in today's digital technologies that you'll encounter in daily life. It follows a general plan put forth in Microsoft's Digital Literacy Standard Curriculum, Version 3. You can find details about it here: `http://www.microsoft.com/about/corporatecitizenship/citizenship/giving/programs/up/digitalliteracy/eng/curriculum3.mspx`.

Microsoft's Digital Literacy program is not only a set of standards, but also an online curriculum and proficiency exam. If you take the online course for it, you'll study these five areas:

- Computer Basics
- The Internet and the World Wide Web
- Productivity Programs
- Computer Security and Privacy
- Digital Lifestyles

The book you are holding in your hands is based on this same curriculum and covers all the same topics. It provides an alternate method for achieving digital literacy to completing the online course.

This book uses certain conventions to highlight important information and help you find your way around:

- ✔ **Tip icons:** Point out helpful extras, such as effort-saving shortcuts, designed to enhance your knowledge or productivity.

- ✔ **Note icons:** Provide interesting side commentary and extra information, such as the origin of a term or an exception to a general rule presented in the main text.

- ✔ **Warning icons:** Point out potential pitfalls and workarounds. For example, if there's a chance that you'll encounter an error message, this icon points out the instructions that will help you know how to deal with it.

- ✔ **Capitalization:** Although some applications use lowercase in options and on buttons, I capitalize their names for emphasis. For example, you might see *Save now* onscreen, but I'll write it as Save Now. It doesn't make much difference on a short name, but when you have something like the Don't Ask for Credentials Again check box, it does help clarify things.

- ✔ **Bold:** I use bold for figure references and also when you have to type something onscreen using the keyboard.

- ✔ **Italics:** Technology always comes with its own terms and concepts, and when I introduce a new term, I italicize it for emphasis.

- ✔ **Figure labels:** Some figures have labels or other markings to draw your attention to specific areas. For example, if I'm referring to a certain button, a label points it out.

- ✔ **Website addresses:** If you bought an e-book, website address are live links. In the text, website addresses look like this: www.dummies.com.

Foolish Assumptions

I assume that you have some sort of computer and are interested in learning more about how it works and how it interacts with other computers. That's really all you need to get started and to get some benefit from this book.

Certain chapters require you to have specific software, but you can skip those chapters if you don't have it, or just skim them for informational purposes. They are:

Chapter 4, "Windows 8.1 Basics," and Chapter 7, "Sending and Receiving Email," assume you have Windows 8.1. If you have Windows 8, you can download a free update to Windows 8.1 through the Windows Update utility. Chapter 7 also assumes that you have one or more email accounts.

Chapter 6, "Working with the Web," assumes you have Internet Explorer, which is the browser that comes free with Windows. You can use Windows Update to make sure you have the latest version.

Chapters 10, 11, 12, and 13 assume that you have Microsoft Word, Excel, PowerPoint, and Access 2013, respectively. These are all part of the Microsoft Office suite.

Chapter 17 assumes that you have a digital camera, and optionally a printer for printing digital images.

Icons Used in This Book

The Tip icon marks tips (duh!) and shortcuts that you can use to make using your computer easier.

Remember icons mark the information that's especially important to know. To siphon off the most important information in each chapter, just skim through these icons.

The Warning icon tells you to watch out! It marks important information that may save you headaches.

Beyond the Book

    ✔ **Cheat Sheet:** This book's Cheat Sheet can be found online at www.dummies. com/cheatsheet/digitalliteracy. See the Cheat Sheet for Windows 8.1 and Office 2013 keyboard and mouse shortcuts.

✔ **Dummies.com online articles:** Companion articles to this book's content can be found online at www.dummies.com/extras/digitalliteracy. The topics range from learning how to set up wireless network security to finding out how to customize Microsoft Office applications.

✔ **Updates:** If this book has any updates after printing, they will be posted to www.dummies.com/extras/digitalliteracy.

Where to Go from Here

Scan the table of contents or the index for a topic that interests you most. Or just turn the page and start at the beginning. It's your book!

Part I
Computer Basics

getting started
with

Digital Literacy

Check out www.dummies.com/extras/digitalliteracy for more great content online.

In this part . . .

- ✔ Learn how computers connect people, businesses, and processes all over the world, and how you can participate in that.

- ✔ Find out how to select and buy a computer and how to set it up.

- ✔ Find out about the various operating systems out there and what computer types they work best on.

- ✔ Take a tour of Windows 8.1 and find out how to use it to run applications and manage files.

Chapter 1

It's a Digital World

*T*he world has changed dramatically in the last few decades, thanks to computer technology. Every second of every day, billions of bits of electronic data are whizzing around the globe and bouncing off satellites to deliver data to businesses and individuals.

This chapter provides a look at the most popular computing devices in use today and how they fit together to make up the digital world in which we live. You'll learn about the types of computers and software, the networks used to enable them to connect, and what you can accomplish by using them.

PCs: Discovering the Personal Computing Connection

When most people think about computers, they picture a *personal computer,* or *PC*. It's designed for only one person to use at a time. Most of the computers you and your friends and family have are probably personal computers.

The term *PC* has different meanings in popular culture. On one hand, it means any computer designed for personal use. That's the meaning it has in this chapter. On the other hand, it is also sometimes used to refer specifically to a computer that runs Microsoft Windows, as in "Which is better: Macs or PCs?"

Personal computers fall into several categories, differentiated mainly by their sizes:

- ✔ **Desktop:** A *desktop computer,* shown in Figure 1-1, is designed to be used at a desk and seldom moved. It consists of a large box called the *system unit* that contains most of the essential components. The monitor, keyboard, and mouse all plug into it using cables (or in some cases, using a wireless technology). Desktops offer a lot of computing power and performance for the price, and they're flexible because you can connect whatever monitor, keyboard, and mouse you want to it, as well as install additional storage drives, memory, and expansion cards that add new capabilities.

Figure 1-1:
A desktop computer.

- ✔ **Notebook:** A notebook, as its name implies, is a portable computer designed to fold up like a notebook for carrying and storage. As shown in Figure 1-2, its cover opens up to reveal a built-in screen, keyboard, and pointing device, which substitutes for a mouse. A notebook can run most of the same software as a desktop, and is similar to it in performance. Some people call it a laptop. Notebooks allow you to take your computer with you almost anywhere. They're more expensive than desktops of the same level of performance, however, and not very customizable or upgradable.

Figure 1-2:
A notebook
computer or
laptop.

✔ **Netbook:** Short for *Internet notebook*, a *netbook* is a smaller and less powerful notebook computer designed primarily for accessing the Internet. A netbook is usually cheaper than a notebook or desktop, and is lighter and more convenient to carry around, but may not have enough memory and a powerful enough processor to run all desktop applications.

✔ **Tablet:** A tablet is a portable computer that consists of a touch-sensitive screen mounted on a tablet-size plastic frame with a small computer inside. There is no keyboard or pointing device; a software-based keyboard pops up onscreen when needed, and your finger sliding on the screen serves as a pointing device (see Figure 1-3). Tablets are extremely portable and convenient, but usually do not run desktop computer applications and have limited memory and storage capabilities.

✔ **Smart phone:** A smart phone, like the one shown in Figure 1-4, is a mobile phone that can run applications and has Internet capability. Smart phones usually have touch-sensitive screens. Many have a variety of location-aware applications, such as global positioning system (GPS) and mapping programs and local business guides. Smart phones have a lot in common with computers, but they lack the power and flexibility of larger computing devices.

Figure 1-3:
A tablet
computer.

Figure 1-4:
A smart
phone.

The Business End: Multi-User Computer Systems

Multi-user computers are designed to serve groups of people all at a time, from a small office to a huge international enterprise. Here are some types of multi-user computers to be aware of:

- **Server:** A *server* is a computer that is dedicated to serving and support-ing a group of network users and their information needs. There are dif-ferent kinds of servers, varying greatly in size and power and performing different functions. For example, a *file server* stores files in a central loca-tion where multiple people can access them. A *database server* stores a database, such as a product inventory, and allows users to look up information in the database from their own computers. A *print server* manages a group of shared printers, controlling and prioritizing print jobs. Servers can be various sizes and designs. A *tower server* looks a lot like a regular desktop computer (Figure 1-1). *Rack servers* are stacked in multiples on storage racks, and accessed via a network interface rather than having their own keyboards and monitors.

- **Mainframe:** A *mainframe* is a large, powerful computer capable of pro-cessing and storing large amounts of business data. The main difference between a mainframe and a server is that the mainframe functions as the processing brain for multiple individual user terminals; it's not just a helper, but the primary processing device. For example, a mainframe might run several dozen cash registers in a large department store.

- **Supercomputer:** A *supercomputer* is the largest and most powerful type of computer. It can occupy a large room, or even an entire floor of a building. Supercomputers are used when a job requires a huge amount of processing power, such as molecular modeling, weather forecasting, or *cryptanalysis* (code-breaking). They are found in high-tech academic, government, and scientific research facilities.

Computer Software

All the computer types you've learned about so far in this chapter have been *hardware* — that is, the physical computing devices you can see and touch. But it's actually the *software* — the instructions given to the hardware — that makes things happen. Without software, the hardware, no matter how grand and expensive it is, would be a useless lump of metal and plastic.

Here's a quick look at the software that makes a computer do what it does.

BIOS

The hardware has a small amount of software permanently built into it on a chip, just enough to help it start up when you apply power to it. This basic startup software is called the *Basic Input Output System*, or *BIOS* (pronounced *buy-ohss*). Because this software is permanently installed, it occupies a somewhat gray area between hardware and software, so it is sometimes called *firmware*. You can mostly ignore it. However, sometimes if you are having problems with a device, the manufacturer will tell you that you can fix the problem by updating the firmware (or BIOS) and will provide you with a utility to do so.

Operating system

The *operating system* manages all the computer's activities after the BIOS has finished its startup routine. It provides the user interface, runs applications, manages file storage, and communicates with the hardware on your behalf. Microsoft Windows, shown in Figure 1-5, is the most popular operating system, but there are also others, including Mac OS X and Linux for desktop computers, and iOS and Android for tablets and smart phones. You will learn more about operating systems in Chapter 3.

Figure 1-5:
Microsoft
Windows.

Utilities

Utility programs work in partnership with the operating system to keep the computer healthy and running well. Some utilities come with the operating system, and others are purchased as add-ons. Utility programs assist with a wide range of maintenance and security functions, such as checking storage disks for errors, blocking security and privacy threats, and backing up important files.

Applications

Last but not least, we get to the reason you own a computer: the applications. An *application* is software that is designed to help you do something productive or fun — something of interest to a human user.

Many computers come with some applications already installed, and you can buy more, either through an online store or on a CD or DVD in a retail store. You will learn more about applications in Chapter 9.

It's All Connected

When computers were first developed, they were mostly standalone units; networking came later, and for years networking of all kinds remained cumbersome and slow, making it not-so-appealing for information sharing. Nowadays, though, connection is the norm. Many good networking technologies have been developed that transfer data from computer to computer quickly and easily, without a lot of complex setup and maintenance.

Here are some of the buzzwords you may hear about computer connectivity and what they mean. Many of these are discussed in much more detail in later chapters.

✔ **The Internet:** The Internet is the big, worldwide network of interconnected computers. When people talk about being "online," they generally mean the Internet. The Internet is the network that enables the World Wide Web (also known as the web), which you'll learn more about in Chapter 6, and email, covered in Chapter 7.

✔ **Ethernet:** *Ethernet* is a network type, but you'll more likely hear the term when someone is referring to the port in your computer that you can plug a network cable into. Although technically most networks today use Ethernet technology, the term Ethernet has lately come to informally mean the wired type of networking, where an Ethernet cable connects an Ethernet port on a computer to a router, switch, or some other type of networking equipment, as in Figure 1-6.

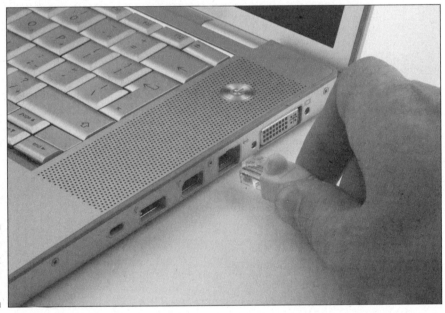

Figure 1-6:
An Ethernet port and cable.

- ✔ **Wi-Fi:** *Wi-Fi* is the technology used to connect your computers, tablets, and smart phones to wireless networking access points. It's an abbreviation of *Wireless Fidelity*, which is itself a play on the phrase "high fidelity" that used to be used to describe vinyl records. It refers to the wireless type of Ethernet networking, and is also known by its official standard: IEEE 802.11. There are various versions of it, like 802.11g or 802.11n, and you'll see those on the boxes if you buy networking hardware.

- ✔ **Private networks:** Besides the Internet, many companies and even homes also have private networks that allow their own computers to communicate with one another. Most of these private networks are Ethernet, and you use the same networking hardware to participate in the private network that you do to connect to the Internet.

✔ **3G and 4G:** These stand for 3rd Generation and 4th Generation, respectively, and are standards for cellular phone networking technology. A 3G or 4G network is a data network that operates through the same system of cell phone towers that carry your voice calls and text messages. Smart phones use these networks to gain Internet access (especially when a Wi-Fi network is not available). Most people don't use 3G/4G networks as their primary means of Internet connectivity because it uses up their phone's data plan quickly, and because the data speeds are not as high as with Wi-Fi or wired Ethernet connections.

✔ **Bluetooth:** *Bluetooth* is a short-range type of wireless networking used to connect computers to external devices such as microphone headsets, wireless mice and keyboards, and printers. If your computer has a Bluetooth adapter, you can pair it to a wireless Bluetooth device and they can communicate as long as they are in close proximity to one another (about 10 feet).

Discovering What's Out There

If you're relatively new to being online (that is, on the Internet), you might be wondering what all the fuss is. What's out there to be discovered? Plenty! Here's a whirlwind tour of the joys that await a digitally literate person online.

Shopping

Ecommerce (buying and selling online) is one of the main reasons the Internet is so popular — and so well-funded. Hundreds of thousands of online stores compete for your business on the web. Giant online retailers like Amazon.com (Figure 1-7) sell a wide variety of merchandise, but there's a place for small merchants too. Mom-and-pop stores in small towns all over the world can put their products up for sale globally. You can have your purchases delivered right to your home, saving you a trip to the mall, and if you catch the right deal, shipping might even be free.

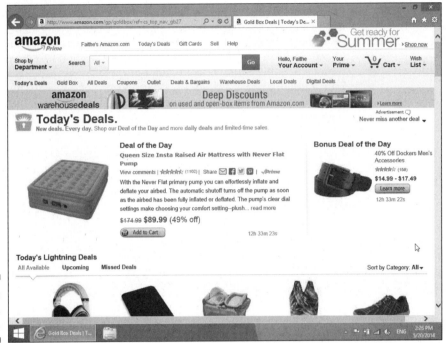

Fun and games

Most people will tell you they use computers to be more productive and efficient, but most of people also use computers to play games, from simple Solitaire games to the fanciest 3D shoot-em-up action adventures. You can buy games online and download them to your computer, or buy them on CDs or DVDs in stores. Some games are for individual use, whereas others have a collaborative component that lets you use the Internet to play with (or against) other players all over the world.

Communicating online

Keeping in touch with your friends, family, and co-workers has never been easier. Here are some of the ways you can communicate online:

✔ **Email:** With electronic mail, you can exchange private messages with individuals. Email is a store-and-forward type of communication; your email is sent to a mail server, where it waits for the recipient to pick it up. In other words, it's not instant communication; it's more like an electronic post office system. You'll learn more about email in Chapter 7.

✔ **Instant Messaging**: You can have private text conversations in real-time with individuals via an instant messaging (IM) service such as Yahoo! Messenger (shown in Figure 1-8) or AOL Instant Messenger (AIM). Some of these services also offer voice and video chat through the same interface, blurring the lines between those offerings.

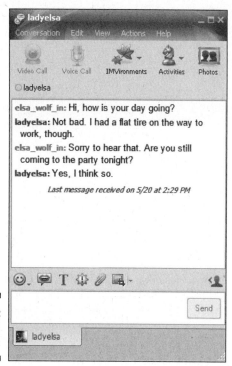

Figure 1-8:
Yahoo!
Messenger.

✔ **Video chat:** Services like Skype enable you to have voice and video person-to-person conversations. All you need is a computer with a webcam (an attached or built-in video camera) and a microphone.

✔ **Video conferencing:** For business use, multi-person and multi-point video conferencing takes video chat to the next level. Not only can multiple people participate in the call, as shown in Figure 1-9, but you can share computer screens, notes, documents, and whiteboards in a single interface.

Figure 1-9:
A video
conference.

Social networking

With the Internet, you'll never be lonely unless you want to be. Millions of people are reaching out to others in every conceivable way online. Social networking is covered in Chapter 8 in more detail, but here are some starting points for finding like-minded people:

✔ **Social networking websites:** Sites like Facebook and Pinterest provide users to create their own pages and spaces to share their hobbies and interests with others. On some social networking sites, you can also play online games.

✔ **Twitter:** Although Twitter has a web interface (www.twitter.com), it's probably best known for being a smart phone app. With Twitter, you can post very short status updates, and anyone who subscribes to your feed will immediately receive them on their computer or phone. You can follow your family and friends, celebrities, and companies. Beware, though, that if you have some friends who post a lot of *tweets* (Twitter posts), it can get exhausting to read.

✔ **Dating sites:** If you're looking for a date (or possibly a lifetime partner), there are many dating websites that want to help you find one. You can create a profile on one of these sites and describe yourself there, and others can browse you, decide you are the best thing since sliced bread, and send you a message. Where you go from there is up to you.

✔ **Forums:** A *forum* (sometimes called a *community*) is a web-based message board, usually open to the public. On a forum you can post questions and comments and other people can reply with answers. Forums are usually narrowly focused on a particular topic. For example, a computer manu-facturer may host a support forum on their website to handle customer questions, as shown in Figure 1-10.

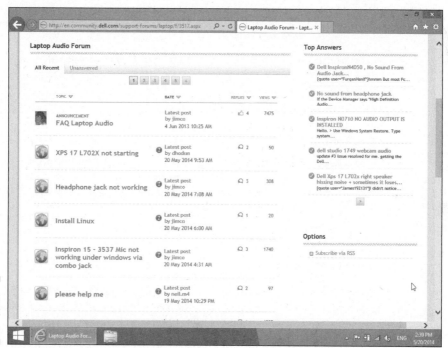

Figure 1-10:
An Internet
forum.

✔ **Internet Relay Chat (IRC):** This is a somewhat older technology, but still very popular. You use IRC software to log into a group of servers that host chat rooms, which are like text-based instant message services except they are public. Anyone may jump into a chat room and start par-ticipating by typing text. Chat rooms are not only for socializing; orga-nizations have their meetings in chat rooms too. For example, there are hundreds of chat rooms that focus on addiction recovery.

Information, please

There's more information available online than you can possibly imagine, and most of it is available for free. There are online encyclopedias and dictionaries, archives of scholarly papers and medical research journals, and even thousands of entire books you can download for free. Here are just a few information websites to get you started:

- ✔ **Encyclopedia Britannica (www.britannica.com):** The encyclopedia that your school probably had in its library is now available online (in expanded and updated form, of course).

- ✔ **Wikipedia (www.wikipedia.org):** This is a wiki, which means it's publicly updated. Therefore the information in it isn't authoritative. It's a great place to start for basic facts, though, and the breadth of topic coverage is staggering.

- ✔ **Dictionary.com (www.dictionary.com):** Your one-stop shop for settling arguments over a word's definition.

- ✔ **Oxford English Dictionary (www.oed.com):** If the dictionary argument ends with one person saying "Yeah, well that's not what it *used* to mean," you can settle *that* argument with the OED, which provides historical meanings for the last thousand years for more than 600,000 words.

- ✔ **Project Gutenberg (www.gutenberg.org):** When books go out of copyright, they become public domain, and many of them become available here, in this library of over 45,000 ebooks, available in plain text, EPUB, or Kindle format.

Education

You say you want an education? You could spend the rest of your life doing nothing but learning online, both at free sites and at formal educational institutions. Here are some basic categories:

- ✔ **Online universities:** Most bricks-and-mortar institutions now have an online segment where you can take college classes online and earn real credits toward a degree. The enrollment process for online classes is probably similar to that of the school's regular classes — and the tuition may also be similar as well. Some universities are even offered entirely online, with no offline classrooms. Figure 1-11 shows a college course at Indiana University that runs through a proprietary web interface.

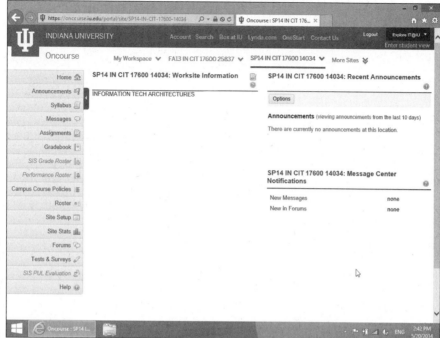

Figure 1-11:
An online
course at
Indiana
University.

✔ **Free education:** If you aren't ready to commit to spending the money on real college classes, that doesn't mean you can't learn. Hundreds of sites offer free classes that are more informal in nature. You won't get a degree, but you can get much the same education as you would get by pursuing a degree. For example, check out Open Yale (`http://oyc.yale.edu`), which offers free and open access to a selection of introductory courses taught by teachers at Yale University.

✔ **Educational videos:** Want to pick and choose what lectures to hear and what subjects to learn about? Try a site such as FreeVideoLectures (`www.freevideolectures.com`), which is full of online courses and lectures on every academic subject you could study at a real university. You can also find interesting educational and how-to videos at general video sites like YouTube (`www.youtube.com`).

✔ **Test preparation:** If you are getting ready to take an important test, such as a college entry exam like the SAT, you can find study help online. Practice tests and sample questions are widely available, as well as online tutoring and peer-to-peer advice and help.

Chapter 2

Buying and Setting Up a Computer

*W*hether it's your first time buying a computer or you're replacing an older model, choosing the right computer can be an intimidating task. Armed with a little information about what makes up a computer and why one model costs more than another, though, and you'll be able to make that decision with confidence.

In this chapter, you find out about the parts of a computer and how they work together. You discover why one computer costs more than another, and how to select the right one for your needs. Finally, you learn how to start up and set up a new computer right out of the box.

Understanding Computer Hardware

Your computing experience is made up of interactions with hardware and software. The *hardware* is all the tangible computer equipment, such as the monitor, central processing unit, keyboard, and mouse. The *software* is what makes the hardware work or lets you get things done, such as writing documents with Microsoft Word or playing a game of solitaire.

The main body of a computer is the *system unit*. The system unit's case houses a number of essential components, including

- ✔ A **motherboard**, which is a rather large circuit board into which all the other components connect.
- ✔ A **central processing unit (CPU)**, also called the processor. This is a very high-tech silicon chip that acts as the brains of your computer. It's installed in a special socket on the motherboard.
- ✔ **Random access memory (RAM)**, a set of data storage chips that act as a temporary holding area for the software as it runs.
- ✔ A **hard drive**, which is a storage unit that holds the operating system files, application files, and data files.

There may be other components too inside the system unit, such as circuit boards that add other capabilities like sound and network support.

In this chapter, I take a closer look at these essential components.

Understanding the CPU

The CPU is responsible for processing most of the computer's data, turning input into output. As you might imagine, the speed and performance of the CPU is one of the biggest factors that determines how well a computer works. A CPU is a very small, thin silicon wafer that is encased in a ceramic chip and then mounted on a circuit board, as shown in Figure 2-1.

CPU speed is measured in *gigahertz (GHz)*. The higher this measurement, the faster the CPU can operate. A hertz is a cycle per second; a gigahertz is 1 billion cycles per second. CPU speed is not the only measurement of its performance, though; different CPUs have efficiency-boosting technologies built into them that can increase data throughput in a number of ways. A fairer comparison between two different CPUs is the number of *instructions per second* they can perform.

There are two main manufacturers of CPUs for personal computers: Intel and Advanced Micro Devices (AMD). Neither is better than the other, although some technical geeks have strong preferences for one or the other. Intel's CPUs tend to be slightly more expensive for the same level of performance.

Most CPUs have multiple *cores*, which means there are multiple sets of the key components inside the chip, so the chip can process multiple actions at once. If the CPU runs at 1.8 GHz, for example, and is quad-core (that is, it has four cores), it can process up to 4 times as much as a single-core CPU could process at 1.8 GHz.

Figure 2-1:
A CPU.

Understanding memory

Memory consists of computer chips that hold data. One type of memory, called *Random Access Memory (RAM),* forms the central pool of memory that a computer uses to operate. The more RAM a computer has, the more applications it can have open at once without the computer's performance starting to bog down. More RAM can also make some applications perform better in general.

Memory capacity is measured in gigabytes (GB), which is a billion bytes. Most basic computers have at least 4GB today, with higher end systems having 16GB or more. Like the CPU, memory consists of small, thin silicon wafers, encased in ceramic chips and mounted on circuit boards. The circuit boards holding memory are called DIMMs, which stands for *dual inline memory module.* Figure 2-2 shows a DIMM.

Figure 2-2:
A DIMM.

© iStockphoto.com/aguirre_mar, © iStockphoto.com/mkos83

Understanding hard drives

A hard drive stores software. When the computer is turned off, whatever is on the hard drive remains there, so you don't have to reload software every time you turn on the computer. The operating system and your applications load from the hard drive into memory, where they run.

Hard-drive capacity is also measured in gigabytes (GB), like memory. A typical hard drive might be 500 GB or even 1 terabyte (1,000 GB) or more. Most hard drives sold today are the traditional mechanical type that use metal platters to store data with magnetic polarity, but a newer type, called a *solid state hard drive (SSHD),* uses a type of memory, resulting in a fast, quiet, and reliable (but expensive) storage alternative.

Understanding input devices

In addition to the components in the system unit, a computer may come with one or more input devices:

- ✔ **A keyboard,** which is similar to a typewriter keyboard. In addition to typing words, you can use a keyboard to give the computer commands such as selecting, copying, and pasting text.

- ✔ **A mouse,** which you also use to give your computer commands. You move the mouse around your desk with your hand, which moves a pointer around onscreen. Using this pointer, you can click an item — an onscreen button, for example — that causes an action, or click the screen and drag the mouse to select text or an object to perform an action on it (such as deleting the text or making it bold).

- ✔ A **trackball**, shown in Figure 2-3, which is like a mouse except it's stationary. You roll a ball on the top of the trackball to move the onscreen pointer.

- ✔ A **touchpad**, shown in Figure 2-4, which is a rectangular touch-sensitive pad with buttons adjacent to it. On many notebook computers, a touchpad is a built-in mouse substitute. You drag your finger on the pad to move the pointer onscreen.

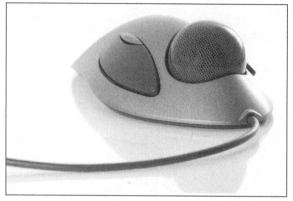

Figure 2-3:
A trackball.

© iStockphoto.com/epixx

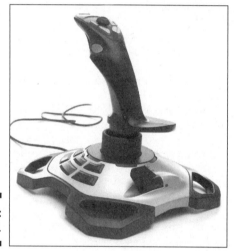

Figure 2-4:
A touchpad.

© iStockphoto.com/chrisboy2004

Understanding display screens

Each computer has some type of display screen. Depending on the type of computer, the display screen may be built-in, or may be a separate unit called a *monitor* with its own power cord, as in Figure 2-5. Some displays are *touchscreen*, so you can use your finger on the screen to provide input to the computer.

Figure 2-5:
A CPU
monitor.

Display size is measured in diagonal inches, the same as TVs. A typical size for a notebook computer display is from 14" to 18". A typical monitor for a desktop computer might be anywhere from 17" to 25". Some computers (especially desktops) can support multiple monitors.

Display quality is measured in *resolution* — that is, the number of pixels (individual colored dots) that comprise the display at its highest resolution. A typical resolution for a notebook PC is 1920 × 1080, for example. The first number is the horizontal resolution and the second one is the vertical resolution.

The *aspect ratio* of a display is the ratio of its width to its height, expressed in pixels. Displays may either be standard aspect ratio (4:3) or widescreen (16:9). For example, a small device might have a maximum resolution of 800 × 600; if you simplify that to a fraction, it comes out to 4/3.

Understanding optical drives

Most desktop and notebook computers come with an *optical drive,* which is a drive that will read CDs, DVDs, and/or Blu-ray discs. Optical drives get their name from the way data is written and read on the disc. A laser light shines on the surface, and a sensor measures how much light is bounced back from a certain spot.

Some laptop computers come without DVD capabilities because you can download and install software or play videos and music from the *cloud* (that is, via the Internet), so it's possible to get along just fine without the ability to play DVDs. However, most desktop computers still come with a DVD drive.

The optical drives in computers vary according to these factors:

- ✔ **Which disc types will it support?** The best drives support all three types: Blu-ray, DVDs, and CDs. Lesser drives may support only DVDs and CDs.

- ✔ **Does it write discs, or only read them?** Writeable drives enable you to buy blank discs and save data to them. Some blank discs can be written to only once (such as DVD-R); others can be rewritten multiple times (such as DVD-RW).

Understanding Internet connectivity options

Whatever computer you have, you will probably want to use it to connect to the Internet. That means you will want it to have a *network adapter* in it. That capability may be built into the computer, or it may be added to the computer via an expansion board or a device that plugs into a port.

Internet connectivity can be either wired or wireless. A wired connection requires you to connect a cable from the computer to the device that supplies your Internet connection (such as a cable modem). That type of cable and connection is known as *Ethernet*.

A wireless connection allows the computer to communicate with the Internet connection device through radio waves. The type of wireless connection used for Internet connectivity is called *Wi-Fi*, or wireless Ethernet.

If high-speed Internet service is not available in your area, you may need to use a *dial-up modem* to connect using your home telephone line. Dial-up modems are nobody's first choice — they are old, slow technology and they tie up your phone line.

Understanding Software

Software (also known as *programs* or *applications*) is installed on your computer hard drive, which resides in the computer casing (either in your laptop or, for a desktop computer, in the computer tower or monitor in all-in-one PCs).

You use software to get your work done, run entertainment programs, and browse the Internet. For example, Quicken is a financial management program you can use to balance your checkbook or keep track of your home inventory for insurance purposes.

Some programs come preinstalled on your computer. For example, a computer always has an *operating system* because the operating system runs all the other programs. Also, some programs are included with your operating system, such as WordPad, a simple word-processing program that comes with Windows 8. Skype, a program with which you can make online phone calls using your computer, is an example of a popular program that you can find on the Internet and install on your computer for free. You can also buy and install other programs as you need them.

The *operating system (OS)* is the software that allows you to start and shut down your computer and work with all the other software programs, manage files, and connect to the Internet.

Microsoft Windows is the most popular computer OS, and this book mainly focuses on its features. There have been several versions over the years; the version covered in this book is Windows 8.1. The previous version, Windows 7, was very popular and is still widely in use.

The second-most-popular computer operating system is Apple's *Mac OS X*. This operating system is for Apple Macintosh computers, although recent versions can also run on the same hardware that Windows runs on. Mac OS X uses names for its versions rather than numbers; the current version is called Mavericks.

Both of these operating systems use a graphical user interface (GUI) that allows the user to interact with the operating system by clicking on pictures with the mouse. The differences between them are mainly cosmetic; some people prefer one over the other. There is more software available for Windows than for Mac OS X.

Choosing a Computer

Just as there are many styles of shoes or mobile phones, you can find several types of computers. Some are small and portable, some use different operating systems to make everything run, and some excel at certain functions such as working with graphics or playing games. The following are some considerations when choosing a computer.

Computer sizes

Computers are also differentiated by their size and portability. As you learned in Chapter 1, a *desktop PC* is a large box into which the various components connect, such as keyboard, mouse, and monitor. It is not designed to be portable. Desktop PCs are popular in offices and with people who want the most computing power for their money and don't care about portability.

A *notebook*, or *laptop*, is a portable computer that folds up like a notebook for storage and transport. It weighs between 3 and 8 pounds, on average, and has a built-in display, keyboard, and touchpad. You can also connect external peripherals to it (for example, if you want an external monitor or a different keyboard or pointing device).

A *tablet* is a portable touch-sensitive screen with computer electronics behind it. You can tap or drag your finger on the screen to enter data and commands; a software simulation of a keyboard appears onscreen for typing text when appropriate. Tablets weigh only a few pounds and are very portable.

A *smartphone* is a cell phone with some computer capabilities. It may have a touch screen and resemble a tablet in some ways, running applications and accessing the Internet as well as making calls.

Operating system

If you have a preference in operating systems, make sure that the computer you choose has the right operating system installed on it. For a desktop or notebook computer, you may be able to buy an operating system separately to put on it, but you will pay more that way. A tablet PC or smartphone doesn't give you a choice of operating systems; it comes with the OS that it can run, and you can't change operating systems on it later. For example, an iPad only runs the Apple iOS operating system.

What do you get for your money?

Computers are available in every price range, from just a few hundred dollars to several thousands. What does the extra money buy you, beyond the basics?

- ✔ **Complex applications will run better and faster.** Any computer can do basic word processing and Internet surfing, but if you use 3D drawing programs, video editors, or graphics-intensive games, you will notice that the programs run much better on a computer with a faster CPU and more memory.

- ✔ **The screen may be larger and easier to see.** Large high-resolution monitors typically cost more than smaller ones.

- ✔ **The hard drive may be higher capacity.** The more hard drive space you have, the more applications and data you can store. Most systems' hard drives are more than adequate for the average user's needs, but users who store a lot of music and videos, for example, or business data, may need more.

- ✔ **The optical drive may be better.** An optical drive (such as CD, DVD, or Blu-ray) is included in some computers. On a higher-end computer that drive may be able to read and write Blu-ray discs; a lower-end computer might only support CDs and DVDs, or might not have an optical drive at all.

- ✔ **The display adapter may be better.** High-end systems have display hardware that processes complex graphical data faster and better, so you might notice better video performance in a game, for example.

- ✔ **Sound support might be better.** Most computers have basic sound support, but with a higher-end system, music and application sounds might be louder and crisper and might support Surround Sound external speakers.

- ✔ **It might have a higher-end edition of the operating system.** Windows 8.1 comes in several different editions; a basic computer will have the basic edition, but a higher-end computer might have Windows 8.1 Pro, which offers some extra features for networking and security.

- ✔ **The warranty may be longer.** A typical basic computer warranty is one year, but extended warranties are also available — for a price.

Think about how often you will use your computer. If you'll be working on it eight hours a day running a home business, you will need a better-quality computer to withstand the use and provide good performance. If you turn on the computer once or twice a week, it doesn't have to be the priciest model in the shop.

Next, consider the features that you need. Do you want (or have room for) a 20-inch monitor? Do you need the computer to run very fast and run several programs at once, or do you need to store tons of data? (Computer speed and storage are covered later in this chapter.) Understand what you need before you buy. Each feature or upgrade adds dollars to your computer's price.

Shop wisely. You can shop in a retail store for a computer or shop online using a friend's computer (and perhaps get his help if you're brand new to using a computer). Consider researching different models and prices online and using that information to negotiate your purchase in the store if you prefer shopping at the mall. Be aware, however, that most retail stores have a small selection compared to all you can find online.

If you walk from store to store or do your shopping online, you'll find that the price for the same computer model can vary by hundreds of dollars at different stores. See if your memberships in organizations such as AAA, AARP, or Costco make you eligible for better deals. Consider shipping costs if you buy online, and keep in mind that many stores charge a restocking fee if you return a computer you aren't happy with. Some stores offer only a short time period, such as 14 days, in which you can return a computer.

Setting Up a Computer

Your new computer has arrived and is sitting in a cardboard box in the middle of your living room floor. Now what?

Unpack the computer

First, you carefully remove the computer from its packing materials. If you are using a knife to open the box, make sure you don't cut too deeply into the box and scratch the computer.

Save all the packing material; don't tear it up and throw it in the trash right away. If the computer doesn't work and needs to be returned, you will need the packing materials to return it.

Save all disks and instruction manuals that come with the computer and put them in a safe place. You won't need them right away, but you might need them if you have to reset the computer at some point.

Connect the monitor, keyboard, and mouse

A desktop PC comes with a system unit, a keyboard, and a mouse, and it may also come with a monitor. (If you already have a monitor from a previous computer, you can use it, so you don't have to buy a new one.)

Before you power on a desktop computer, you'll need to connect the monitor, keyboard, and mouse to it. The monitor connects either to a VGA or DVI port on the back of the system unit. Figure 2-6 shows a USB connector being plugged in; the 15-pin directly above it is a VGA port for a monitor.

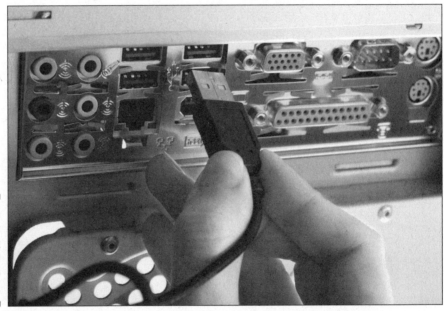

Figure 2-6: The ports on the back of a typical desktop computer.

The keyboard and mouse connect to USB ports. Your computer probably has multiple USB ports, and you can use any of them for those devices. Figure 2-6 shows some USB ports.

Some computers have different speeds of USB ports. They are all backward-compatible with earlier speed standards, and keyboards and mice have very low requirements for speed, so any USB port will do for them. However, if your computer has some USB ports that are blue, those are high-speed USB 3.0 ports; try to avoid wasting them on the keyboard and mouse.

A notebook or tablet computer does not require any external devices; you won't need to connect a monitor, keyboard, or mouse to either of these. However, a notebook or tablet PC may need to have its battery charged before you can work with it on battery power. Plug its power cord into a wall outlet before you start using it so that the battery power doesn't go out in the middle of the device's initial setup.

Set up the device

The first time you power on your new computer, you will be prompted to walk through a setup process. Follow the steps onscreen, entering information as prompted. The process is different for different models and types of computers. You might be prompted to enter a network password, for example, to create a user ID and password, and/or to choose an appearance theme.

Using Input Devices

If this is your first time at a computer, you might need a bit of a tour of the input interfaces to get you up to speed. Here's a quick overview of what to expect.

Using a pointing device

A *pointing device* moves the onscreen pointer in a graphical user interface such as Windows or Mac OS X. The most common pointing device is a mouse, but as you learned earlier in this chapter, there are others too, such as a trackball and a touchpad.

First things first: moving the onscreen pointer. The pointer moves in direct relation to the direction and amount that you interact with the pointing device. For a mouse, position the mouse on a flat surface such as your desk, or on a mouse pad (a soft cushiony pad designed for rolling a mouse), and then drag the mouse around. For a trackball, roll the ball with your fingers to move the pointer. For a touchpad, drag one finger across the surface of the touchpad to move the pointer.

After the pointer onscreen is touching something you want to interact with, such as a button you want to select or a text box into which you want to type, you use one of the buttons on the pointing device.

Each pointing device has a primary and a secondary button. By default, the primary button is the left one and the secondary is on the right. That's because most people are right-handed and the dominant finger (the index finger) is toward the left on the right hand. However, you can switch the buttons in the operating system's configuration options so that a left-handed person can use her dominant finger on the right mouse button.

The most basic operation is *click*. That means to press and release the primary button (the left button) once. Clicking usually selects whatever it is that the pointer is pointing at.

Double-click means to press and release the primary button twice in quick succession. Double-clicking usually activates something, such as opens a file or starts an application.

To *right-click* means to press and release the secondary (right) button.

To *drag* means to press and hold down the primary button and then move the pointer to another spot, and then release the button. Dragging usually moves an object onscreen from one place to another.

Some pointing devices have a *scroll* feature. Depending on the application you are using, scrolling may move up or down in a multi-screen document you are reading on the screen, or it may zoom the display in or out. On a mouse, the scroll feature is often a rubber wheel between the two mouse buttons that you can turn with a finger.

Work with a touchscreen

With a touchscreen computer or tablet device, your finger replaces a mouse click. You can tap the screen to select something, to activate features with buttons, and to make a field active so you can type content. Touchscreen-enabled operating systems also offer an onscreen keyboard that touchscreen users can work with to enter text with the tap of a finger.

You can also use your finger to swipe to the right, left, up, or down to move from one page to another (for example, from one web page to another or from one photo to the next in the Gallery app) or to move up or down on a page.

Windows also offers some gestures you can make with your fingers, such as moving your fingers apart and then pinching them together to minimize elements on your screen, or swiping down from the top of the screen to close an app. If you do own a touchscreen and want to learn more, visit `http://windows.microsoft.com/en-us/windows7/using-touch-gestures` for more information.

Understanding the keyboard layout

Besides the ordinary letter, number, and symbol keys, a computer keyboard has some special keys. Some of these can be assigned to certain operations in the software, such as pressing F1 to get help in most programs. Other keys are modifiers, which means they change the meaning of some other key when pressed in conjunction with it, the way the Shift key changes a lowercase to a capital letter. Figure 2-7 shows a typical desktop keyboard and identifies some of the key types.

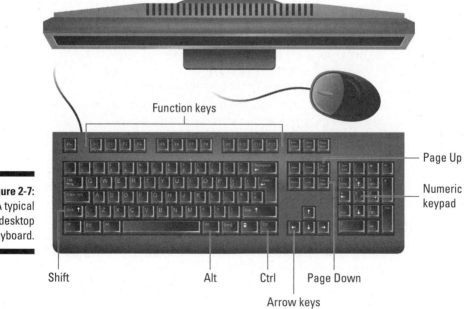

Figure 2-7: A typical desktop keyboard.

Function keys

Page Up

Numeric keypad

Shift   Alt   Ctrl   Page Down

Arrow keys

Some of the keys you may have on your keyboard include

- ✔ **Function keys:** These keys begin with the letter F and are numbered 1 through 12. Some of these keys have default assignments in the operating system and some don't. Most of them have special assignments in certain applications too, such as in Microsoft Office applications.

- ✔ **Fn key:** On a notebook computer, an Fn key, located near the bottom on the left, modifies certain keys to perform different operations. This is done because a notebook computer has a smaller area for keyboard keys, so some of the keys that a normal desktop keyboard would have are omitted. Notebooks also require some special keys that other computers don't, such as keys to change the display brightness or switch to an external display. To identify Fn keyboard actions, look for additional symbols on a key, such as a sunburst with an up arrow over it for Increase Brightness.

- ✔ **Windows key:** A Windows key has a four-paned window symbol on it; it's used in the Windows operating system for various tasks. For example, it opens the Start screen (Windows 8) or Start menu (Windows 7 and earlier).

- ✔ **Arrow keys:** The arrow keys can be used to move the cursor onscreen in some applications. For example, in Excel, it changes the active cell, and in Word, it moves the text insertion point.

- ✔ **Numeric keypad:** If your keyboard has a numeric keypad, you can use it to enter numbers the way you would on an adding machine. You can press the NumLock key to toggle the numeric keypad between its normal functionality and operating as an arrow keypad (see arrow keys mentioned in the previous bullet).

- ✔ **Modifier keys:** Keys such as Ctrl, Alt, and Shift modify the functionality of other keys. For example, pressing Alt+F4 is a shortcut for shutting down the active application. Keyboard shortcuts, covered in the next section, make extensive use of modifier keys.

- ✔ **Positioning keys:** Keys such as Home, End, Page Up and Page Down are used to move the insertion point in some applications.

Using keyboard shortcuts

A *keyboard shortcut* refers to a key or combinations of keys that you press and hold to perform an action. Many shortcuts involve the Windows key (it's the one near the left-bottom corner of your keyboard that sports the Windows logo). For example, you can press and hold the Windows key plus C (Win+C) to display the Charms in Windows 8.

In Windows 8, keyboard shortcuts can be very helpful to those who don't have a touchscreen computer. Table 2-1 lists some handy shortcuts to know.

Table 2-1	Common Windows 8 Keyboard Shortcuts
Key(s)	*Result*
Windows key	Displays the Start screen
Win+B	Displays the desktop
Win+C	Displays the Charms bar
Win+E	Displays File Explorer
Win+F	Displays the Files search field
Win+I	Displays the Settings panel
Win+L	Displays the Lock screen
Atl+D	Displays the Address field in Internet Explorer 10
Win+Tab	Displays recently used apps

Starting Up and Shutting Down

To start up your computer just press its power button. The operating system loads automatically. At that point, the operating system's desktop (or other interface) may appear, or you may be prompted to sign in.

Signing in

Depending on the operating system and the way it's set up, you may be prompted to sign in by selecting a user account. If that account is password-protected, you will also be asked for the password.

Understanding user accounts

Where do user accounts come from? Well, one of them may be created automatically. The first time you turn on a new computer, part of the setup process may involve creating a user account. (That's what happens with Windows systems, for example.) From that point on, you can sign in with that same user account each time you turn on the computer.

If more than one person uses the same computer, you may want to create additional user accounts. To do so, sign in with an existing account and then use the procedure in your operating system for creating new accounts.

In Windows 8.1, you can create either a Microsoft account or a local account. A *Microsoft account* is linked to an email address; a local account is not. A Microsoft account has some advantages, such as the ability to access OneDrive online storage and to use the same settings (such as desktop colors) on different computers. A *local account* is private; it is on one computer only, with no record of it anywhere else.

Windows 8.1 user accounts can also have one of two levels of authority: Standard or Administrator. A *Standard account* can run applications and can make changes that do not affect other users, such as choosing a different background image. An *Administrator account* has full permission to make changes that will affect other users too, such as to install and remove software and update device drivers.

Not all operating systems allow multiple user accounts or require you to sign in; the operating systems on tablets and smartphones usually don't, for example.

To create a new user account in Windows 8.1, follow these steps:

1. **Select the Settings charm and click Change PC Settings.**
2. **Click Accounts.**
3. **Click Other Accounts.**
4. **Click Add an Account.**
5. **Enter the person's email address and click Next.**

   Follow the prompts to enter any other information requested and complete the account setup.

Shutting down

When you are finished with your computer session, you can do any of the following:

- ✔ **Shut down:** This completely turns off the computer's power; when you restart, the operating system must completely reload.

- ✔ **Sleep:** The computer goes into a low power-consumption mode that keeps only the memory powered; it appears to be off, but when you turn it back on again, it comes back up faster because the memory has remained powered.

✓ **Hibernate:** The computer's memory content is copied to a holding area on the hard disk and then the computer's power is shut off. When you turn it back on again, the stored data is copied back into memory; the computer starts up faster than from a complete shutdown, but not as fast ask from Sleep mode.

✓ **Sign Out:** Using this command signs out your user account and displays a prompt for someone else to sign in.

In Windows 8.1, you can access the Sleep, Hibernate (if available), and Shut Down commands from the Power icon in the upper right corner of the Start screen, and then choose the desired command, as shown in Figure 2-8.

To sign out, you can click the currently signed-in user name in the upper-right corner of the Start screen, and then choose Sign Out from the menu, as shown in Figure 2-9.

Figure 2-8:
Making a
choice from
the shut-
down menu.

Figure 2-9:
Signing out.

Chapter 3

Understanding Operating Systems

In This Chapter

▶ Discovering what an operating system is

▶ Understanding the types of operating systems available

▶ Choosing the right operating system for a desktop or notebook PC

▶ Identifying some operating systems for tablets and smart phones

▶ Finding out how operating systems communicate with hardware

*W*hen you think about using a computer, you probably envision performing some useful task with it, like writing a letter or calculating a budget. Behind the scenes, however, is the software that keeps the computer up and running: the operating system.

This chapter explains what an operating system actually does back there behind the scenes, and why your choice of operating system matters. You'll learn about the operating systems used on different kinds of computers, and which ones are best suited to certain tasks and situations.

What Is an Operating System?

An *operating system* (OS) is software that starts up a computer and keeps it running and responding to your commands. Operating systems have several important jobs. An operating system

  ✔ Runs applications (useful programs like word processors, calculators, and so on) and enables you to interact with them.

  ✔ Creates and maintains the user interface that you see onscreen, such as the icons you click and the dialog boxes you see.

  ✔ Controls and manages the file storage system, so you can save and open data files in your applications and manage the files that run your applications.

> ✔ Communicates with the hardware, giving it instructions to accomplish
> the tasks you request, such as printing your work.

Don't look to the operating system for fun or productivity — that's not its
job. For example, you can't use it to produce a newsletter, send an email,
draw a picture, or look something up online. However, the operating system
contributes to all those activities because it enables applications to run that
can do all those things.

Types of Operating Systems

Each OS is optimized for the hardware it runs on and the tasks the user is
likely to want to perform. For example, the OS on a tablet computer is compact
because there's not much storage space for it, and it's easy to use because
most tablet users aren't computer professionals. On the other hand, the operating system for a server is designed to give a computer professional many
options for managing and configuring a network and its devices, and neither
compactness nor ease-of-use are major factors in that.

Some operating systems are designed to run on just one specific platform. A
platform is a type of hardware. For example, most Windows-based computers run on the *Intel platform*, sometimes called the *IBM-compatible platform*.
Several other operating systems can also run on that platform, including
Linux and recent versions of Mac OS X. On the other hand, most tablets and
smart phones support only one operating system — the one they come with.

An operating system can have either a *graphical user interface (GUI)* or a
command-line interface. GUI interfaces are the norm in operating systems
designed for personal computing devices like desktops, notebooks, tablets,
and smart phones. Users interact with the graphics they see onscreen by
using a keyboard, mouse, or touchscreen. In a command line interface, you
type each command manually; the area of the screen where your typing
appears is the *command prompt.* You have to memorize the commands to
use, or keep a reference book handy.

Why on earth would anyone want to type commands at a command prompt,
if they had any other choice? Well, primarily because it's easier to do certain
things at a command line than it is to do them in a graphical environment.
Most such things are pretty technical and only IT professionals do them.
That's why a command line interface is found primarily in operating systems
designed to be used on servers, such as UNIX and Linux. Figure 3-1 compares
a GUI OS with a command-line OS.

Figure 3-1:
A GUI OS
(left) versus
a command-
line OS
(right).

Operating Systems for Desktop and Notebook PCs

There are two main operating systems for desktop and notebook computers: Apple and Intel (IBM-compatible). A third OS, Linux, is somewhat of a specialty item, but has a small, devoted following.

Mac OS X

The Apple Macintosh platform uses the Apple operating system: Mac OS X (pronounced *Mac O-S-X*, although the X technically is the Roman numeral ten). This OS has an easy-to-use GUI interface. Mac O X versions have code names as well as version numbers. Figure 3-2 shows the Mavericks version (version 10.9) of Mac OS X.

Apple has lately started making Mac hardware that can also run the Windows operating system. However, because Macintosh hardware is more expensive than IBM-compatible hardware, most people who buy an Apple computer do so because they want to run Mac OS X.

Macintosh computers have a reputation for being the choice of graphics and page layout professionals, and in most large commercial publishing and printing offices, Mac computers are the standard. Are they really better for these tasks? That's a matter of opinion. They used to be because the best high-end page layout and graphics editing software was written for Macs. Nowadays, however, with the same applications available for both, it's largely a matter of past history continuing to affect public perception.

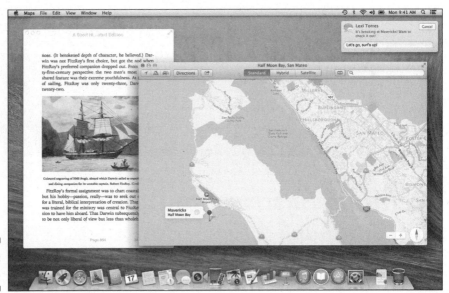

Figure 3-2:
Mac OS X.

Microsoft Windows

Microsoft Windows is by far the most popular operating system in the world, with an estimated 90 percent of all computers in use today running some version of Windows. It is also a GUI interface and is easy to use. Because it's the most popular, more applications are available for it. You'll very seldom run into an application that doesn't have a Windows version.

Windows 8.1 has two interfaces. The Start screen, which was new with Windows 8, is where you go to launch most applications. You can pin shortcuts to your favorite applications there for easy access, as shown in Figure 3-3. The desktop is the more traditional Windows interface, shown in Figure 3-4, with a taskbar at the bottom of the screen and applications appearing in rectangular windows. You learn much more about Windows 8.1 in Chapter 4.

Figure 3-3:
The
Windows 8.1
Start
screen.

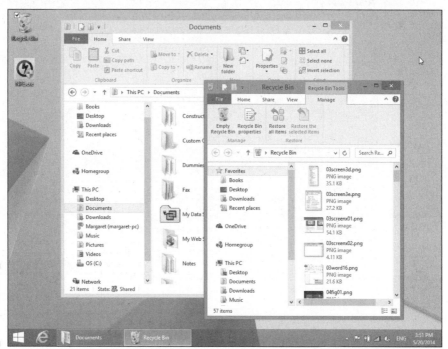

Figure 3-4:
The
Windows 8.1
desktop.

Linux

Linux is a free operating system that runs on a variety of platforms, including IBM-compatible PCs, servers, tablets, and smart phones.

Linux was developed by a guy named Linus Torvalds. The name Linux is a combination of *Linus* and *UNIX*. Linux is *open-source*, which means that Mr. Torvalds retains ownership of his original code, but it is free to the public to use in any way they see fit. Users are free to modify the code, improve it, and redistribute it. Developers are not allowed to charge money for the Linux *kernel* (that is, the main part of the operating system), but they can charge money for distributions (distros for short), which are packaged collections of add-ons, shells, and utilities for Linux. Some of the most popular distros include Ubuntu Linux and Red Hat Linux.

At its most basic level, Linux is a command line OS, but you can install a *shell* for it that places a GUI environment over the top of it so you can interact with it like you would Windows or Mac OS X. A variety of different shells are available. Figure 3-5 shows the Ubuntu Linux shell, for example. Linux is very flexible and customizable that way; you can customize it to run servers too, and even handheld devices. (Android, a popular OS for smart phones and tablets, is a variant of Linux.)

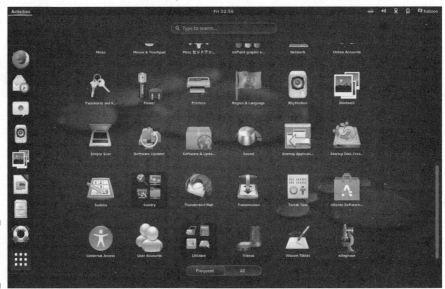

Figure 3-5:
The Ubuntu
Linux shell.

Linux is a little more difficult to install and configure than either Windows or Mac OS X, and there are fewer applications that run on it, so having Linux on a desktop or notebook PC is mostly the domain of computer experts who are either trying to pinch pennies by not paying for one of the commercial operating systems or unhappy with Microsoft and using their choice as a protest.

Operating Systems for Netbooks

Recall from Chapter 1 that a netbook is a small notebook computer with lesser specs than most, used primarily to access the Internet. On a netbook, you don't need or want a big bulky operating system — you want an operating system that is going to run fast on minimal hardware. In other words, you want a *thin client*.

Chrome is the name of both an operating system and a web browser, both produced by Google. Chrome OS is a very popular thin client that is a variant of Linux. This simple operating system comes preinstalled on many netbooks. It contains a simple file manager, the Google Chrome web browser, and a media player. It doesn't run most applications designed for other operating systems. Figure 3-6 shows a Chrome OS screen.

Chrome is far from the only thin-client OS. Several other open-source operating systems include Haiku, openThinClient, and Thinstation.

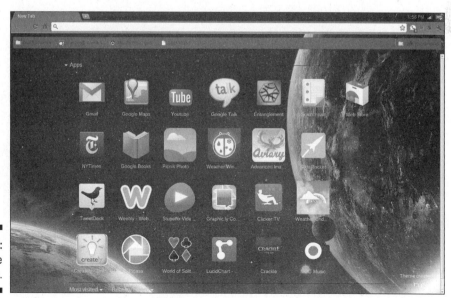

Figure 3-6:
The Chrome
OS screen.

Operating Systems for Tablets and Smart Phones

Tablets and smart phones have special operating-system needs. They use solid state storage, which is expensive, so the amount of storage space is limited. Therefore a large operating system is impractical; the OS must be simple, easy to use, and above all, compact in size. The OS comes prein-stalled on a static memory chip on tablets and smart phones, so these plat-forms are often referred to as *system-on-chip (SoC)*. A separate memory chip (or group of chips) is used to hold the data you create and the extra applica-tions you install.

Portable Apple devices (iPhone and iPad) use an operating system called iOS. Its main advantage is popularity — because it's so popular, thousands of apps are available for it via the Apple Store. Figure 3-7 shows an iPad screen with iOS as the operating system.

Figure 3-7:
An iPad
running iOS.

The main competitor to iOS is *Android*, an open-source OS created by Google. Android is popular on low-end tablets because it is free, and because many apps are available for it, and most of them are free. Many smart phones also use a version of Android.

Microsoft has two different versions of Windows for portable devices. For tablets, there is Windows RT, which looks a lot like the Start screen from Windows 8.1 but lacks the desktop component; it is designed to run on SoC devices such as tablets. Most desktop applications won't run on a Windows RT system. For smart phones, there is Windows Phone, an OS designed specifically for phone use. Figure 3-8 shows a Windows Phone display.

Figure 3-8:
The
Windows
Phone.

Learning How Operating Systems Talk to Hardware

As I mentioned at the beginning of this chapter, one of the jobs of an OS is to communicate with hardware. The problem with that, though, is that each piece of hardware speaks a different language, and they are all different from the language that the operating system itself speaks. *Device drivers* help the operating system and the hardware communicate. They are files that translate the operating system's requests into the language of a particular device, and then translate back again when the device sends a message in return. Each device driver is designed for one specific device and one specific operating system version, although it may work, fully or partially, with other similar devices or operating system versions.

A device driver can make or break a device's performance, and often when a device appears to be malfunctioning, it's actually the driver's fault. For example, if you are playing a game and big white patches appear on the display in certain parts of the game, the display adapter's driver is probably at fault. It might be corrupted, but more likely it is just out of date or incompatible with the game. Downloading and installing an update for the driver might correct the problem.

When you install a new piece of hardware, the operating system uses a technology called plug-and-play to identify the device and locate a driver for it if possible. Thanks to plug-and-play, users can set up most devices by simply connecting them, and perhaps running a software utility that came with the hardware.

Over time, new versions of drivers become available online. Different operating systems have different means of keeping drivers up to date. In Mac OS X, for example, driver updates are downloaded automatically along with OS updates. In Windows 8.1, you can view driver versions and install new drivers in the Device Manager utility. You can also roll back an updated driver to the previous version if system problems occur after you install an update.

Chapter 4

Windows 8.1 Basics

● ●

In This Chapter

▶ Finding your way around in Windows 8.1

▶ Running Windows applications

▶ Controlling application windows

▶ Managing files

▶ Using a home network

● ●

*W*indows 8.1 is the operating system that comes preinstalled on most new computers today. You can think of Windows as the taskmaster of your computer — you tell Windows what you want to do, and it directs your computer to do it. You don't typically talk to your computer to get it to do something (although a few grumbles now and then don't hurt); instead, you make selections from what you see onscreen using the computer's mouse, keyboard, or touchscreen.

In this chapter, you learn the basics of Windows 8.1, including how to run programs and manage files with it. Armed with this knowledge, you'll be able to use applications in Windows to do what you want to do, whether it's play games, write letters, use the Internet, or listen to music and watch videos.

Getting Around in Windows 8.1

Windows 8.1 has two main interfaces: the desktop and the Start screen. Depending on how your computer is set up, one or the other of these appears automatically when you start your computer.

Understanding the Start screen

The *Start screen* is like a bulletin board that contains pinned shortcuts to applications. A *shortcut* is a graphical object (usually a picture or a rectangular block) that opens a particular file, folder, or application when you click it.

The Start screen starts out with a default set of shortcuts pinned to it, but you can pin shortcuts to your own favorite applications to it, and unpin shortcuts that you don't use. The Start screen replaces the Start menu in earlier Windows versions.

Each pinned item on the Start screen appears as a rectangular *tile*. Figure 4-1 shows the Start screen; yours may have different tiles on it, or the tiles may be different sizes.

Figure 4-1:
The
Windows 8.1
Start
screen.

The Start screen might appear automatically at startup; if it doesn't, you can access it by pressing the Windows key on your keyboard. Or, if the desktop appears, you can click the Start button in the lower-left corner of the desktop to access the Start screen.

If there are a lot of shortcuts pinned to the Start screen, you might not be able to see them all at once. Use the scroll bar at the bottom of the screen to scroll to the right to see the rest, or if you are using a touchscreen, swipe (drag your finger) from right to left to scroll the display.

Understanding the desktop

The desktop, along with the Start screen, forms the main interface of Windows 8.1. By default, the desktop is rather bare. It consists of a graphical background with a single icon on it. (An *icon* is a picture that represents an object, such as a file, folder, or application.) The desktop also includes a taskbar. The *taskbar* is the thin horizontal bar at the bottom of the screen. It serves multiple purposes, as shown in Figure 4-2:

Figure 4-2:
The Windows 8.1 desktop.

✔ The taskbar contains the Start button, which opens the Start screen. You can also right-click the Start button to open a shortcut menu of common commands and locations.

✔ You can pin shortcuts to the taskbar. By default, there are two there: Internet Explorer and File Explorer. Pinned shortcuts appear at the left end of the taskbar.

✔ When applications are running, icons for them appear immediately to the right of the pinned shortcuts. For example, in Figure 4-2, there are two applications running: Calculator and Notepad. Notice that the icons for these two appear with a lighter background than the background of the taskbar itself; this indicates that those icons are for running programs, not just pinned shortcuts.

✔ At the far-right end, the current date and time appear.

✔ To the left of the date and time are icons for utilities or features that are running in the background, such as the volume control, the battery monitor (on a portable PC), and the network connection indicator. This area is called the *notification area*, or system tray.

Using the Charms bar

The Charms bar is a pop-up vertical bar along the right side of the screen that displays five special icons, called *charms*. See Figure 4-3. You can display the Charms bar, move the mouse pointer to the bottom right corner of the screen, or if you have a touchscreen, swipe in from the right.

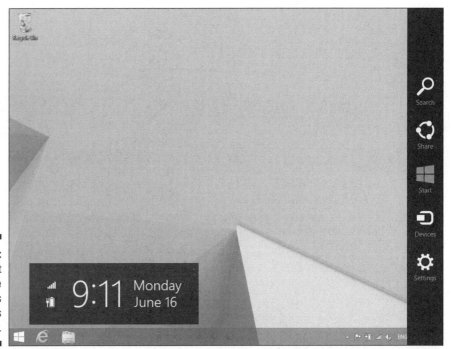

Figure 4-3:
On the right side of the screen is the Charms bar.

Each of the charms performs some special function that Windows 8.1 users frequently need. From top to bottom, they are

- **Search:** Opens a Search screen, from which you can search for any applications, settings, or files on your computer or online.

- **Share:** Enables you to share links, photos, and more with your friends and social networks without leaving the app you're in.

- **Start:** Takes you to the Start screen, or if you're already on the Start screen, back to the last app you were working with.

- **Devices:** Enables you do things like sending files and streaming movies to printers and TVs.

- **Settings:** Provides access to many common system settings, such as brightness, volume control, and notifications, as well as access to the Control Panel. You also can shut down your PC from here, as you discovered in Chapter 2.

The exact options that appear when you click a certain charm depend on the context — that is, they depend on what's on the screen at the moment. For example, when you choose the Settings charm with the desktop displayed, you get different choices than when you choose it with the Start screen displayed.

Running Applications

Computers exist for one basic reason: to run applications. An *application* is a program that performs some useful function. For example, there are applications that create spreadsheets, play games, edit photos, and access email, to name only a few. The applications installed on your PC determine the down-to-business tasks you can perform with it, as well as the entertainment options you have available (games, movies, music, and so on).

There are two kinds of applications in Windows 8.1. *Desktop applications* are traditional-style applications designed to run on the Windows desktop in windows that are typically resizable. Windows 8 apps are applications that only run on Windows 8 and 8.1. They typically run full-screen. Their interfaces are different, as you will learn later in this chapter.

Starting an application

If the application you want to start appears on the Start screen, you just click or tap its shortcut. If it doesn't appear there, click the down-pointing arrow at the bottom of the Start screen to display the Apps list, shown in Figure 4-4. This is a list of all installed applications.

Figure 4-4:
A list of
installed
apps in
Windows 8.1.

To pin an application to the Start screen, right-click it on the Apps list and choose Pin to Start.

You can also start applications from their pinned shortcuts on the taskbar or the desktop. Click a pinned taskbar shortcut icon, or double-click a pinned desktop shortcut icon, to start the application.

After you start an application, one of two types of interfaces opens, depending on the type of application it is. Traditional desktop applications run in a window, with the desktop as a background. You can move and resize the window (covered later in this chapter), and you can have lots of windows open at once, arranged so you can see all of them. (See Figure 4-5.) Desktop applications typically have a menu system or some toolbars or a ribbon at the top of the window for issuing commands.

A Windows 8 app, on the other hand, typically fills the entire screen, and may not have any visible controls. Right-click to display a command bar at the top or bottom of the screen with commands you can execute. See Figure 4-6, which has a command bar at both the top and the bottom. Windows 8 apps are designed to work well with touch screens; their controls and commands are larger and simpler than those in desktop applications.

Figure 4-5:
Multiple
windows
open at
once.

Figure 4-6:
A command
bar.

Switching among applications

When there are multiple applications open at once, you can switch among them freely. There are many ways to do this, depending on the types of applications and whether you prefer to work with the keyboard, mouse, or touchscreen.

For desktop applications, you can switch to an application's window by clicking any visible part of the window, or by clicking the application's icon on the taskbar. You can point the mouse pointer at an icon to see a thumbnail preview of the application. See Figure 4-7. Windows 8 apps also have an icon in the taskbar (if you have Windows 8.1 or higher), so you can switch to them that way too.

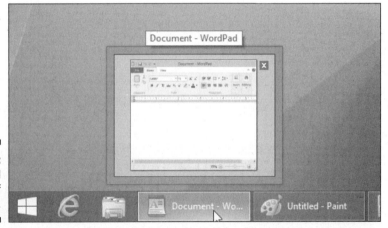

Figure 4-7: A thumbnail preview of the app.

For Windows 8 apps, you can swipe the touchscreen from the left to switch to a different app. (The desktop is considered an app itself, so you can toggle between your Windows 8 apps and the desktop this way, but not between specific open desktop apps.)

With the mouse, you can manage open Windows 8 apps by moving the pointer to the upper-left corner. When you see a thumbnail image appear there, move the mouse pointer down the left edge of the screen until a bar appears with thumbnails of running apps. From there, you can click the app you want to switch to.

For all types of apps, you can hold down the Alt key and tap the Tab key. A bar appears in the center of the screen with thumbnail images of the open apps. Each time you tap Tab, a different one is selected. When the desired app is selected, release the Alt key.

Closing an application

For traditional desktop apps, you can easily close the application window by clicking the Close (X) button in the upper-right corner of the window. You can also right-click the app's icon on the taskbar and choose Close window. If the application has a menu system, there is probably also an Exit or Close command on the leftmost menu.

For Windows 8 apps, you can move the mouse pointer to the top of the screen to make a title bar appear, and then click the Close (X) button in the title bar. (That works in Windows 8.1 and higher only.)

If you have a touchscreen, you can drag from the top of the window all the way down to the bottom of the screen to close a Windows 8 app. You can do the same thing with a mouse by dragging (with the left mouse button held down) from the top of the app window to the bottom of it. You can also move the mouse to the top of the screen, so that a title bar appears for the app, and then click the Close button (X) on it.

Working in a desktop application

Desktop applications, as a general rule, have a menu bar or a ribbon. On a menu bar, click a menu name to open a menu, and then click a command on the menu. Some menu-based applications also have one or more tool-bars, which are rows of graphical icons that represent common commands. Figure 4-8 shows an application with both a menu and a toolbar. In some applications, the menu bar is hidden by default; you can make it appear by pressing the Alt key.

In applications that use a ribbon instead of a menu bar, click a tab to display the desired set of buttons, and then click the button that represents the command you want to execute. See Figure 4-9.

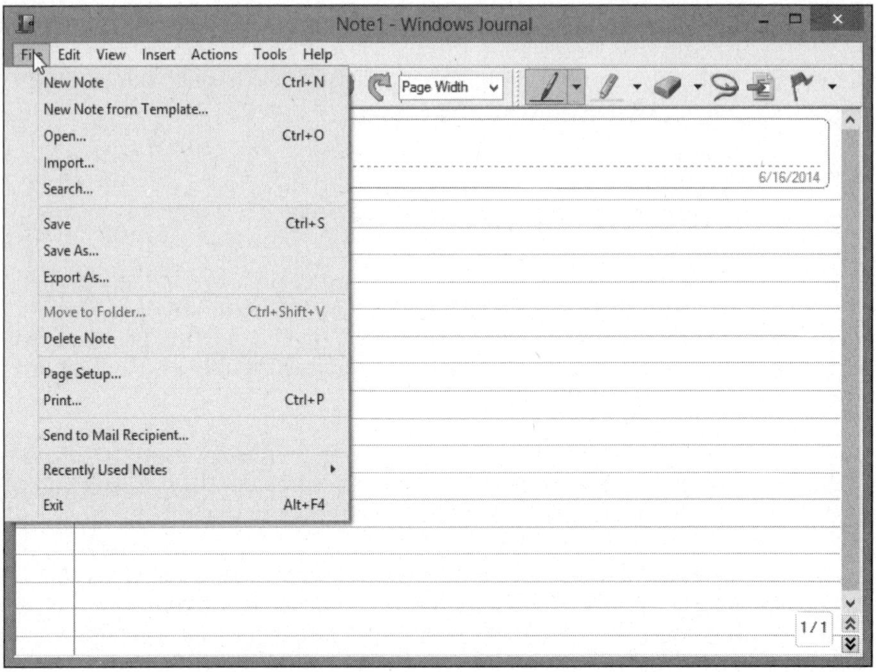

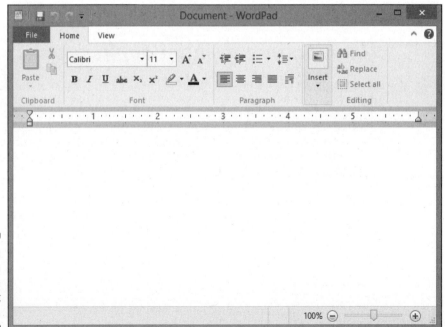

Figure 4-8:
An application with a menu and a toolbar.

Figure 4-9:
Click a tab to display a desired set of buttons.

Working in a Windows 8 application

Windows 8 applications have their own unique control methods. At first, new users may be taken aback by Windows 8 app because it lacks any of the familiar components of a Windows desktop application. For example, it's not in a resizable window, there are no window controls in the upper-right corner, and there is no ribbon or menu system. It's not obvious how to proceed.

Here's a giant clue when it comes to Windows 8 apps: *When in doubt, right-click.* Right-clicking usually brings up a command bar with buttons for issuing commands such as starting a new data file, saving your work, or setting options.

Controlling Application Windows

Application windows are different in Windows 8.1 depending on whether you are working with a desktop app or a Windows 8-style app. (Sensing a pattern yet? Windows 8 apps are very different from anything else you have probably encountered in the Windows world.)

For desktop applications, all the same window-control commands and buttons are the same as they've been for the last decade's worth of Windows versions. You can minimize a window so that it shrinks to just an icon on the taskbar, maximize a window to fill the screen, or restore a window to a resizable rectangular area that can be moved around on the desktop and resized as needed.

For Windows 8 applications, there are no windows in the traditional sense. Each app fills the entire screen when it is active. However, as you will learn later in this chapter, you can run two Windows 8 apps side by side.

Managing desktop windows

Windows that appear on the desktop can have any of three states:

- **Maximized:** The window fills the entire desktop. Maximize a window when you want to concentrate on the program or document in that window and nothing else.
- **Restored:** The window is open but not inflated to full-screen size.
- **Minimized:** The window is still open, but it's hidden from view. An icon for the application appears on the taskbar.

You choose the window's state with the buttons in the window's upper-right corner, as shown in Figure 4-10. The leftmost button is Minimize. The center button is either Restore or Maximize, depending on the window's current state. (When the window is already maximized, the button is Restore; when the window is already restored, the button is Maximize.)

Figure 4-10:
The
Minimize,
Restore, and
Maximize
buttons.

The rightmost button (X) is Close. This button closes the window, and closes the application too.

When a window is not maximized, you can move and resize it on the desktop. To move a window, drag its title bar. To resize a window, drag anywhere on its border (except at the top, because that's where the title bar is). Dragging a corner enables you to resize both dimensions at once. When you position the mouse pointer over the border of a window, the pointer changes to a double-headed arrow when it is positioned correctly for resizing.

Arranging Windows 8 apps

Windows 8 apps are designed to run full-screen. They can't be windowed like the traditional desktop applications.

However, you can use the Snap feature to make a Windows 8 app occupy only one side of the screen, rather than filling it completely. You can then do the same to another app, so that the two of them are side by side and you can see them both at once. Figure 4-11 shows the People app and the Calendar app.

To snap an app, start dragging the top of it downward, as if you were going to close it, but instead of dragging all the way to the bottom, pause in the center of the screen. The app appears as a thumbnail image, and a vertical bar appears onscreen. Still holding down the mouse button, drag to the left to make the vertical bar appear on the left, or drag to the right to make the vertical bar appear on the right. Then release the mouse button to drop the app into the space between the vertical bar and the edge of the screen.

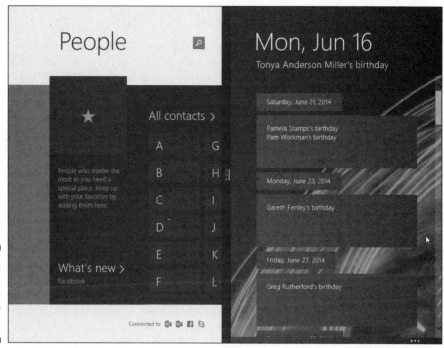

Figure 4-11:
The People
app and the
Calendar
app.

After you've got one app snapped into place, go back to the Start screen and open another. The second app nestles itself into the remaining space next to the first app.

You can drag the divider line between the two apps to change their respective shares of the screen space.

The desktop itself is seen as an app in the eyes of the Windows 8 interface, so you can place it side-by-side with a Windows 8 app if you like. Just drag down from the top of the desktop until the desktop turns into a thumbnail image, and then drag it left or right to snap it into place, just like you would a Windows 8 app.

Managing Files with File Explorer

File Explorer is the primary tool for working with files in Windows 8.1. No matter which folder or drive you are viewing at the moment, the same basic File Explorer interface is in effect. In the following sections, you will learn how computer storage is logically organized and how to use File Explorer to work with it.

Understanding file storage

Your computer has hundreds, maybe even thousands, of files on it. They're nicely organized into folders to keep track of them. For example, you have a Windows folder that holds the system files needed to keep Windows up and running, and you have a Program Files folder that stores the files you need to run your installed apps.

Your hard disk drive is the main storage unit. It holds the operating system files, the files for the installed apps, and probably a lot of your own personal files too, such as your word processing documents and spreadsheets. Your main hard-disk drive is probably internal, meaning it's inside the computer box. You can also have other hard disk drives besides the main one, and the other drives can be either internal or external.

In addition to hard disk drives, you can also store and retrieve files from optical discs (like CDs and DVDs) and flash RAM drives that you connect to your computer's USB port.

A file can be stored directly at the top level of a drive's organizational system, or it can be stored in a folder on that drive. The top level of a drive is called the *root directory*; it's like the lobby of a building. It's the entryway to the disk. On a small-capacity drive, like a USB flash drive, you might be able to get away with storing most (or all) files in the root directory because you're working with a limited number of files. The list is not unmanageable to browse. However, when you start getting into higher capacity drives, like your main hard-disk drive, folders are a necessity because they help you keep things sorted.

File locations on a disc are described as a *path*. A path begins with the drive letter and a colon, followed by a slash sign (\). If the file is in the root directory, the file name appears immediately after the slash, like this: C:\myfile. txt. If the file is in a folder on the disk, the path shows the folder name, then another slash, and then the file name, like this: C:\schoolwork\myfile.txt.

You can have folders within folders to further organize and segment your file storage. For example, within the C:\Windows folder on your hard disk is a Help folder, and within that folder there's a Windows folder, and within that folder there's a ContentStore folder, and within that folder is an en-US folder, and within that folder is a file called art.mshc. The path to this file can be written as follows:

C:\Windows\Help\Windows\ContentStore\en-US\art.mshc

Paths are represented in Windows 8.1 in several different ways. You may see a path in an Address bar shown with right-pointing triangle arrows between each folder, as in Figure 4-12.

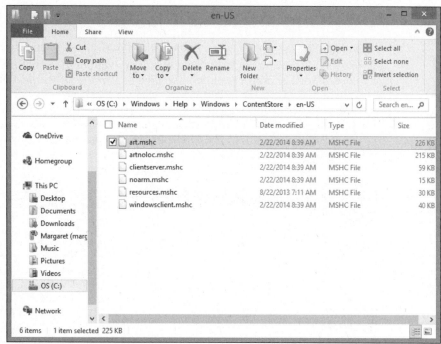

Figure 4-12:
The file path
shows up in
the Address
bar.

Paths are also sometimes represented by *folder trees*, which are visual representations of the hierarchy of the folder system. The navigation pane shows a partial folder tree of the previously referenced path in Figure 4-13 (from the Help folder downward). Notice how the folders directly involved in the path being illustrated have black triangles next to them, indicating those levels of folders are expanded in view at the moment. The white triangles indicate a collapsed folder.

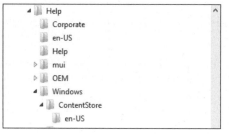

Figure 4-13:
The hierarchy of the
Windows
folder
system.

Browsing drives and folders

To open File Explorer, click the File Explorer shortcut pinned to the taskbar in Windows 8.1, or right-click the Start button and choose File Explorer. The File Explorer interface consists of two main panes. On the left is the navigation pane, which provides shortcut links to various locations you can browse and a folder tree of the entire local drive system (under This PC). On the right is the content pane, which shows the names of the files and folders in the currently selected location. At the top is an address bar, which shows the current location's path. See Figure 4-14.

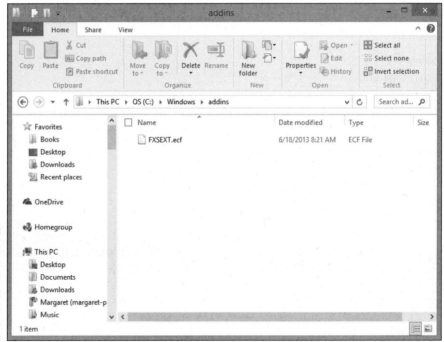

Figure 4-14: The address bar shows the current location's path.

To browse to a certain location, click the shortcut for it in the navigation pane. The Favorites section of the navigation pane contains shortcuts for the most common destinations; you can add your own shortcuts there too by dragging and dropping a folder onto that list. Below the shortcuts, there are icons for OneDrive, HomeGroup, and This PC.

If there's no shortcut readily available for the location you want to browse to, start by clicking This PC in the navigation pane, and then choose the drive, and then choose the folder, and so on, until you arrive at your destination.

You can also move between locations by using the triangle arrows on the address bar. Clicking one of them opens a drop-down list of other locations at that same level in the folder hierarchy. For example, in Figure 4-15, I'm clicking the arrow that follows the C: drive, and I'm seeing a list of other folders that are on that drive.

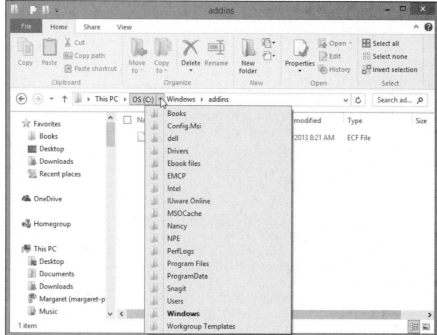

Figure 4-15:
Click the arrow after the C: drive to see what folders are on that drive.

Creating a new folder

Besides the folders already on your disk drives, you can also create your own folders. For example, you might create a folder called Books to store the data files for the books you are writing, or you might create a folder called Taxes to store the data files from your tax preparation software.

You can create the new folders anywhere you like. You might want to create them in the root directory of the C: drive, for example, so that they will appear on the top-level list of folders when you browse the C: drive's content. Alternatively, you might create them in the My Documents folder, or on some other drive, such as a USB flash drive you plan to share with others or take to another computer.

To create a new folder, use any of these methods:

- ✔ Click the New Folder button in the Quick Access Toolbar of the File Explorer window. The Quick Access Toolbar is the set of icons at the left end of the File Explorer window's title bar. Figure 4-16 points them out.

Figure 4-16:
The Quick Access Toolbar (top of figure).

- ✔ Press Ctrl+Shift+N.
- ✔ Right-click an empty area of the content pane, point to New, and click Folder.

Selecting files and folders

Windows has many commands you can issue to do things to files and folders, but first you must select the file(s) or folder(s) you want the commands to affect.

Selecting a single file or folder is simple: Just click it. The file or folder name becomes highlighted, indicating it is selected.

To select a group of contiguous items, click the first one, hold down the Shift key, and click the last one. Everything in-between becomes selected too, as well as the two items you clicked. To select a group of non-contiguous items, click the first one, hold down the Ctrl key, and click each individual item to include in the selection; then release the Ctrl key.

In File Explorer, you can select items only in the content pane, and only from the currently displayed location. So, for example, you can select three files at once that are in the same folder, but you cannot select three files that are in three different folders.

Changing the file listing view

You can change the way the files and folders appear in the content pane of File Explorer by selecting a different view. The Details view, which was shown in Figures 4-12 and 4-14, shows the file's name, its date modified, and its type. You can also choose to show them in List view (same as Detail but without the details), or as small, medium, large, or extra large icons.

In the lower-right corner of File Explorer are two icons for quickly switching to Details and Large Icons views. If you want some other view, click the View tab, and then select the desired view from the Layout group. See Figure 4-17.

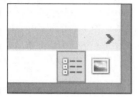

Figure 4-17: The icons for switching views.

Searching for files

If you can't easily locate the file(s) you seek by sorting and grouping, you might want to try searching for them. Searching creates a filter, and displays only files that meet the filter criteria.

You can perform a quick keyword search by clicking in the Search box (in the upper-right corner of File Explorer) and typing the word there that you want to find. Windows will search not only the file and folder names, but also within files, and if you have a Microsoft email program such as Outlook, it will search within email messages and contacts too.

If you want more control over the search, click in the Search box and then click the Search tab. (The Search tab becomes available when you click in the Search box.) On the Search tab, you'll find options for specifying where to search and what properties the found content must have (such as date modified, size, or type of file).

Copying or moving a file or folder

You can move and copy files freely from location to location. However, be careful in doing so because if you move the files that an app needs to run, the app won't work anymore. That includes Windows itself too; if you move any files out of the Windows folder, Windows might decide not to work anymore too. When you aren't sure whether a file is needed in its current location in order for something to function, your best bet is to copy it rather than move it.

Data files, on the other hand, are generally safe to either move or copy. Any files you have created yourself in an app can be moved or copied anywhere you like without any adverse effects to the program.

There are many different ways to move or copy files and folders in Windows 8. The simplest is to just drag-and-drop the item(s) where you want them.

You have to have two File Explorer windows open at once to drag-and-drop between locations — one for the original location and one for the destination. To open an additional copy of File Explorer, hold down Shift as you click the File Explorer icon, or as you double-click a folder in an existing File Explorer window. For some locations, you can also right-click a shortcut to the location and choose Open in New Window.

Does drag-and-drop move, or does it copy? That all depends on where you are drag-and-dropping to and from. If going from one location to another on the same disk drive (that is, the same drive letter), drag-and-drop moves. If going to a different disk drive, drag-and-drop copies. If you want something other than the default behavior, you can get it, though: To ensure a move, hold down Shift as you drag. To ensure a copy, hold down Ctrl as you drag.

You can also use the Clipboard to move and copy. The Windows Clipboard is a temporary storage area in memory. When you issue a Cut command, you move the selection to the Clipboard; when you issue a Copy command, you copy the selection to the Clipboard. Then you display the destination location and issue the Paste command.

Yet another way to move and copy is with the Move To and Copy To buttons on the Home tab. Select the items to be moved or copied, and then use one of these buttons to select a destination location from among recently viewed locations, or click Choose location to select a location not on the list.

Deleting and recovering files

Here are some ways to delete a file or folder (or a group of them, if you've selected multiples):

✔ Press the Delete key.

✔ Drag the selection to the Recycle Bin icon on the desktop.

✔ Right-click the selection and click Delete.

✔ Click the Delete command on the Home tab.

Deleting a file removes it from the location where it is stored. Depending on your system settings, it may not be gone forever, though; by default, deleted files on the hard disk drive go to the Recycle Bin, a temporary holding area. You can retrieve deleted files from the Recycle Bin at any time. The Recycle Bin retains deleted files until you empty the bin, delete specific files from the bin, or run out of room on your hard disk.

Using a Home Network

Networking: *it's a good thing*, to borrow a phrase from Martha Stewart. Networked computers can share files and printers with one another, and can share an Internet connection. You can also use your network to share music and video files between computers, transfer TV shows from your home theater system to your PC (with the right software to do so), and access your handheld and gaming devices from your computers.

A *network* is a group of computers and other devices that can share data with one another. There are many types of networks, from very small to very large. A network in which all the computers are physically located in the same place is a *local area network (LAN)*; a network in which the computers are geographically spread out is a *wide area network (WAN)*. If you create a network in your own home or office, it will likely be a LAN.

Some use cables to make the connections (*wired networks*); others use radio waves or infrared (*wireless networks*). Your network can consist of either wired or wireless connections or a combination of the two.

The most common technology for computer networking today is called *Ethernet*. It's so common that you can generally assume that any computer network you encounter is Ethernet unless told otherwise. The term Ethernet technically refers to both wired and wireless types, but in popular usage, the term Ethernet has come to mean the wired type, whereas the wireless type has come to be called *Wi-Fi*.

There are actually several other types of networks besides Ethernet you may encounter, although you might not think of them as networks. If you connect a Bluetooth headset to a cell phone, for example, you've just created a Bluetooth network. And if you access the Internet on a smartphone or tablet via your cell phone provider's service, you're participating in a 3G or 4G network.

Big businesses do networking on a large scale, with certain computers set aside to be *servers* — that is, to provide services to the other computers, rather than being used by an individual person. The computers that individual people use are called *clients* in that environment, and that type of network is known as *client/server*.

The type of network you will probably want for your own home, though, is one in which each computer is used by an individual, and there aren't any servers. This type of network is called a *workgroup*, or a *peer to peer (P2P) network*.

Assessing your current network

Your computer may already be connected to a network. If you already have Internet connectivity on your PC, and there are multiple PCs in your household that all share that connection, your network is probably already good to go.

Take a moment to identify your current networking and Internet equipment. Find your broadband modem, to start with: that's the box with the flashing lights that delivers your Internet service (via cable, DSL, satellite, or some other method). The broadband modem is probably connected to another box, also with flashing lights. That's the router. Sometimes the router and the broadband modem are a single, dual-purpose device, so you might not have two separate boxes.

Each of your computing devices connects to the router, either with a cable (wired access) or wirelessly. If you have a wired connection, then you have an Ethernet cable that plugs into your computer. An Ethernet cable, used for wired Ethernet connections, looks like a telephone cable but it's thicker, and the plug is slightly wider. The other end of the cable looks the same, and plugs into your router.

Look in the notification area for a Network icon, and then point the mouse at it to see a pop-up message telling you your current connection status. The more white bars, the stronger the connection. Point to the icon and read the tooltip, as in Figure 4-18.

Figure 4-18: Pointing to the icon brings up a tooltip.

You may see one of these messages:

- ✔ **Internet Access:** You have an Internet connection.
- ✔ **No Internet Access:** You have local network access, but no Internet. That probably means you don't have an Internet service hooked up to your router, or that the one you have isn't working.

✔ **Not connected — Connections are available:** There are wireless networks available, but you haven't connected to one yet. Along with this message, you may see a star on the network icon.

✔ **Not connected — No connections are available:** Your computer can't find any networks to connect to. There may not be any, or your computer's wireless network adapter may be disabled or malfunctioning. Along with this message, you may see a red X on the network icon.

For a wired connection, there's no need to do anything to enable the connection in Windows; the connection begins when you plug in the cable. For a wireless network, you must connect to the network — at least the first time. You can indicate that you want this connection to be reestablished automatically whenever you're in that network's range, so you have to manually connect only once.

Setting up network hardware

If you failed to detect an existing network in the previous section, you might need to buy some hardware and create one. To create a network, you'll need the following:

✔ An *Ethernet adapter* (wired) or *Wi-Fi adapter* (wireless) in every computer that will participate in the network. Most computers have some type of built-in adapter. Desktop PCs usually have the wired type, and all types of portables usually have the wireless type.

✔ A *router*, which is a box into which you connect each of the computers, either with a cable or wirelessly with Wi-Fi. If you have some wireless devices to include in your network, get a wireless router. (Wireless routers support a limited number of wired connections too.)

A router has several ports on it. The one that looks different from the other (different color, separated from the others, or in some other way, and possibly labeled WAN or Modem) is for your Internet connection. The rightmost port in Figure 4-19 is the different one, for example. Run an Ethernet cable (which probably came with the router) from your broadband modem to the router to share the Internet connection with all the computers on the network. The other ports are for wired network connections; connect any computers that have wired network adapters to these ports. If it's a wireless router, it may also have an antenna on it, enabling wireless devices to connect with the router.

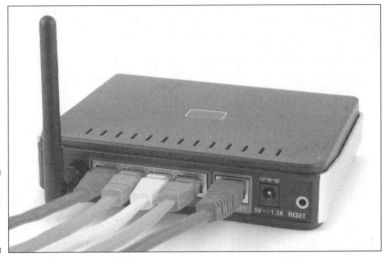

Figure 4-19:
Routers
have mul-
tiple ports.

A wireless router won't have any security set up initially; you'll need to do that yourself if you want it. Security prevents others from using your wireless connection without your permission. If you plan on sharing files on your local network, you will want security. Follow the steps in the manual that came with the router to enable it. If you have a choice of types, choose WPA2 with AES. Make a note of the password you assign when you set up the security.

Connect each computer to the router in some way — either with a cable or by using a wireless connection through the computer's operating system.

Connecting a computer to a wireless network

With a wired connection, once you run the cable to the router, you're good to go. With a wireless connection, however, you have to establish the connection manually (at least the first time). In Windows 8.1, here's how to connect to a wireless network:

1. **In the notification area on the desktop, locate the wireless networking icon, as shown in Figure 4-18.**

2. **Click the wireless networking icon. A pane appears listing all the available wireless network connections, as in Figure 4-20.**

   The ones with a shield and an exclamation point on them are open networks (no security).

Figure 4-20:
A list of
available
network
connections.

3. **Click the desired network; a Connect button appears.**

4. **(Optional) Select the Connect Automatically check box. If you do so, Windows will reestablish this connection automatically in the future, so you won't have to go through these steps again.**

5. **Click the Connect button.**

6. **If prompted for the network password, type it and press Enter.**

7. **Click away from the panel to close it.**

After perhaps a minute of setup, you are connected to the wireless network —
or a message appears that you can't connect, along with a Help Me Solve
Connection Problems hyperlink. Click that to troubleshoot if needed.

If your network connection isn't working, for whatever reason, right-click the wireless networking icon in the notification area and choose Troubleshoot Problems. Then follow the prompts to use a Windows troubleshooting utility.

Getting better wireless signal strength

A typical wireless router can transmit signals throughout a 100-meter radius when you set it up indoors. Walls and floors, especially thick ones like those in older homes, decrease that range significantly.

Here are some tips for wireless router placement to help optimize signal strength throughout your house:

- **Closer is better.** Place the router as close as possible to the rooms where you use computers with wireless network access the most often.

- **Don't put the router in a closet.** Remember, walls degrade signal strength, and a closet is just another layer of wall barrier.

- **Experiment with antenna positions.** If your router has antenna that rotate, try different angles to see which one works best. You can also buy an antenna booster kit to increase the effectiveness of your antenna.

- **Place the router higher up to possibly get a better signal strength.** Try placing the router on a tall bookshelf or on top of your refrigerator.

- **Keep the router away from any other devices that also use RF (radio frequency) signals.** Cordless phones, baby monitors, and wireless stereo speakers are RF devices. Don't locate the router near a microwave oven because when the oven is operating, it can interfere with the RF signal.

Sharing files and folders on a network

If you want to share your personal folders on the network (Documents, Pictures, and so on), an easy way to do so is to create a Homegroup. Homegroup is a feature of Windows 7 and higher that enables you to quickly create a small trusted network of local computers. Any computer on your network can initiate the Homegroup. Then other computers can join the Homegroup by typing the password (automatically generated when the Homegroup is created).

Being part of a Homegroup is optional; you don't need a Homegroup to share files and printers on your network. Only Windows 7 and Windows 8 computers can be part of a Homegroup, and if you have both of those on the same network, you must create the Homegroup from one of the Windows 8 computers.

Follow these steps to create a Homegroup on a Windows 8.1 computer:

1. **Right-click the networking icon in the notification area and choose Network and Sharing Center.**

2. **In the lower-left corner of the screen that appears, click the HomeGroup hyperlink.**

3. **If you are not already a member of a Homegroup, you will see either a Create button (if there is no Homegroup) or a Join Now button (if there is already a Homegroup on your network). Click whichever one appears to begin the process.**

4. **Click Next to access the Share with Other Homegroup members list.**

5. **Open the Permissions drop-down list for each library or folder to be shared and choose Shared or Not Shared. See Figure 4-21.**

6. **Click Next.**

7. **If prompted for the Homegroup password, type it. You can get the password by going to any PC that is already in the Homegroup, following steps 1–2, and then clicking View or printing the Homegroup password.**

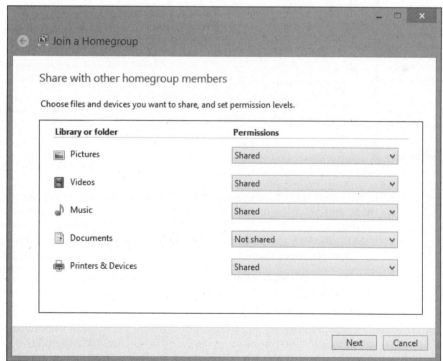

Figure 4-21:
Choose
Shared or
Not Shared
from the
drop-down
box.

You can also share individual folders with your Homegroup. To do so, right-click any folder in File Explorer and choose Share With, and then select Homegroup (view and edit) for full privileges, or select Homegroup (view) for read-only access. See Figure 4-22.

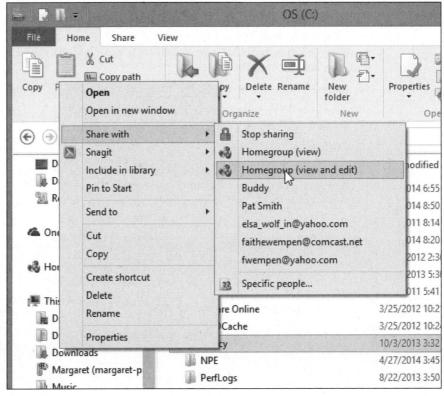

Figure 4-22:
Share a
Homegroup
for full
privileges
or read-only
access.

If you aren't using the Homegroup feature, you can share a folder by following these steps:

1. **Right-click the folder in File Explorer, point to Share With, and click Specific People.**

2. **To share it with everyone on your network, type** `Everyone` **in the text box and then click Add.** Then click Everyone on the Name list and choose a permission level (Read/Write or Read). See Figure 4-23.

    Or, to share with an individual user, click that user's name on the Name list and then choose a permission level (Read/Write or Read).

3. **Click Share.**

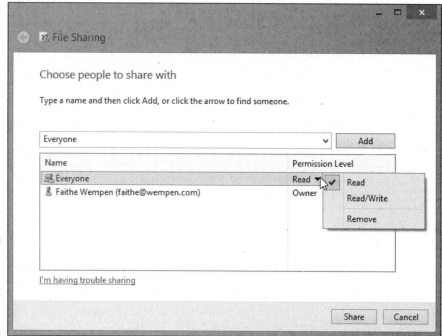

Figure 4-23:
Choose who
to share
your files
with.

Browsing other people's shared resources

When a network connection is established, you can access the network loca-tions that have been made available to you by other users. These can include folders on a dedicated file server (in a large company, for example) or folders on individual PCs that the owners have chosen to share. The network loca-tions available depend on the PC's network connectivity. Depending on your network type, you may see PCs, network storage devices, network-aware printers, media devices, and other resources.

One way to access a network location is to browse for it. You can do this by opening File Explorer and then clicking the Network link in the Navigation pane; a list of computers appears that are part of your workgroup or domain. From there, you can see what a computer is sharing by double-clicking the computer's icon.

Using a shared printer

If you have a local printer (that is, a printer that is directly attached to your computer), you can share it with other people on your network, so that they can send print jobs to the printer just as if the printer were locally connected.

Two types of printers can be available on a network: those that are truly network-aware, and those that are shared with an individual PC. A network-aware printer can be connected directly to the network's router, so that it doesn't rely on any particular PC being active in order to be available. A shared printer is dependent on the PC to which it's attached. When the PC sharing is turned off or disconnected from the network, the printer becomes unavailable to network users.

The Add Printers utility enables you to install either local or network printers. If you choose to install a network printer, it scans the network and presents you with a list of the available printers, both network-aware ones and shared ones. You can tell the difference because a network-aware printer has an IP address (a numeric address) listed for it; whereas a shared printer has a network path containing the name of the PC to which it's attached. To access the Add Printers utility, open the Control Panel, and under the Hardware and Sound heading, click View Devices and Printers.

Sharing your printer with others

You can make your own local printer available to other network users so that they can set it up on their PCs. A shared printer shows a sharing symbol on its icon, the same as with a shared folder.

If the other network users also run the same version of Windows, the needed driver is copied to their PCs automatically when they set up the printer. If other people on the network have other versions of Windows and would like to use the shared printer, however, you must make drivers available for those versions, or those users must supply their own drivers for the printer.

To share your printer, open the Control Panel, and under the Hardware and Sound heading, click View Devices and Printers. Right-click the printer to share, choose Properties, and click the Sharing tab. On the Sharing tab, choose Share this Printer. See Figure 4-24. You can change the share name if you like, or you can just click OK to share using the default name.

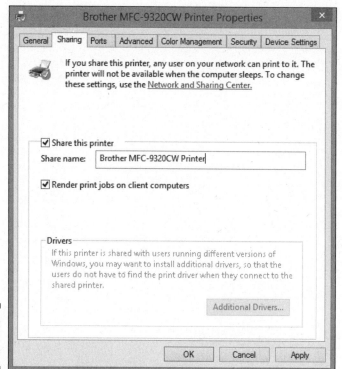

Figure 4-24:
Sharing a
printer.

Part II
The Online Experience

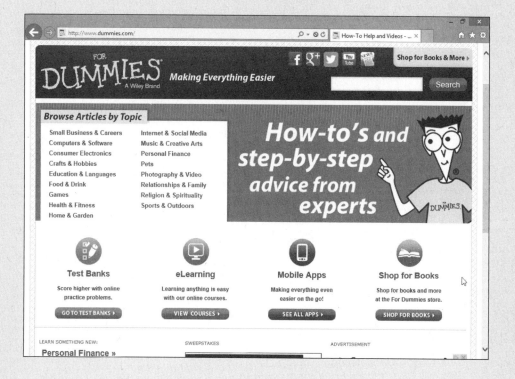

Check out www.dummies.com/extras/digitalliteracy for tips on how to shop smart online.

In this part . . .

- ✔ Learn about your options for connecting a computer to the Internet and choose the best method for your situation
- ✔ Find out how the web works and how to use web browser software to explore it
- ✔ Set up your computer to send and receive email and learn how to compose and manage messages
- ✔ Learn how cloud-based applications and storage work and how they can benefit you

Chapter 5

Understanding Internet Basics

· ·

In This Chapter

▶ Understanding what the Internet is

▶ Exploring different types of Internet connections

▶ Setting up an Internet connection

▶ Troubleshooting Internet connectivity

· ·

*F*or many people, going online is the major reason to buy a computer. You can use the Internet to check stock quotes, shop, play interactive games with others, and file your taxes, for example. The Internet can provide wonderful ways to keep in touch with family and friends located around the country or on the other side of the world via email or instant messaging. You can share photos of your family or connect with others who share your hobbies or interests.

But before you begin all those activities, it helps to understand some basics about the Internet and how it works.

This chapter helps you understand what the Internet and World Wide Web are, as well as some basics about connecting to the Internet and how to troubleshoot problems with your Internet connection.

What Is the Internet?

The "Internet," "links," the "web," the "cloud" . . . people and the media bounce around many online-related terms these days, and folks sometimes use them incorrectly. Your first step in getting familiar with the Internet is to understand what some of these terms mean.

The *Internet* is a large network of computers that contain information and technology tools that anybody with an Internet connection can access. The Internet is the "big tent" under which all the individual technologies reside.

One of the main features of the Internet is the *World Wide Web* (or web for short), a huge collection of documents with links to one another. An individual document is a *web page*. A related group of web pages published by the same person or company is a *website*. To get around on the web, you use an application called a *browser*. Browsers offer tools to help you navigate from website to website and from one web page to another. Chapter 6 covers the web in more detail.

Websites have many purposes: For example, a website can be informational, function as a retail store, or host social networking communities where people can exchange ideas and thoughts. When you conduct business online, such as buying or selling items, it's known as *e-commerce*. E-commerce includes business-to-business transactions such as banks exchanging data with one another, business-to-consumer transactions like a person buying something at an online store, and consumer-to-consumer transactions like an individual selling an item on an online auction site or creating a classified ad.

A *cloud* is a password-protected area of the web in which registered users can safely store and retrieve files, run applications, and look up information that may not be available to the public. For example, Microsoft's OneDrive service, which is free to anyone who signs up for a Microsoft account, offers free, secure online file storage, as well as access to web-based versions of popular Microsoft applications such as Microsoft Word, Excel, and Outlook. Clouds are becoming more and more popular these days; you'll learn more about them in Chapter 8.

An *intranet* is an information storage and retrieval system that works on the same technologies as the Internet does, but is private inside a certain company. Employees can access private company information on the company's own servers using the familiar interface of a web browser.

Besides the web, the Internet also enables several other types of online activity. For example, you can send and receive email, participate in video conferencing, and exchange instant text messages with others. You will learn about some of these technologies in Chapters 7 and 8.

Figure 5-1 shows the relationships between some of the terms you just learned, so you can keep them straight in your mind. Notice that technologies like email and instant messaging overlap somewhat with the web. That's because they are essentially separate from the web technologically, but there are optional web interfaces available for them that make them seem like part of the web.

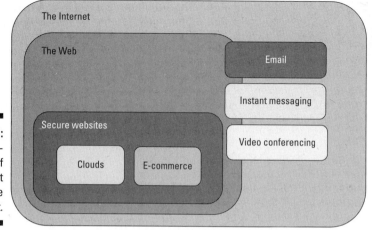

Figure 5-1:
The rela-
tionship of
different
parts of the
Internet.

Exploring Different Types of Internet Connections

Before you can connect to the Internet for the first time, you have to have certain hardware in place and choose your *Internet service provider* (also referred to as an *ISP* or simply a *provider*). An ISP is a company that owns dedicated computers (called *servers*) that you use to access the Internet. ISPs charge a monthly fee for this service.

You can choose a type of connection to go online. The type of connection you want determines which companies you can choose from to provide the service. For example, a DSL connection might come through your phone company, whereas a cable connection is available through your cable TV company. Not every type of connection is necessarily available in every area, so check with phone, cable, and local Internet providers rather than national or international providers to find out your options and costs (some offer discounts to AARP members, for example).

Here are the most common types of connections, each of which offers pros and cons in terms of the quality of the signal and potential service interruptions depending on the company and your locale, so do your homework before signing on the dotted line:

✔ **Digital subscriber line (DSL):** This service is delivered through your phone land line, but your phone is available to you to make calls even when you're connected to the Internet. DSL is a form of broadband communication, which may use phone lines and fiber-optic cables for transmission. You have to subscribe to a broadband service (check with your phone company) and pay a monthly fee for access.

- ✔ **Cable:** You may instead go through your local cable company to get your Internet service via the cable that brings your TV programming rather than your phone line. This is another type of broadband service, and it's relatively fast. Check with your cable company for monthly fees.

- ✔ **Satellite:** Especially in rural areas, satellite Internet providers may be your only option. This requires that you install a satellite dish. DISH and Comcast are two providers of satellite connections to check into.

- ✔ **Wireless hotspots:** If you take a wireless-enabled laptop computer, tablet, or smart phone with you on a trip, you can piggyback on a connection somebody else has made. You will find wireless hotspots in many public places, such as airports, cafes, and hotels. If you're in range of such a hotspot, your computer usually finds the connection automatically, making Internet service available to you for free or for a fee.

- ✔ **Cell phone networks:** If you use a smart phone to connect to the Internet, you can access the Internet through your phone provider's 3G or 4G network. Some tablets also can connect this way, and you can buy add-on devices that allow other computers to use a cell phone network too. And if you need Wi-Fi access for other devices where there is no wireless hotspot, you may be able to create a temporary wireless hotspot using your phone.

  Unless you have an unlimited data plan on your cell phone, be careful of using your cell phone service for Internet access because you can easily go over your data plan limit and be subject to additional charges.

- ✔ **Dialup:** With a dialup connection, you use a dialup *modem* to connect to an Internet service provider using your home phone line. With this type of connection, you can't use a phone line for phone calls while you're connected to the Internet. This is the slowest connection method and is most people's last resort.

Internet connections have different *bandwidths* (speeds) that depend partially on your computer's capabilities and partially on the connection you get from your provider. Faster speeds allow you to send data faster: for example, to download a photo to your computer. In addition, web pages and images display faster. Before you choose a provider, it's important to understand how faster connection speeds can benefit you.

Dialup connection speeds run at the low end, about 56 kilobits per second, or Kbps. Most broadband connections today are around 500 to 600 Kbps. If you have a slower connection, a file might take minutes to upload. (For example, you upload a file you're attaching to an email.) This same operation might take only seconds at a higher speed.

Broadband (which means high-speed) services typically offer different plans that provide different access speeds. These plans can give you savings if you're economy minded and don't mind the lower speeds, or offer you much better speeds if you're willing to pay for them.

Depending on your type of connection, you'll need different hardware.

- ✔ A broadband connection such as cable or DSL requires a *broadband modem* designed for that type of service and a cable TV or telephone line. The provider will usually rent you a modem, so you don't have to buy it.

- ✔ If you need to use dialup service, you'll need a *dialup modem* and a telephone line. Some computers have a built-in dialup modem (sometimes called a *telephony modem*); you can also buy them separately.

If you want to share the Internet connection with multiple computers in your home, you will also need a router (unless you have a broadband modem with router features built into it). Each computer in your home will then connect to the router to get Internet access, either via an Ethernet cable or wirelessly.

Each computer will need some type of network adapter. Many computers have that built into them, either wired (more common on a desktop PC) or wireless (more common on a notebook, tablet, or smart phone). The wired type uses an *RJ-45 jack*, also called an Ethernet jack, which looks like a telephone connector except it's wider.

If this all sounds like Greek to you, review your computer's user guide for information about its networking capabilities, and then visit a computer or major office supply store and ask representatives for their advice about your specific hardware.

Many providers offer free or low-cost setup when you open a new account. If you're not technical by nature, consider taking advantage of this when you sign up.

Setting Up an Internet Connection

If you have a properly configured broadband modem and router (for example, one set up by the installer when you order cable or DSL service), you might not have to do anything to set up an Internet connection. You can just connect your computer to the modem with an Ethernet cable and the Internet automatically becomes available to you. You can open a browser and view a few web pages to confirm that your service is working.

Or, for a wireless connection, you can just connect your computer wirelessly to the router (or modem with router capabilities). To do that, follow these steps in Windows 8.1:

1. **In the notification area (the icons near the clock in the lower right corner of the screen), click the wireless networking icon, as shown in Figure 5-2.**

   The Networks pane appears, as in Figure 5-3.

Figure 5-2:
Click the
wireless
networking
icon.

2. **If one of the wireless networks says Connected under it, as in Figure 5-3, you are already connected to the wireless network. If not, click the wireless network you want to connect to.**

   Networks with a shield icon on them are unsecure networks. Anyone may connect to them. Networks without the shield are secure and require a password.

3. **If the network you connect to requires a password, and this is the first time you have connected to it, a prompt appears. Enter the network password and press Enter.**

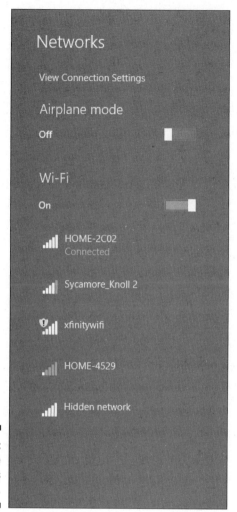

Networks

View Connection Settings

Airplane mode

Off

Wi-Fi

On

HOME-2C02
Connected

Sycamore_Knoll 2

xfinitywifi

HOME-4529

Hidden network

Figure 5-3:
The
Networks
pane.

Troubleshooting an Internet Connection

If you can't view web pages or send and receive email, your Internet connection is probably to blame.

This section walks you through some troubleshooting help, but there's one important thing to know upfront: Sometimes it's not your equipment's fault that the Internet isn't working. Service providers can have their own problems that result in temporary outages, ranging from a few seconds to a few hours. In addition, sometimes the data traffic on the Internet, or on the segment of it that affects your service, gets bottlenecked, and things run more slowly than usual. If you just wait it out for a few hours, a lot of times the problems go away.

That said, here are some things to try when troubleshooting, in the approximate order to try them:

- ✔ Restart your computer.

- ✔ Power-cycle the modem (and router, if they are separate units). That means to turn the device off or unplug it for 30 seconds, and then turn it back on again. Some modems take several minutes to fully come back up after a power cycle; this is normal.

- ✔ If you are using a wired connection, check to make sure the cables are plugged in snugly.

- ✔ If you are using a wireless connection, check to make sure that your computer's wireless networking feature is turned on. On some notebooks, there's a button somewhere near the keyboard that toggles the wireless networking on/off. If you accidentally press that button, your wireless turns off. If you look for the wireless icon in the notification area and it has a red X on it, as in Figure 5-4, that's a pretty good clue that the wireless networking is turned off on the device.

Figure 5-4:
Wireless networking is turned off for this device.

- ✔ Right-click the networking icon in the notification area and choose Troubleshoot Problems. Then follow the prompts to walk through a Windows Network Diagnostics utility, shown in Figure 5-5, which will ask you questions about your problem and try various fixes.

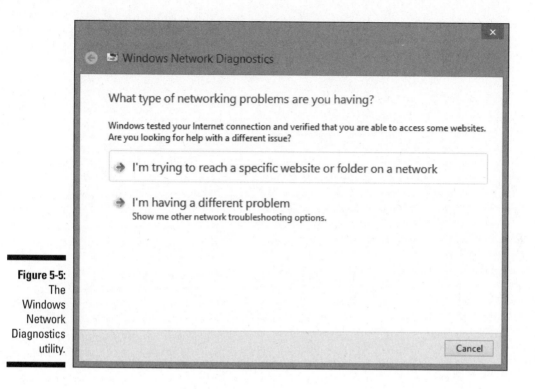

Figure 5-5:
The
Windows
Network
Diagnostics
utility.

Chapter 6

Working with the Web

A *browser* is a program that you can use to move from one web page to another, but you can also use it to perform searches for information and images. Most browsers, such as Internet Explorer (IE) and Mozilla Firefox, are available for free. Macintosh computers come with a browser called Safari preinstalled with the operating system.

In this chapter, you discover the ins and outs of using the web. You'll be introduced to Internet Explorer, Windows 8's default browser. You'll find out how to browse the web, go to a certain address, save your favorites, and use secure sites. You also discover how web content is created and published.

Discovering How the Web Works

First, I want to get some vocabulary out of the way. The *web* is a part of the Internet; it is a system of interconnected pages of information stored on publicly accessible servers. A *web page* is a document created in a programming language known as *Hypertext Markup Language (HTML)*. It's stored on a *web server* somewhere on the Internet, and it has an address, called a *Uniform Resource Locator (URL),* that can be used to access it. (You will learn more about URLs in the next section.)

A collection of related web pages, such as all the pages for a particular company's web presence, is known as a *website*.

A *browser* is software that enables you to display web pages on your computer. Internet Explorer is the browser that comes free with Windows. That's the browser you will work with in this chapter.

One way to view a particular web page is to type its URL into the browser. Suppose you have the URL of a web page you want to view. Maybe you got the address from a magazine article or a billboard, or a friend sent it to you. You type the URL into the browser's Address bar and press Enter, and the browser goes out to the Internet, retrieves the page, and displays it for you. See Figure 6-1.

Figure 6-1:
Type a URL into the browser to view a web page.

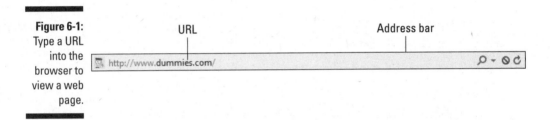

URL   Address bar

http://www.dummies.com/

Another way to access web pages is to follow a *hyperlink*, which is a clickable link to another web page. A hyperlink can be either text or a graphic. When you hover the mouse pointer over a hyperlink, the pointer turns into a pointing hand, indicating it's over a clickable hyperlink, as shown in Figure 6-2. Sometimes text hyperlinks are underlined or in a different color from the rest of the text to make them more obvious. You can click a hyperlink on one page to move to another page, and then click a hyperlink on *that* page to move to another, and so on, bouncing your way across the web from link to link.

Figure 6-2:
Your mouse pointer turns into a hand when it's hovering over a hyperlink.

Hyperlink

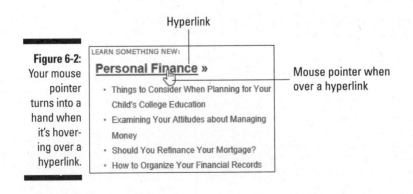

LEARN SOMETHING NEW:

Personal Finance »

· Things to Consider When Planning for Your Child's College Education
· Examining Your Attitudes about Managing Money
· Should You Refinance Your Mortgage?
· How to Organize Your Financial Records

Mouse pointer when over a hyperlink

Understanding Web Addresses

A web URL (address) looks something like this:

```
http://www.dummies.com/Section/Store.id-321213.html
```

Here's a breakdown of that:

- **http** stands for HyperText Transfer Protocol. It's a standard that governs how web content is transmitted.

- **www** stands for World Wide Web. This indicates that on the server you are going to be accessing, you want the section that contains the web content. This is sometimes called a *subdomain*.

- **dummies.com** is the *domain name*. That's the name of the website you are visiting.

- Everything that comes after the domain name is a path on the server to the content you want. For example, **Store.id-321213.html** is the filename containing the content you want, and **Section** is the folder in which it is stored.

- The forward slashes (/) in the address are separators.

Figure 6-3 summarizes all that as a quick reference.

Figure 6-3: The breakdown of a URL.

The last part of a domain name (the part after the last decimal point, like com in dummies.com) is called the *top-level domain*. There are only a limited number of top-level domains, and each one has a special meaning that describes the type of domain. For example, com is short for "commercial." Table 6-1 lists some of the most common top-level domains. You can use that information to tell at a glance what type of site a certain domain name represents.

Table 6-1	Top-Level Domains	
Domain	*Type*	*Site Type*
com	Commercial	Commercial businesses
net	Network-related	Commercial sites that deal in networking or the Internet itself
org	Organizations	Non-profit organizations
mil	Military	U.S. military
gov	Government	U.S. government
edu	School	Educational institutions of all levels
uk	United Kingdom	Sites located in the United Kingdom
ca	Canada	Sites located in Canada
Other country codes (there are many)	Country-specific	Sites located in the country represented by the code

Domain names are human-friendly versions of web addresses. They are easy to remember, and easy to understand. But behind the scenes, domain names have another face: a numeric one. Each domain name has an equivalent Internet Protocol (IP) address.

All across the Internet, there are special servers that translate between domain names and IP addresses. These are called *Domain Name Server (DNS) servers*. When your browser sends out the request over the Internet to get a particular page you've requested, a DNS server intercepts that request and looks up that domain name's IP address in a giant database. It then uses the IP address to route the request to the server that contains the requested information.

There are two kinds of IP addresses: IP version 4 (IPv4) and IP version 6 (IPv6). The Internet currently uses only IPv4 addresses, but at some point in the future, it's going to switch over to IPv6 addresses, a newer type of addressing that has more possible addresses.

An *IPv4 address* (pronounced *I-P-V-4*) is four numbers, each of which is between 0 and 255, separated by decimal places, like this:

```
203.55.28.4
```

An IPv6 address is six numbers, written in hexadecimal (base 16) numbering, separated by colons. Here's an example:

```
2001:0:9d38:6abd:287e:1e9c:9d23:4e72
```

You'll probably never need to know any more — or even that much — about IP addresses, unless you find yourself in the unfortunate position of trouble-shooting a network problem or talking to tech support for your Internet service provider. (Well, actually both of those situations do come up fairly frequently in life, so now you're equipped for those possibilities.)

Checking out Internet Explorer's Interface

Windows 8 contains two different versions of Internet Explorer (IE). One is accessed from the Start screen and has the tablet-style interface; the other is accessed from the desktop, and has the traditional desktop application interface. Here's how they differ:

- ✔ **Desktop IE:** This version is much like any other desktop application. It has an Address bar across the top of the screen, and buttons for accessing favorites and tools (see Figure 6-4).

- ✔ **Start screen IE:** This version was designed along the lines of Windows 8 apps (see Figure 6-5) with a few buttons and an address field along the bottom of the screen.

Figure 6-4: A web page in desktop Internet Explorer.

Figure 6-5:
A web page viewed in the Start screen version of IE.

In this chapter, all the examples and steps use the desktop version. It's good to know that the Start screen version exists, though, for three reasons. One, if you accidentally open it, you'll know what's going on, and won't panic. Two, if you are using a touchscreen device, you might find the Start screen version easier to use. Three, if you're using a Windows tablet device, the Start screen version is the only version available to you because Windows tablets don't include the desktop.

To start the desktop version of IE, click the IE icon that's pinned to the task-bar on the Windows desktop. It looks like a lowercase e, as shown in the bottom center of Figure 6-6.

Figure 6-6:
The Internet Explorer icon.

Internet Explorer icon

When you open IE, the *home page* appears, which is whatever page has been set to be your startup default. If you haven't changed it, it's `http://t.msn.com`, which is the MSN news site.

To choose a different home page, display the desired page and then click the Tool icon (the gear cog) in the upper right corner of the browser window, click Internet Options, and on the General tab of the Internet Options dialog box, click Use Current.

To display a specific page, enter its URL in the Address bar at the top of the window and then press Enter. See Figure 6-7. Or, to display a page from one of the hyperlinks on the home page, click the hyperlink.

URL   Address bar

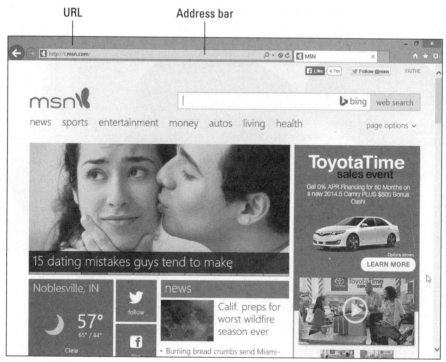

Figure 6-7: Access a page by typing its URL in the Address bar or clicking a hyperlink.

After you've navigated to a different page, you can click the Back button (the left-pointing arrow) to return to the previously viewed page. You can click the Back button as many times as there are pages to be gone back to. You can also click and hold the Back button to display a menu of previously viewed pages, and select from that menu, as in Figure 6-8. After you've used Back, the Forward button becomes available (the right-pointing arrow). You can click it to move forward again. If a page doesn't load correctly, you may need to reload it. You can do so by clicking the Refresh button at the right end of the Address bar, or by pressing the F5 key on the keyboard.

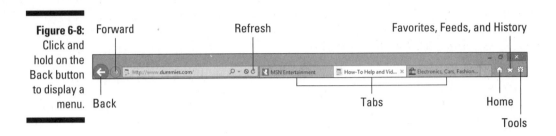

Figure 6-8: Click and hold on the Back button to display a menu.

Forward • Refresh • Favorites, Feeds, and History

Back • Tabs • Home • Tools

The three buttons in the upper right corner of the window, from left to right, are

- ✔ **Home:** Returns you to your Home page at any time.

- ✔ **View Favorites, Feeds, and History:** Opens a menu system with three tabs: Favorites, Feeds, and History. You'll discover more about this menu system later in the chapter.

- ✔ **Tools:** Open a menu of settings you can adjust for Internet Explorer.

Internet Explorer uses *tabs* to enable you to have more than one web page open at the same time. In Figure 6-7, there is only one tab open (MSN), but in Figure 6-8, there are three tabs open. You can switch back and forth between tabs by clicking the tab.

To open a new tab, click the New Tab button, which is the blank square to the right of the rightmost tab. You can also open a hyperlink in a new tab by right-clicking the hyperlink and choosing Open Link in New Tab.

When you are done with a tab, you can close it. To do so, click the X on the tab, or right-click the tab and choose Close Tab.

Performing Web Searches

You might occasionally have a specific address of a page you want to view, or you might stumble across a hyperlink that looks interesting to check out, but you will probably find the majority of the web sites you visit by doing searches.

A *search engine* is a web-based utility that searches a huge index of web page content based on keywords you specify. It then returns pages full of search results consisting of hyperlinks and brief descriptions of the sites they represent. There are many different search engines, each one owned by a large company with huge, powerful servers that maintain their databases. Performing the same search with different search engines will likely produce similar but not identical results.

One way to use a search engine is to display its web page and enter the desired keywords in the Search box on that page. For example, to use Google, one of the most popular search engines, go to `www.google.com/` and start your search from that page. Table 6-2 lists some popular search engines you may want to explore.

Table 6-2	Popular Search Engines
Search Engine	*URL*
Google	www.google.com
Bing	www.bing.com
Yahoo!	www.yahoo.com
AOL	www.aol.com
Ask	www.ask.com
Web Crawler	www.webcrawler.com
Dog Pile	www.dogpile.com

Internet Explorer has search capability built into its Address bar, so you don't have to visit a search engine's website in order to search. Simply type the desired keywords directly into the Address bar and press Enter, and IE will use your default search engine to perform the search.

 Unless you have changed it, Bing is the default search engine in Internet Explorer. To make a different search engine your default, click the down arrow on the Address bar to open its menu, and then click the Add button. On the web page that appears, choose another search engine add-on, and follow the prompt to install it. From that point on, you can switch default search engines by clicking a search engine icon at the bottom of the Address bar's menu.

Regardless of the interface you use for your search (that is, whether you go to a search website or search using the Address bar), your results will come back as a list. In Figure 6-9, for example, I've done a Bing search of rhubarb pie recipes.

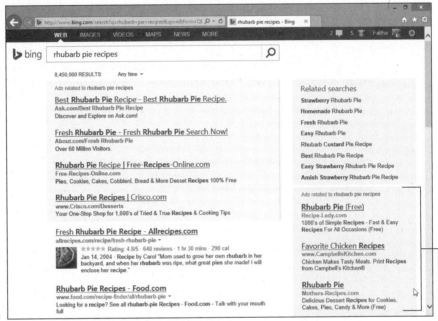

Figure 6-9:
Bing search
results.

Sponsored links

The search results appear in order of relevance, with the sites most relevant to your search at the top. However, the results will probably also contain ads, or *sponsored links*. These are links for sites that have paid the search engine company for high placement on the list. In Figure 6-8, for example, the sponsored links appear on the right. Not all search engines make such a clear distinction between the best results (most relevant to your search) and the ones where the most money has been paid for the placement.

To check out an entry, click its URL or title. Or, to open it in its own tab, right-click the hyperlink and choose Open in New Tab.

You might find that a search using only one or two keywords returns a huge number of results, so many that you could spend days wading through them. The key to smart web searching is to use many keywords to narrow down what you want. You can even type real-language sentences as searches, such as *What is the best dishwasher brand?*

Not all websites contain reliable and objective information, even those that purport to do so. Some sites may have a political or religious bias, or be designed to sell you a product or service. Be aware of the potential agendas of the site owners, and don't be fooled into believing that something is true just because it's on the web.

Some search engines allow you to use some special syntax for more control over your searches. For example, you might be able to enter - (a minus sign) before a word to have the search exclude that word. Say you want to find pages about badgers, but your search results keep turning up lot of pages devoted to the Wisconsin Badgers sports team. Using *badger -Wisconsin* would eliminate all results that featured the word *Wisconsin* in them. Table 6-3 lists some common advanced search syntax. Not all search engines support all the syntax listed.

Table 6-3	Syntax for Advanced Searching	
Syntax	*Description*	*Example*
Quotation marks	Put quotation marks around phrases to be found exactly as written	"Imagine all the people"
- (minus sign)	Excludes a keyword	-Wisconsin
NOT	Excludes a keyword	NOT Wisconsin
*	Represents an unknown value	"A * saved is a * earned"
OR	Searches for either of two words	Olympics 2014 OR 2016
.. (two periods)	Searches within a given range	cars $10,000..$15,000

Using a Secure Site

A *secure site* is one that uses encryption to guard the communication from being snooped on. Ordinarily, web traffic is quite unsecure, and anyone with the right spying software can wiretap your communications and steal any information you send, like passwords or credit card numbers. Communication with a secure site, though, scrambles the communication before sending it, and the receiving computer unscrambles it using an agreed-upon code.

Secure sites are useful for performing transactions online that contain personal information, such as bank account numbers and financial data. At a secure site, you log on using a username and password, and then any activities you do on that website after logging in are secure.

How do you tell if a site is secure? Look in the Address bar. A secure site will show a padlock symbol there, and instead of http, the URL will begin with https. Depending on the browser, the background of the Address bar may also appear green. See Figure 6-10.

Figure 6-10:
The URL of a
secure web-
site starts
with https.

Padlock

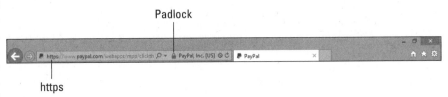

https

Viewing Your History

IE maintains a *history* of where you've been, so you can revisit a website that you've recently looked at.

There are two ways to look at history. One is to click the down arrow on the Address bar to see a drop-down list of recently visited sites. Then click the one you want to revisit. See Figure 6-11.

Figure 6-11:
Click the
down arrow
to see a list
of recently
visited sites.

The other is to click the View Favorites, Feeds, and History button (the star) in the upper right corner of the window. Then click the History tab to see a more complete history. You can click Today to see the sites you have visited today, click Last Week to see sites from last week, and so on. Figure 6-12 shows today's history from an example PC.

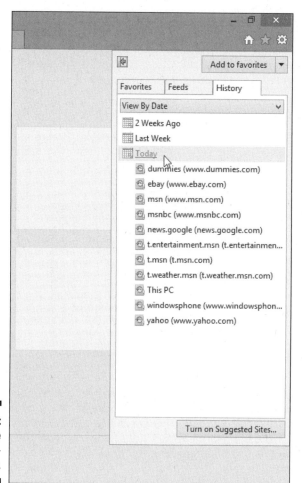

Figure 6-12:
An example
web brows-
ing history.

If you don't want others snooping to find out what sites you have visited, clear your history list. To do so, click the Tools button (the gear cog), point to Safety, and click Delete Browsing History. In the dialog box that appears, make sure the History check box is marked, and then click Delete. You can delete other types of stored information from this same dialog box, such as temporary Internet files, cookies, and passwords. When deciding what to delete, balance your need for privacy against the convenience of having the browser remember informa-tion for you so you don't have to retype it, like passwords and form data.

Saving and Organizing Favorites

If there's a site you intend to revisit, you may want to save it to IE's Favorites folder so you can easily go there again.

While you are viewing the page to save, click the View Favorites, Feeds, and History button (the star) in the upper right corner of the window. Then click the Add to Favorites button. The Add a Favorite dialog box opens, as shown in Figure 6-13. Change the name in the Name box if you want; this name will appear on your Favorites list. Then click Add.

Figure 6-13:
Save frequently visited websites as favorites.

Notice in Figure 6-13 that you have a choice of where to store the favorite. By default, the Create In setting is Favorites, which means the top level of organization of the Favorites list. But you can also create and use folders to further organize your favorites into categories. Choose a folder from the Create In list when adding a favorite, or click the New Folder button there to create a new folder for it.

Then, when you want to reopen one of your favorites, click the View Favorites, Feeds, and History button again, click the Favorites tab (if needed), and click the desired favorite to revisit. If a favorite is stored in a folder, click the folder to open it. In Figure 6-14, the Computers folder contains two favorites, for example.

You can keep the Favorites list open all the time if you like. Open up the list and then click the Pin the Favorites Center icon, which is the green arrow icon in the upper left corner of the pane.

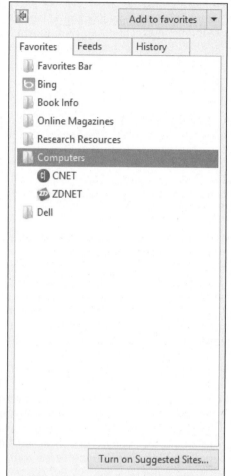

Figure 6-14:
You can
organizes
favorites in
folders.

If you want to change the organization of the Favorites list, click the down
arrow on the Add to Favorites button to open a menu, and then click
Organize Favorites. The Organize Favorites dialog box opens. From here, you
can move, rename, and delete favorites.

Creating Your Own Web Content

After you've been using the web for a while, you might think to yourself,
"Wow, it seems like anyone can create a website." And you're absolutely right.
Anyone can. It's not hard. (It's hard to create a large, professional-looking
site, but that's not what we're talking about here.)

As I mentioned earlier in the chapter, web pages are created in HyperText Markup Language (HTML). It's a very simple programming language that marks up plain text with bracketed codes called *tags* that inform the browser how to format it. For example, the <i> tag makes text italic, so here's how you would write the sentence "I had a *great* time."

```
I had a <i>great</i> time.
```

Most tags are two-sided, meaning there's an opening tag and a closing tag and the text to affect is placed between them. In the above example, </i> is the closing tag.

There are hundreds of tags in HTML, but there's really only about a dozen that you need to create a simple web page, like <p> for paragraphs, <h1> for headings, and <ul> for bulleted lists.

For more information about HTML, check out the book *Beginning HTML5 and CSS3 For Dummies* by Ed Tittel and Chris Minnick (Wiley).

You can write HTML pages in a plain text editor like Notepad, but hardly anyone ever does that anymore because there are so many good applications that create web pages much more easily, such as Dreamweaver and Web Easy Professional. These programs shield you from having to create the tags yourself; they work a lot like a word processing program such as Word.

After you create the page, what then? Here's the basic process:

1. Find a server that will host it. Your ISP may offer some server space for free with your Internet service, and there are lots of free hosting sites on the web. If you want to really get serious about it, you can also register your own domain name (it's not that expensive, only about $20 a year) and pay an online *hosting company* to host your site for you.

2. Upload your file(s) to the server. You can do this using the web-based interface of the company you've chosen to host your site, or you can use a file transfer utility program.

3. Let your friends and family know the URL of your uploaded page, or wait for the world to discover it on their own.

Want something even easier than that? There are many ways you can publish your own content online without having to create the web pages yourself. Hundreds of places will host your content for free, as long as you don't mind using their own format. (And, if you're new at this, using a predesigned format with easy input may actually be quite a relief for you.)

Here are some sites where you can put up your own content for free:

- ✔ **WordPress:** A blogging site, suitable for online journaling. They have free accounts, but for a small fee, you can get an account with more features and flexibility.

- ✔ **Pinterest:** You can create your own online bulletin board here and pin interesting things to it for your friends to check out.

- ✔ **Facebook:** This large social networking site is great for posting short updates, pictures, and status messages for friends and family to share.

- ✔ **Weebly:** This site lets you create your own web pages using a proprietary interface and host them for free.

- ✔ **OneDrive:** Microsoft's free file storage system enables you to make files available to the public or to certain invited users. If you have files you want to share with others but they aren't in web page format, this may be your simplest route.

Chapter 7

Sending and Receiving Email

An email program is a tool you can use to send messages to others. These messages are delivered to the recipient's email inbox, usually within seconds. You can attach files to email messages and even put images within the message body. You can get an email account through your Internet provider or through free email sites such as Yahoo! and Outlook.com.

In this chapter, you discover some email basics, including how to get an email account and what settings you need to set it up in an email application. You also find out how to send and receive email using the Mail app that's included with Windows 8.1. If you want to use a different email application than that, no worries; you learn some tricks for setting up email accounts in any email application too.

Understanding Email

Electronic mail, or email for short, is an online message delivery system. It delivers private messages to individuals and groups.

Email addresses and mail servers

To participate, you need an *email address*. You can get this for free from your Internet service provider or from one of the many free web-based email services such as Gmail, Yahoo! Mail, and Outlook.com. Your email address is unique in all the world, like your postal address or phone number is unique.

An email address might look like this:

myemailname@myprovider.net

The first part (myemailname) is your user name on the mail server. The @ sign indicates the break between the username and the domain name. Everything after the @ sign is the domain name, which indicates the mail server.

Email is quick, with messages usually being delivered within a minute or two of sending, but it's not instantaneous communication like texting and instant messaging. Email relies on *mail servers*, much like postal mail delivery relies on the local post offices at each end of the transaction. When you send email, it goes to the mail server belonging to the company that issued you your email address (for example, Comcast or Google). That mail server forwards it to the recipient's mail server, where it is stored until the recipient logs in and picks it up.

Most mail servers provide a web-based interface that you can use to send and receive mail. If you use the web interface, your mail is available from any computer, as long as you have Internet access.

You can also send and receive mail using an *email client*, which is an application that sends and receives email. Microsoft Outlook is an email client, for example, as is the Mail app in Windows 8. If you use a mail client, your previously sent and received mail is accessible even when no Internet access is available.

Types of email accounts

There are several different email account technologies, and you should know which type you have (or what kind you want, if you're still looking for an email provider) because the setup and the choices of email programs you can use are different for each:

✔ **Web-based:** This type of email account is designed to be used primarily with a web-based interface. Many of the free email services are this type, including Gmail, Hotmail (now part of Outlook.com), and Yahoo! Mail. This is the easiest, most no-fuss type, and it's what I recommend for casual users who don't send many messages and don't want to fool with setting up an email program.

✔ **POP3:** This type of email account is designed to be used with an email client, although the provider may also allow web access too. This type of account downloads your received messages to your local PC when it connects to the mail server. A POP3 account is tethered to a particular computer where the received mail is stored; it's best for someone who uses the same computer all or most of the time. POP3 stands for Post Office Protocol version 3.

✔ **IMAP:** This type of email account, like POP3, is also designed to be use with an email client. It does not download received messages, though; it reads them from the server, like web-based email does. That way, you can browse your mailbox from multiple computers and still see the full set of emails. The downside is that you can't browse your mail if you aren't connected to the Internet. IMAP stands for Internet Mail Access Protocol.

✔ **EAS:** This type is similar to IMAP except it is used by Exchange servers. It is a popular type of account for groupware and corporate accounts, as well as for mail delivered to smart phones. EAS stands for Exchange ActiveSync.

Signing Up for an Email Account

This section is for people who don't have an email account yet, or who want another one. You can skip this section if you already have an email address that works for you and you aren't interested in others.

If you have Internet service, you probably also already have an email address, whether you realize it or not. Most Internet service providers (ISPs) require that you have one, so they can send you administrative messages. So, your first task is to track down the information you got when you signed up for your Internet service and see if there's anything in that paperwork about your email account.

You can use one email address for everything, or you can have multiple email addresses. Most ISPs allow you to have several email addresses for no extra charge. That means everyone in your family can have their own, or you can have separate accounts for different activities. For example, you might have one email account that you use for nothing except signing up for online mailing lists.

To get a web-based email address, visit one of these websites and follow the prompts to register:

- **Yahoo! Mail:** http://mail.yahoo.com
- **Gmail (Google):** http://mail.google.com
- **Outlook.com:** www.outlook.com

Hotmail.com and Live.com, Microsoft's previous web-based email services, both redirect to Outlook.com now.

To get a POP3 or IMAP email address, check with your ISP to find out how to create one. The process may be different depending on your ISP.

Email accounts come with certain features that you should be aware of. For example, each account includes a certain amount of storage for your saved messages. (Look for one that provides 10 gigabytes or more.) The account should also include an easy-to-use address book feature to save your contacts' information. Some services provide better formatting tools for text, as well as calendar and to-do list features.

Whatever service you use, make sure it has good junk-mail filtering to protect you from unwanted emails. You should be able to modify junk-mail filter settings so that the service places messages from certain senders or with certain content in a junk-mail folder, where you can review the messages with caution or delete them.

Make sure your username is a safe one: If possible, don't use your full name, your location, age, or other identifiers. Such personal identifiers might help scam artists or predators find out more about you than you want them to know.

As you are making the decision of what type of email account to sign up for, here's something to consider: Windows 8.1 doesn't support POP3 accounts in its Mail app. The Mail app is not a great mail app, so don't feel like you have to use it, but it is a handy app if you use a touchscreen, such as on a tablet.

Setting Up an Account in Your Email Client

This section is for people who have an email account but don't yet have a way to access it, or don't know whether they do. It shows you how to use three different methods to access your email account. You might want to try each one and see which interface you like the best, among the ones that work with your account.

The exact steps for setting up an email account vary depending on the email client, but generally speaking, the software walks you through a setup process.

In this chapter, I show you how to set up three different email clients. The first one is the Mail app in Windows 8.1. (It doesn't work with POP3 accounts.) The second is not really a client at all, but a website: Outlook.com. It has many of the features of the standalone application Microsoft Outlook, including the ability to support POP3 accounts, but Outlook.com is free. The third is Microsoft Outlook 2013, a great, full-featured email program that comes with most versions of Microsoft Office 2013.

For POP3 accounts, my top choice is Microsoft Outlook 2013 for when I'm home and Outlook.com when I'm on the road. I like having a POP3 account because I like keeping offline records of all my email in a client program. However, most of my friends have Gmail or Yahoo! Mail accounts as their main email providers, and they love the convenience, so it's up to you. If you go with one of those web-based services, you can use the web interface all the time, and you don't need an email client.

Setting Up an Account in Mail in Windows 8.1

If you have a web-based email account from one of the major email services (Google, Yahoo!, Outlook.com, Hotmail, Live.com, or AOL), or an IMAP or EAS account, follow these steps to set up your email account to use in the Mail app in Windows 8.1:

1. **From the Start screen, click Mail. The Mail app opens.**

2. **Select the Settings charm to open the Settings pane, shown in Figure 7-1.**

   To select the Settings charm, you can move the mouse to the bottom-right corner of the screen until the Charms bar appears and then click the Settings charm, or you can swipe in (on a touch screen) from the right and then click Settings.

3. **Click Accounts.**

   A list appears of the mail accounts already set up, plus the account you use to sign into your Windows account (regardless of whether you use it to send and receive email on this PC).

4. **Click Add an Account.**

   A list of some of the most common email services appears, as shown in Figure 7-2.

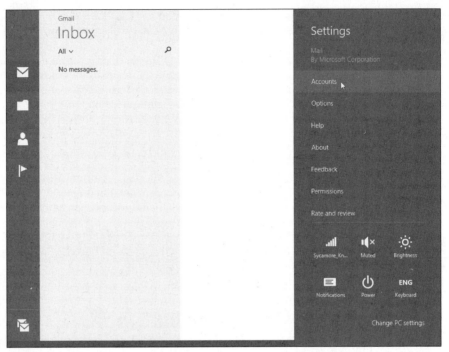

Figure 7-1:
The Settings
pane.

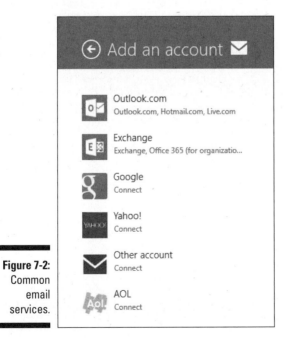

Figure 7-2:
Common
email
services.

5. **If your email provider appears on the list, click it and then follow the prompts to finish setting up your account.** If you have a Hotmail or Live address, choose Outlook.com as the provider.

OR

If you have an EAS or IMAP account, click Other Account and then follow the prompts to finish setting up your account.

Setting up an account at Outlook.com

Outlook.com is a very useful website. You can not only use it to access any of your Microsoft-sponsored email accounts (any account that ends in outlook.com, live.com, or hotmail.com), but you can also set up your POP3 accounts so you can send and receive mail from them on the website.

The sign-in for Outlook.com is the same as for your Microsoft account (the one you use to sign into Windows 8). If you don't have a Microsoft account, you're prompted to create one when you visit www.outlook.com for the first time.

When you're logged in, follow these steps to set up a POP3 email account to send and receive mail through Outlook.com. (These steps assume you are using the desktop version of Internet Explorer.)

1. **Click the Settings button (the cog icon) in the upper-right corner of the screen to open a menu, and then click Options. See Figure 7-3.**

2. **Under Managing your account, click Your Email Accounts.**

3. **Click Add a Send-and-Receive Account. See Figure 7-4.**

4. **Follow the prompts to complete the setup. Outlook.com will ask you for the information it needs.**

If you get an error when you try to set up the account by just entering the email address and password, click the Advanced hyperlink, which opens extra options you can set. For example, you may need to set a certain incoming or outgoing mail server or port. Check with your provider if you don't have that information or don't know what that is.

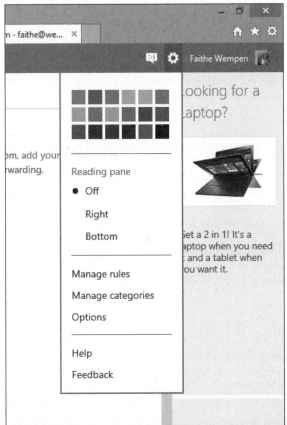

Figure 7-3:
The
Settings⇨
Options
menu.

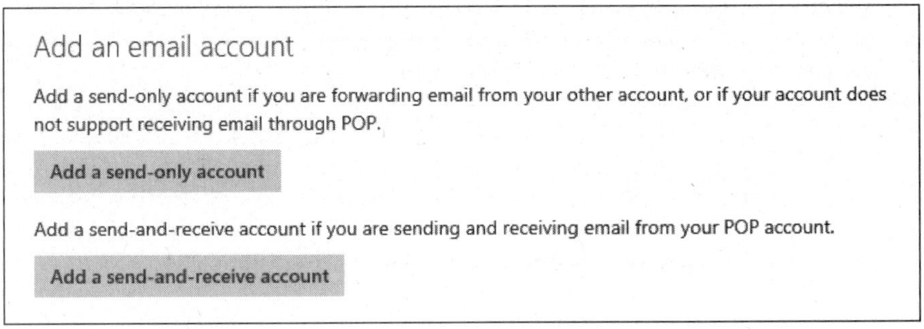

Add an email account

Add a send-only account if you are forwarding email from your other account, or if your account does not support receiving email through POP.

Add a send-only account

Add a send-and-receive account if you are sending and receiving email from your POP account.

Add a send-and-receive account

Figure 7-4:
Adding a
send-and-
receive
account.

Setting Up an Account in Microsoft Outlook 2013

The first time you run Outlook 2013, you may be prompted to set up your email account. If that happens, follow the prompts to get started.

If not, you can manually initiate the process of setting up your account in Outlook by doing the following:

1. **Click File and click Add Account. The Add Account dialog box opens, as in Figure 7-5.**

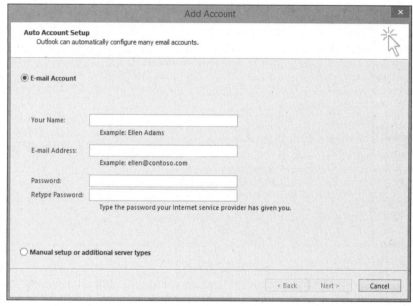

Figure 7-5: The Add Account dialog box.

2. **Fill in the information requested (name, email address, and password) and click Next.**

   Outlook tries to detect the server settings and log into it with an encrypted connection.

3. **If Outlook is successful, a message appears to that effect; click Finish and you're done. If it is not successful, a message appears that reads Click Next to attempt using an unencrypted connection. Click Next to do that.**

4. **If Outlook is successful, click Finish and you're done. If it is not successful, click to mark the Change account settings check box and then click Next.**

5. **Click the button for the type of account you have (for example, POP or IMAP) and click Next. Then fill in the information requested and follow the prompts to complete the setup.**

   For example, for a POP account, you will see the screen shown in Figure 7-6.

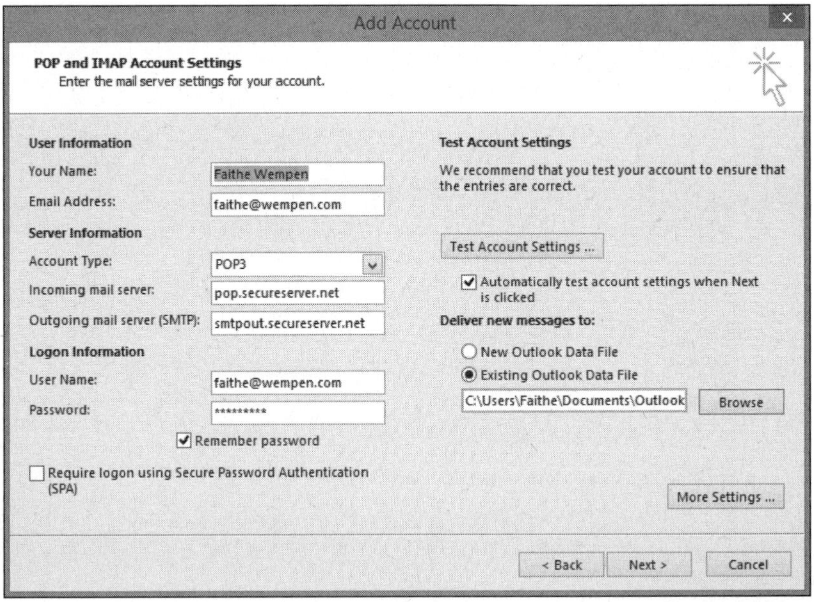

Figure 7-6: The POP and IMAP Account Settings screen.

Check with your provider if you are asked for any information you don't have, such as incoming or outgoing mail server. For a POP3 account, if the test message doesn't send correctly, you might need to click More Settings and enter some special settings for the server. Your provider will tell you what those are if needed.

Composing and Sending Email

Okay, we took the long way to get here, but at least you have some sort of email account set up, right? Good. Then it's time to start composing and sending email.

In whatever email client or web-based app you are using, look around for a button or hyperlink that creates a new message. It may be called New, New Email, Create, or some other wording, or it may just be a plus sign. Here's what to look for the in the three programs I talked about earlier:

- ✔ **Mail (Windows 8.1 app):** Click the New button (looks like a plus sign).
- ✔ **Outlook.com:** Click the New button. (It also looks like a plus sign, but the word New also appears with it.)
- ✔ **Microsoft Outlook 2013:** On the Home tab, click New Email.

From this point on in the process, the differences between the various programs are mostly cosmetic; the fields to be filled out may appear in a different order or in different places onscreen, but they request the same information. Figure 7-7 shows it for the Mail app.

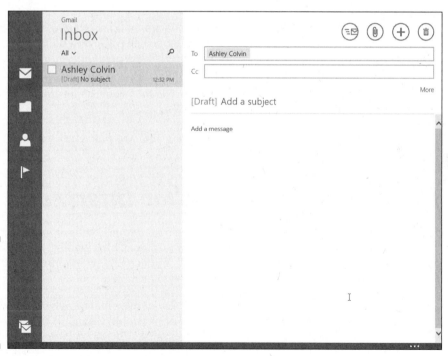

Figure 7-7: The compose message screen for the Mail app.

The first thing you'll want to do is enter one or more recipients in the To box. If there is more than one recipient, you can separate the addresses with semicolons. You can choose email addresses from a stored address book if you like. To access that, click the word To to the left of the To field.

You can optionally specify additional recipients to receive a copy or a blind copy of the message by entering them in the Cc and Bcc fields, respectively. A *blind copy* is one that none of the other recipients are aware of.

Next, enter a subject in the Subject (or Add a subject) field. This subject will appear in the recipient's inbox, so make it descriptive.

Finally, enter your actual message in the Message (or Add a Message) area, which is the big blank area on the message composition screen.

Before you send the message, you might want to include an *attachment*, which is a file that travels along with the message. The procedure is a little different in each of the mail programs we're looking at in this chapter:

✔ **Mail (Windows 8.1 app):** Click the Attachments button (which looks like a paperclip) to open a file management interface. Navigate to and select the desired file and then click Attach.

✔ **Outlook.com:** Click the Insert button to open a menu, and then choose Files as attachments. In the Choose File to Upload dialog box, navigate to and select the desired file and click Open.

✔ **Microsoft Outlook 2013:** On the Message tab, click Attach File. In the Insert File dialog box, navigate to and select the desired file and click Insert.

When everything is ready to go, click the Send button to send your message.

Understanding the Inbox Interface

Most email clients send and receive mail automatically at specified intervals (for example, every 10 minutes). You can also manually initiate a send/receive operation in most programs by clicking the Send/Receive button (or some similarly named variant of that).

When a new message arrives, it appears in your *Inbox*, which is the folder designated for arriving mail. It may appear bold when it is unread, to help you visually distinguish the new messages. The Inbox listing shows the date and time of the message (or just the time if it was received today), the sender, and the subject, and perhaps other information too. In Figure 7-8, Microsoft Outlook 2013 shows all that information plus the message size. (Attachments will increase the size.) Notice in Figure 7-8 that one of the messages has a paperclip next to it; that means it has an attachment. That same message also has an exclamation point, indicating a high-priority message.

Another message has an open envelope icon to its left with an arrow on it; that symbol means I have replied to the message. There is one message that appears in bold (the third one); it is the only unread message.

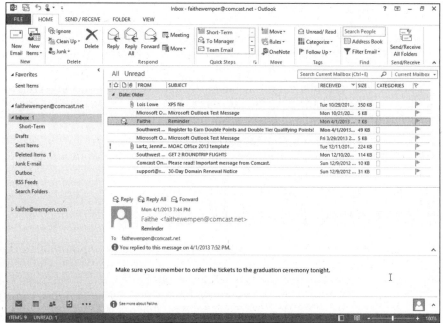

Figure 7-8:
The
Microsoft
Outlook
inbox.

Depending on the mail program, there may be a preview pane that shows the selected message in the Inbox. In Figure 7-8, the preview pane is below the Inbox's message list. On Outlook.com there is no preview pane; when you click a message, the message displays in the browser window. In the Mail app in Windows 8.1, the preview appears to the right of the Inbox.

Replying and Forwarding

To reply to a message, look for a Reply button when you are viewing the message. Clicking it opens a message composition window with the original message quoted below the message body area and with the recipient's address already filled in. Just type your reply and click Send. There will also be a *Reply All* command that does the same thing except it includes all of the original recipients in the reply also, if there were more than just you.

Forwarding a message is like replying but it doesn't fill in the email addresses for you. It sends a copy of the original message along in the body area, but you must choose new recipients for it yourself.

Here's how to access those commands in the mail programs we've been looking at:

- **Mail (Windows 8.1 app):** Click the Respond button, which looks like an envelope with a curved arrow on it. A menu opens, from which you can choose Reply, Reply All, or Forward.

- **Outlook.com:** You can either click the Reply button on the toolbar, or click the down arrow to the right of the Reply button to open a menu, and from that menu you can click Reply, Reply All, or Forward.

- **Microsoft Outlook 2013:** There are three separate buttons on the Home tab: Reply, Reply All, and Forward. Click the appropriate one.

Managing Email Messages

Part of an email program's job is to organize the copies that you keep of sent and received messages. By default, a message remains in the Inbox folder until you dispose of it somehow, by either deleting it or moving it to another folder. You can create your own folders and move messages into them to create a message storage system that makes sense for your needs.

Deleting messages

If you don't need a message any longer, delete it. To do so, select it and press the Delete key on the keyboard, or select it and click the Delete button in the application. (Its exact location varies.)

Deleted messages go to a folder called Deleted Items. You can retrieve them from there if you've made a mistake.

Browsing folders

To organize your received messages, it may be appropriate to create one or more folders.

In the Windows 8.1 Mail app, you won't see the folder list by default. Click the Folders button in the navigation pane on the left to see the folders, as in Figure 7-9. From there, click the desired folder to see its contents.

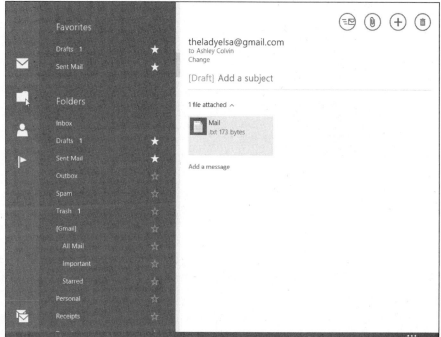

Figure 7-9:
Click a folder to see its contents.

The available folders appear in a navigation pane on the left side of the screen at Outlook.com and in Microsoft Outlook 2013 all the time; you don't have to do anything to access them. You can click any folder at any time to move to that folder.

Creating folders

To create a new folder in Mail, follow these steps:

1. **Display the contents of the folder under which the new folder should appear. For example, if you want the new folder to be a subfolder of Inbox, display Inbox.**

2. **Right-click anywhere. A command bar appears at the bottom of the screen. The button on the far left is the Manage Folders button.**

3. **Click the Manage Folders button. A shortcut menu appears, as in Figure 7-10.**

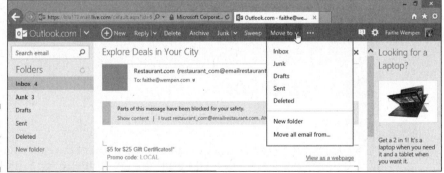

Create folder

Create subfolder

Pin to Start

4. **Click Create Subfolder. A prompt appears for the name.**

5. **Type the name for the new folder and click OK. A confirmation message appears.**

6. **Click OK.**

Now when you click the Folders icon at the left, you see the new folder there.

To create a new folder at Outlook.com, click the Move To button on the command bar, opening a menu, and then choose New Folder, as shown in Figure 7-11.

To create a new folder in Microsoft Outlook 2013, follow these steps:

1. **In the navigation pane on the left, right-click the folder that the new folder should be subordinate to (for example, Inbox) and choose New Folder.**

2. **Type the name for the new folder and press Enter.**

Moving messages into folders

In Mail, here's how to move a message into a different folder:

1. **Click to place a check mark in the check box to the left of the message(s) to be moved.**

2. **Right-click to display the command bar at the bottom of the screen.**

3. **Click the Move All From button. A menu appears. See Figure 7-12.**

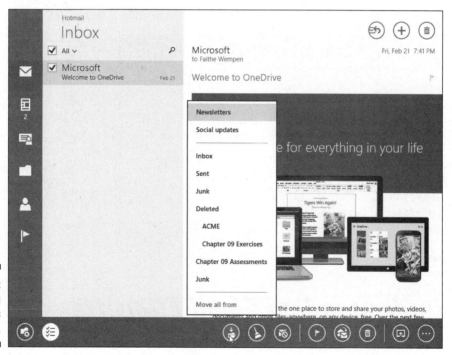

Figure 7-12:
Moving messages into folders.

4. **Click the folder to which you want to move the message.**

In Outlook.com, you can either drag-and-drop the message onto the appropriate folder in the navigation pane, or you can do the following:

1. **Click to place a check mark in the check box to the left of the message(s) to be moved.**

2. **Click the Move To button on the command bar. A menu appears.**

3. **Click the folder to which you want to move the message.**

In Microsoft Outlook 2013, you can also drag-and-drop the message onto the folder in the navigation pane to move it. Alternatively, you can do the following:

1. **Select the message(s) to be moved. To select multiple messages, hold down Ctrl as you click each one.**

2. **On the Home tab, click the Move button, and then click Other Folder. The Move Items dialog box opens. See Figure 7-13.**

3. **Click the desired destination folder, and then click OK.**

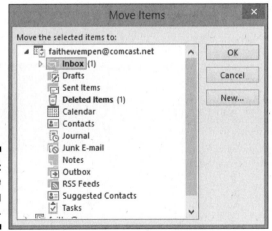

Figure 7-13:
The Move Items dialog box.

Understanding Email Etiquette

We finish up this chapter by looking at a subject that is the same for every email program because it's not a program issue at all: It's a human issue. How do we use an emotionless text medium like email to convey politeness and good will? Here are some tips.

✔ Don't leave a sender hanging if a reply is required. Users understand that email is not instantaneous, but it is polite to reply as soon as you are able.

✔ Don't send email formatted with wild, difficult-to-read colors and backgrounds or extremely large or small fonts.

✔ Don't include large attachments without a good reason. For example, sending a large report to a business colleague is a good reason, whereas forwarding a large video clip of a chicken and a goat playing because you think it is funny is not a good reason.

✔ Don't overuse abbreviations, especially when writing to someone who may not understand them. Remember, email is not subject to length restrictions. There's not a fixed character limit like with texting and tweeting (using Twitter), so spell things out, like "are you" instead of RU.

✔ Use correct grammar, punctuation, and spelling. This is especially important in business correspondence.

✔ In business communications and also in more formal personal communications, it is considered good manners to begin with a greeting and close with your name (and also your title and company if it's for business).

✔ Don't write in all-caps. It is considered shouting. On the other hand, don't write in all-lowercase; it is difficult to read.

✔ Don't say anything in an email that you wouldn't say in person. In other words, don't hide behind the technology to be a jerk. Even though the recipient can't see your face, and can't punch you in the nose immediately if she feels insulted, the insult or hurt is still real.

✔ Don't overuse *emoticons* (smileys), which are little happy face symbols (or frowning face, or a host of other emotions), and don't use them at all in business. And while we're at it, don't overuse LOL (a common texting abbreviation for *laughing out loud*).

Chapter 8

Clouds and Online Communication

• •

• •

*A*s the Internet has gotten faster and more universally adopted, many people have found that it's just as easy — if not easier — to store files and run applications directly from the Internet than it is to do so from an individual computer. That's the basic idea behind *cloud computing*, which means to store, manage, and process data on remote servers on the Internet.

Different companies out there want you to use their online applications and storage systems — and luckily for you, it's all mostly free. (The companies make money by selling advertising on their websites and by selling enhanced packages of features to power-users.) In this chapter, you'll learn about some of the cloud-based applications and storage systems available on the Internet, including Microsoft's OneDrive online storage cloud.

This chapter also looks at some of the many ways you can communicate online (besides email, of course, which we looked at in Chapter 7). I take a tour here through instant messaging, video chatting, blogging, and social networking.

Using Cloud-Based Applications

Certain applications came free with your operating system, and you have probably installed others as well, such as Microsoft Office, a personal finance program, an email client, or a game or two. Today, however, you don't necessarily have to install software in order to have that software's capabilities. Instead you can use the applications online, via a web browser. These are called *cloud-based apps*. At the consumer level, most cloud-based apps are free, but cloud-based does not automatically equal a freebie. Cloud-based apps designed for business use are often leased to companies on a monthly or yearly basis, handling such complex matters as purchasing, accounting, and project management. When a company leases an application like that, it's known as *Software as a Service (SaaS)*.

Here are some examples of free cloud-based apps you can explore:

- ✔ **Microsoft Office Online:** Microsoft offers free, simplified versions of its popular Office applications online (at `https://office.com`). The products available include Word (see Figure 8-1), Outlook, PowerPoint, Excel, and OneNote, as well as a Calendar app and a People app. You can also access the OneDrive storage system from there, which is covered in detail later in this chapter.

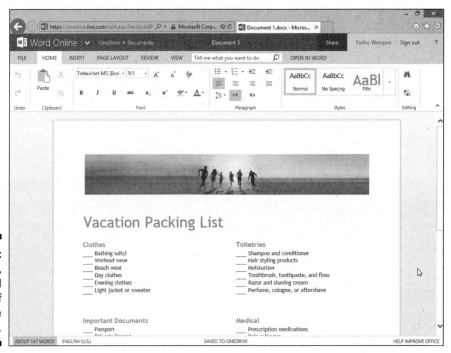

Figure 8-1:
A free,
simplified
version of
Word can be
found online.

- ✔ **Google Docs:** This suite of online software (available at `www.docs.google.com`) includes word processor, spreadsheet, presentation, drawing, and form design software products you can use by logging into a Gmail account. These applications are compatible with popular office software such as Microsoft Word and PowerPoint.

✔ **Email clients:** When you log into a web-based email account, as discussed in Chapter 7, you're using a cloud-based email client.

✔ **Photo-sharing sites:** Sites such as Flickr (`www.flickr.com`) enable you to upload and download photos to them without ever installing an app on your computer. A variation on this is a site such as Viewbook (`www.viewbook.com`), where you can create an online portfolio of art samples or business presentations, for example, to share with others.

✔ **Financial applications:** You might use a site such as CNN Money Portfolio (`https://portfolio.money.cnn.com`) to maintain an online portfolio of investments and generate charts to help you keep track of trends. You can also use online versions of popular money-management programs, such as Intuit's free online service Mint (`www.mint.com`), through which you can access your data from any computer or mobile device.

Working with Microsoft OneDrive

OneDrive (formerly known as SkyDrive) is a Microsoft-owned cloud-based storage space. Each user has his or her own storage area, where they can store private files, share files with certain specific others, or make files publicly available. A certain amount of storage space is free, and you can pay if you want more than what's provided. (The amount of storage space available depends on when you signed up for your account and what type of account you have.) OneDrive is the default storage location for Office Online cloud-based apps, and also for Office 2013 applications.

Using OneDrive as your main document storage area has several consequences:

✔ You can access your files from any computer, whether or not it has Excel installed on it.

✔ You can share your work with other people without having to send them separate copies of it.

✔ Your files are available only when Internet access is available.

You can get around that last drawback by installing the OneDrive app on your PC (free from Microsoft at `www.onedrive.com`), which automatically mirrors the content of your OneDrive on your PC and keeps the copy in sync with the OneDrive's actual content. It's already installed by default as part of Windows 8.1. You can tell whether it's installed by looking in File Explorer in the Favorites list in the navigation pane. If you see a OneDrive shortcut there, you've got the OneDrive app.

There are several ways to access your OneDrive; each of the following sections explains one of the methods.

Signing into the OneDrive web interface

Some OneDrive management activities can only be performed via the OneDrive web interface, so you should know how to access it. To get started, point your browser to `www.onedrive.com`. (The page will redirect to the server where Microsoft is hosting OneDrive at the moment. As of this writing, it is `https://OneDrive.live.com`, but by the time you read this, it may have changed.)

If you already have a Microsoft account and your computer is set up to automatically sign you into it, your OneDrive's content appears automatically. Figure 8-2 shows an example, but you may have different files and folders than shown. From this interface, you can click folders and files to open them or use the buttons on the toolbar at the top of the window to perform other actions.

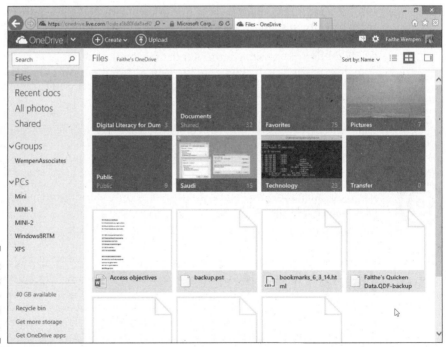

Figure 8-2: Documents and folders on OneDrive.

Installing and using OneDrive for Windows Desktop

To get around the drawback of not being able to access your OneDrive files offline, and to make managing OneDrive files as easy as managing your local files, install the OneDrive for Windows app on your PC.

The OneDrive for Windows app automatically mirrors the content of your OneDrive on your PC and keeps the copy in sync with the OneDrive's actual content. If you are ever unconnected to the Internet, it allows you to work on local copies of your files, and then it automatically uploads the updates to your OneDrive the next time Internet connectivity is available. The OneDrive for Windows app also places a shortcut to your locally mirrored copies of your OneDrive content on the Favorites list in File Explorer (or Windows Explorer) so you can easily access them with one click.

To get OneDrive for Windows, open the OneDrive web interface, as described in the preceding section, and then in the navigation pane at the left, click the Get OneDrive Apps hyperlink. From there, find and follow the link for the Windows desktop apps. Click Download Now and follow the prompts to complete the installation. (I'm being intentionally vague about the steps here because by the time you read this, they may have changed; Microsoft updates its websites frequently.)

After OneDrive for Windows has been installed, you'll see a OneDrive shortcut in the Favorites list in File Explorer (Windows 8) or Windows Explorer (Windows 7). This shortcut points to a folder on your hard drive: C:\Users\ username\OneDrive. This folder is a staging area for your online OneDrive and is automatically synchronized with it.

If you use Word, Excel, and/or PowerPoint 2013, you can access OneDrive from within those applications. When you choose Save As from the File menu, the default save location is your OneDrive. You can click Browse to browse your OneDrive's content, or you can click one of the folder names under Recent Folders to access one of the folders within your OneDrive.

Using the Windows 8 OneDrive app

If you are running Windows 8, you can access the Windows 8 OneDrive app from the Start screen. It's a tablet-style app optimized for touchscreens, like the other new Windows 8 style applications.

Within the OneDrive app you will see your folders listed to the left, as big blue rectangles. To the right of the folders, you'll see tiles for any files that are stored at the top level of your OneDrive's organizational system, not in any particular folder. Right-click to open a command bar at the bottom of the screen and choose commands from it to work with your content. Figure 8-3 shows the command bar open. Using the commands on the command bar, you can do all the basic file management tasks from the Windows 8 OneDrive app, such as uploading and downloading, creating new folders, deleting, renaming, and moving.

Figure 8-3:
The command bar appears at the bottom of the screen.

When you click a file or folder, it opens. If it's a file, it opens in its default program. You choose some other program in which to open the file, click Open With on the command bar and then select the desired app from the menu that appears. To select something without activating it, right-click it.

Participating in Social Networking

In its broadest definition, *social networking* means to participate in an online community in which people interact with one another in various ways. Examples include social networking sites like Facebook, blogs, micro-blogging services such as Twitter, discussion boards (as discussed later in this chapter), and chat rooms. In the following sections, I take you on a tour of some of the most popular social networking forms.

Facebook and other social network sites

A social networking site may offer a variety of communication methods, including private messaging (like email except only on that site), making comments on a friend's page, sharing URLs to other sites, uploading photos, and journaling.

Although most social networking sites are personal and social in nature, such as Facebook and Myspace, social networking sites can also include business and career oriented sites like LinkedIn.

Facebook is the most popular social networking site today, with millions of registered users. To sign up for an account, go to www.facebook.com and click the Sign Up link.

What can you do when you're there? Well, the first thing you may want to do is find your friends and relatives and "friend" them. That means sending them a friend request, which they then accept (hopefully), and from that point on, your accounts are linked in a friend relationship, and you can see each other's posted activities and information. To find a friend, click the Find Friends hyperlink on the shaded bar at the top of the page. If the person has a common name, you may have to sift through multiple listings to find the right person. Figure 8-4 shows my Facebook feed. The *feed* is the ever-changing stream of activity reports that show what your friends are up to.

To post a status update (which is like a micro-blog, explained in the Twitter section later in this chapter), type it in the *What's on your mind?* box near the top of the page, as shown in Figure 8-4.

Figure 8-4:
My
Facebook
feed.

Discussion boards

A *discussion board* is a place where you can post written messages, pictures, and videos on a topic. Others can reply to you, and you can reply to their postings. In a variation on discussion boards, you'll find *blogs* (web logs) everywhere you turn, and you can also post your comments about blog entries.

Discussion boards and blogs are *asynchronous,* which means that you post a message (just as you might on a bulletin board at the grocery store) and wait for a response. Somebody might read it that hour — or ten days or several weeks after you make the posting. In other words, the response isn't instantaneous, and the message isn't usually directed to a specific individual.

You can find a discussion board or blog about darn near every topic under the sun, and these are tremendously helpful when you're looking for answers. They're also a great way to share your expertise — whether you chime in on how to remove an ink stain, provide historical trivia about button styles on military uniforms, or announce the latest breakthroughs in your given field. Postings are likely to stay up on the site for years for people to reference.

To explore a discussion board, follow these steps:

1. **Enter `http://answers.microsoft.com/en` in your browser's address field: to go to the Microsoft Support discussion groups.**

   Some discussion boards require that you become a member, with a username, and sign in before you can read messages, although this site doesn't. You must sign in, however, before you can post.

2. **Under the Browse the Categories heading, click a category.**

   For example, click Windows Phone.

3. **In the topic list that appears, click a sub-topic to narrow down your interest. Continue to click until you get to a specific discussion board, such as the one shown in Figure 8-5.**

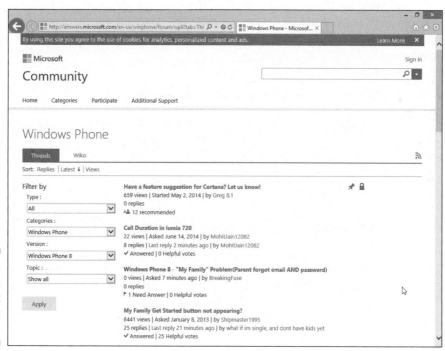

Figure 8-5:
A discussion board about Windows Phone.

4. **When you click a posting that has replies, you'll see that the replies are organized in the middle of the page in easy-to-follow threads, which arrange postings and replies in an outline-like structure.**

You can review the various participants' comments as they add their ideas to the conversation.

There are thousands of discussion boards all over the Internet that you can participate in, for every imaginable topic. Most websites for a product have a Support section, for example, that includes a user-to-user support discussion board.

Blogging

A *blog* (short for *web log*) is an online journal. It can be entirely private, open to invited guests only, or available to the general public. Most blogs are personal in nature, but some companies have corporate-sponsored blogs that employees write to convey information informally to the public. For example, Microsoft encourages many of their employees to blog about new product developments, and it even hosts their blogs on official Microsoft servers. In addition, some independent contractors blog about their work to become more well-known in their field and to share information with others in similar professions.

There are millions of active blogs all over the Internet, so you may just content yourself with reading other people's writings. You might start with a popular blogging site such as WordPress, TypePad, or Blogger, and browse the blogs on the home pages. Or, you might have friends or relatives who blog and you might bookmark their blog pages for regular reading.

If you want to create your own blog, your best bet is to sign up for an account on a blogging website (again, WordPress, TypePad, and Blogger are the popular ones). A basic account is free; you can pay extra for upgrades, but if you're just getting started, you might as well wait and see if you actually like blogging.

After creating your account, you can enter the text for your blog entries directly into the website, or if you prefer, you can use an offline blogging application. Microsoft Word works to compose blogs, but a perhaps easier tool to use is Windows Live Writer, which is part of the Windows Live suite of free apps that Microsoft offers. You can download Windows Live apps from www.microsoft.com/en-us/download/details.aspx?id=8621.

When you run Windows Live Writer for the first time, it prompts you to enter the URL and login information for your blog. After you enter those once, the application remembers them thereafter, and each time you start the application, a new post document starts. Write and format your post as you would in a word processing program, and then click Publish to publish it to your blog. See Figure 8-6.

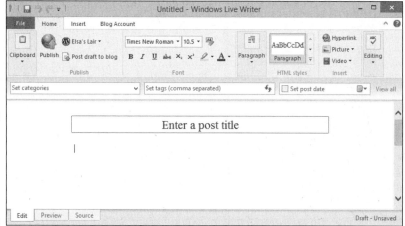

Figure 8-6:
Create a blog post with Windows Live Writer.

Twitter

Twitter is a *micro-blogging* service, where you can post status updates in short, 140-character chunks. Posting a status update is known as tweeting. You can tweet from the Twitter website or, perhaps more commonly, from a Twitter app on a smartphone. As with Facebook, Twitter provides you with a feed that tracks the activity of people that you have chosen to follow (the equivalent of friending on Facebook).

To get started with Twitter, sign up for a Twitter account at `www.twitter.com`. You can optionally check the app store on your smart phone or tablet for a Twitter app to use on the phone. Figure 8-7 shows the Twitter website.

Sending and receiving tweets is fun, but it can be exhausting to keep up with everyone else's tweets, many of which may seem mundane and uninteresting. Do you really want to know what 20 different friends had for dinner, for example? When tweeting yourself, to make sure that your tweets are something that your friends look forward to rather than roll their eyes at, make sure you say something of substance.

Figure 8-7:
The Twitter
website.

Using Instant Messaging

Instant messaging (often called just *IMing*) is the process of exchanging text-based messages in real-time over a computer in a one-on-one conversation (usually, although it is possible to invite multiple people to the same conversation). To do it, you use an instant messaging service such as Yahoo! Messenger or AOL Instant Messenger. Instant messaging is a lot like Simple Mail Service (SMS) text messaging on a cell phone except it is sent over the Internet rather than via cell phone.

To try out Yahoo! Messenger, go to http://messenger.yahoo.com and download the Yahoo! IM client software. (It's free.) Then install it, create an account if you don't have one already, and you're off and running. To add someone as a contact, open the Contacts menu and choose Add Contact. Then to have a conversation with someone on your Contacts list, double-click their name and type a greeting in the message window that opens, as in Figure 8-8.

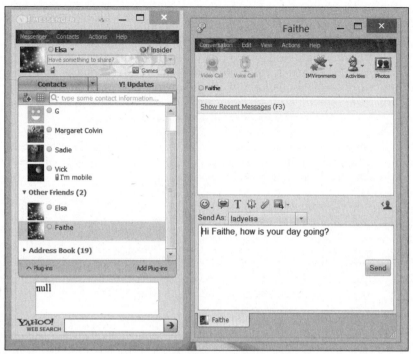

Figure 8-8:
Writing a
message
in Yahoo!
Messenger.

IM is ideal for quick, little messages where you just want an answer without forming a formal email, as well as for touching base and saying hi. This isn't a tool you'd typically use for a long, meaningful conversation, but it's great for quick exchanges.

Instant messages go through a central server maintained by the company that owns the service you are using. Instant messaging services are usually free to the user; the costs are paid by advertisers. Instant message conversations may be logged (saved), but are not necessarily so by default, so this is not the best medium for preserving important conversational records.

Some IM services blur the line between IM and other more sophisticated communication forms such as video chatting. Yahoo! Instant Messenger, for example, offers both webcam and audio chat capabilities as well as text-based communication.

Using a Webcam

A *webcam* is a video camera that is attached to a computer; the computer runs the camera's software, so the camera is essentially a dumb piece of hardware that just feeds data directly into the application. This is different from a standalone video camera, which has its own programming and can function when detached from a computer.

Because a webcam is pretty simple hardware-wise, it's inexpensive, and many computers come with a webcam built into the display frame (especially notebooks, tablets, and smartphones).

Video chatting works in real-time. A webcam works by capturing video of you (or of whoever or whatever is in front of the camera) and then transmitting it immediately across the Internet to a recipient's computer. It doesn't store the video feed locally. That's a good thing because you wouldn't want your hard drive to fill up with all those large video files. Similarly, if the person on the other end broadcasts video to you via his or her webcam, the video appears on your screen in real-time, but isn't saved.

The process of video chatting varies depending on the software you are using. Your webcam may come with its own software, and you can also use a variety of services such as Skype. As I mentioned in the last section, you can also use some IM clients for video chat too. For example, in Yahoo! Instant Messenger, you first start a text conversation with someone, and then click the Video Call button in the chat window to invite the person to participate in video chat.

Do not allow children or teens to video chat with strangers. This can invite the attention of online predators and pedophiles.

If you plan on doing a lot of video chatting (for example, if your sister just moved to a foreign country and you plan on talking to her for hours every week on video chat), you may want to sign up for Skype. *Skype* is a free audio and video chatting service, and the Skype software comes free with Windows 8.1. You may already have it on your PC; if not, you can download it from www.skype.com. If you use Skype on a computer on which you are already signed in with a Microsoft account, you might not even have to create a Skype account; the service may use your Microsoft account as your ID there.

Part III
Productivity Programs

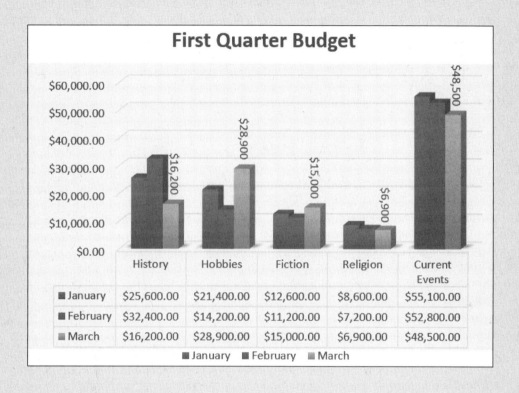

First Quarter Budget

	History	Hobbies	Fiction	Religion	Current Events
■ January	$25,600.00	$21,400.00	$12,600.00	$8,600.00	$55,100.00
■ February	$32,400.00	$14,200.00	$11,200.00	$7,200.00	$52,800.00
■ March	$16,200.00	$28,900.00	$15,000.00	$6,900.00	$48,500.00

■ January   ■ February   ■ March

Check out www.dummies.com/extras/digitalliteracy for alternatives to paying for Microsoft Office.

In this part . . .

✔ Discover how to select, install, and remove applications and how to navigate in an Office application.

✔ Learn to create attractive documents in Microsoft Word with pictures and tables.

✔ Find out how to manage and calculate date with Microsoft Excel, including creating charts.

✔ Learn how to use Microsoft PowerPoint to create presentation graphics that include pictures, transition effects, and sounds.

✔ Learn about databases and how they store data and find out how to create a multi-table database in Microsoft Access.

Chapter 9

Understanding Applications

*A*pplications are programs that enables you to do something useful or fun on your computer. This can include creating documents for business or personal projects, pursuing hobbies, learning, and being entertained.

In this chapter, you find out about the types of applications available and how to install and remove them in Windows 8.1. You will also learn what programs are included in Microsoft Office 2013 and what common features each of the Office applications share.

Types of Applications

Applications are available for just about anything you can imagine doing with a computer. Some broad categories of applications include the following:

✔ **Business productivity:** These applications are designed to help people do serious stuff, such as write a report, calculate a budget, send invoices, store data, and manage projects. Examples include word processors, spreadsheets, databases, presentation graphics, accounting programs, and tax preparation software.

✔ **Graphics:** Graphics can be serious stuff too, or they can be just for fun. Graphics software helps you create and modify artwork of all kinds, including photos, drawings (both technical and creative), diagrams, and clip art.

- ✔ **Video:** Applications are available that play videos on your computer, and also that create and edit your own videos.

- ✔ **Audio:** There are applications that play back all types of audio content, including music, podcasts, audio books, and so on. You can also get applications that enable you to create and edit your own audio recordings.

- ✔ **Education:** You can get applications that will teach you about any subject you are interested in, whether it's learning a new language or learning how to repair computers. You can also participate in academic courses that may have their own applications for delivering the course content, such as a tutorial DVD that comes with a textbook.

- ✔ **Communication:** If you have an Internet connection, you can use various types of communication software to surf the web, send and receive email, chat with friends using instant messaging, have video conversations, and exchange files.

- ✔ **Hobbies and personal enrichment:** Software is available that can help you with whatever hobbies you pursue. Applications exist that can plan your home landscaping, record genealogical information, and much more.

- ✔ **Games:** So many games, so little free time to play them! Whatever type of games you like to play, there are hundreds available for you to try out, from card and board game simulations to shoot-em-up monster action.

- ✔ **Development tools:** Don't like any of the software that's out there? Write your own! Development software provides a programming environment for creating software, if you have the programming knowledge. (Take a class; don't try to learn it on your own.) You can also get development tools for creating web content.

 If you want to see what applications are installed on your computer already, display the Start screen in Windows 8.1 and then click the down arrow at the bottom to display the Apps list. Read about the Apps list and how to run programs in Chapter 4.

Installing and Removing Applications

Each application has minimum system requirements. In order to install the application, your computer must meet or exceed those requirements. For example, the system requirements for Microsoft Office 2013 are as follows:

CPU: 1 GHz clock speed

RAM: 1 GB for the 32-bit version or 2 GB for the 64-bit version

Hard disk space: 3 GB free space

Operating system: Windows 7, Windows Server 2008 R2, Windows 8, or Windows Server 2012

You can find out an application's system requirements on the retail box for the product or on the manufacturer's website online. If your computer doesn't meet the requirements, the application may not install at all, or it may install but run poorly.

Installing an application on a Windows 8.1 PC does these things:

- ✔ It decompresses and copies the needed files to your hard drive.

- ✔ It makes changes in the Windows configuration files (the Registry) so that Windows is aware of the application. This may include changing the default applications for certain data file types.

- ✔ It places a shortcut to the application on the Apps list (accessed from the Start screen).

The procedure for installing an application depends on how you acquired it. If you downloaded the application, the file you downloaded is a setup program. Double-click its icon to run it and follow the prompts to install the software.

If you bought the program on disc, insert the disc into your DVD drive. You may see a message asking you to choose what happens with the disc. If you click or tap that message, you see a list of choices, as in Figure 9-1. Choose to run Setup.exe if that choice is available. If it's not, choose to browse the files on the disc and locate the setup file manually.

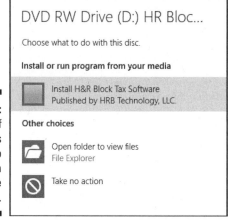

Figure 9-1:
A list of
choices
for what to
do with a
disc you've
inserted.

After an application has been installed, it appears in Windows' list of installed applications on the Start screen's Apps list, which you learned about in Chapter 4, and also in the Programs section of the Control Panel.

To uninstall an application, use the Control Panel interface, as in the following steps:

1. **From the Windows desktop, right-click the Start button and choose Control Panel.**

2. **Under the Programs heading, click Uninstall a program. A list of installed programs appears, as in Figure 9-2.**

Select the application   Choose Uninstall

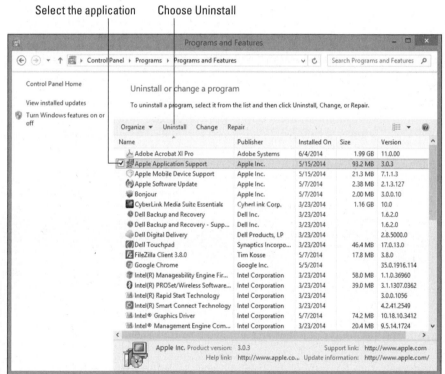

Figure 9-2:
A list of installed programs.

3. **Click the application you want to uninstall.**

   Buttons for the available actions for that program appear in the bar above the list.

   For example, in Figure 9-2, the available actions are Uninstall, Change, and Repair. Some applications only have the Uninstall option.

4. **Click Uninstall. The uninstall process begins.**

5. **Follow the prompts to complete the uninstallation. The steps vary depending on the application.**

What Is Microsoft Office?

Microsoft Office is a suite of applications for business productivity. A *suite* is a group of applications that are designed to work well together and are designed around a common interface. It is less expensive to buy a suite than it is to buy the individual applications separately.

The Microsoft Office 2013 suite comes in several different editions, each with a different combination of applications. Table 9-1 summarizes which applications are available in which editions. Note that some editions are available only through *volume licensing* — that is, when a company purchases a bulk license that allows many copies of the software to be installed. For example, a university might offer Office to all students and teachers through volume licensing.

There are also subscription-based editions of Office called Microsoft Office 365; they are available on a yearly subscription basis online. To see a more complete chart of editions and their included products, including all the Office 365 editions, see `http://en.wikipedia.org/wiki/Microsoft_Office_2013#Comparison`.

Table 9-1	Microsoft Office Editions				
	Home & Student	*Home & Business*	*Profes- sional*	*Standard (Available Only Through Volume Licensing)*	*Professional Plus (Available Only Through Volume Licensing)*
Word	X	X	X	X	X
Excel	X	X	X	X	X
PowerPoint	X	X	X	X	X
OneNote	X	X	X	X	X
Outlook		X	X	X	X
Publisher			X	X	X
Access			X		X
InfoPath					X
Lync					X

Here's a quick description of each application:

- ✔ **Word:** A word processor, used for text-based documents like reports, memos, and letters.

- ✔ **Excel:** A spreadsheet program, used to organize and calculate numeric data like budgets, sales results, and loans.

- ✔ **PowerPoint:** A presentation graphics program, used to create computerized slide shows to accompany all types of public speaking (sales pitches, lessons, informational meetings, and so on).

- ✔ **Outlook:** An email and personal information management program, used to send and receive email, schedule meetings, track to-do lists, and store contact information.

- ✔ **Access:** A database management system, used to store and organize structured data such as inventory and personnel information and customer orders.

- ✔ **Publisher:** A desktop publishing program that enables you to create documents with more complex page layouts than Word, such as brochures and newsletters.

- ✔ **OneNote:** A note organizing program that allows you to store and combine data from many different sources as you would with a cardboard folder or a filing cabinet drawer.

- ✔ **InfoPath:** An application for creating, distributing, and filling out electronic forms.

- ✔ **Lync:** An instant messaging application that can be used with certain types of servers.

In addition to the full applications, Microsoft also offers streamlined, online versions of some applications (Word, Excel, PowerPoint, and OneNote). To access these, log into OneDrive (www.onedrive.com) with your Microsoft ID, and then click the Create button and choose the type of document you want to create. Alternatively, click one of your existing files stored on your OneDrive to open it in the web-based version of its native application.

In this book, I keep things simple, and look at only the basic set of applications: Word (Chapter 10), Excel (Chapter 11), PowerPoint (Chapter 12), and Access (Chapter 13), plus a little bit about Outlook in Chapter 7.

Navigating an Office Application's Interface

The Office 2013 interface in each program consists of a tabbed Ribbon, a File menu, a status bar at the bottom, window controls, and other common features. In the following sections, you become familiar with these common elements. I use Microsoft Word as the example in most cases, but keep in mind that these elements are all basically the same in every Office application.

The Start screen

New in Office 2013, a Start screen appears when you start an application. To bypass it and go to a new blank document, you can press Esc. Alternatively, you can choose to open an existing document or click one of the templates that appears to start a new document based on a template. See Figure 9-3 for the Start screen in Word.

Click a recent file to reopen it.　　Click a template to start a new document

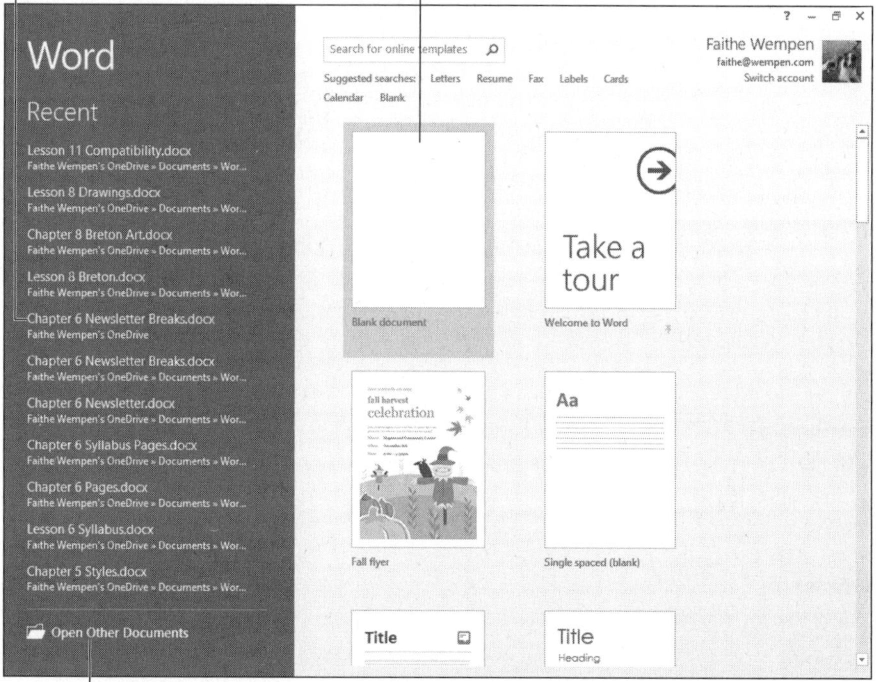

Figure 9-3:
The Start
screen in
Word.

Click here to use the Open dialog box to open a file

Ribbon and tabs

All Office 2013 applications have a common system of navigation called the *Ribbon,* which is a tabbed bar across the top of the application window. Each *tab* is like a page of buttons. You click different tabs to access different sets of buttons and features. Within a tab, the buttons are organized into groups. The group name appears below the buttons.

When you point at a button, a *ScreenTip* appears, telling you the button's name and purpose and showing a keyboard shortcut (Ctrl+L) that you can optionally use to select that command, as shown in Figure 9-4.

Tab   Group

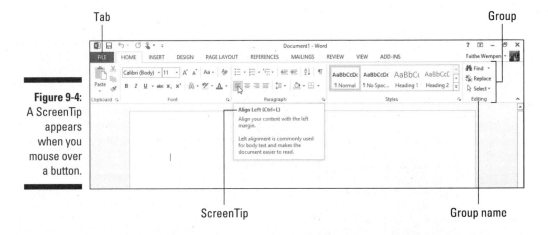

Figure 9-4:
A ScreenTip appears when you mouse over a button.

ScreenTip   Group name

Certain tabs and groups of tabs appear only when you are performing specific actions or working with certain types of content. These are called *contextual tabs.* For example, when you are working with a table, a group of tabs called Table Tools becomes available. There are two tabs in that group: Design and Layout. In this book when I refer to a contextual tab, I include both names. For example, the Table Tools Design tab is shown in Figure 9-5.

Quick Access Toolbar   Contextual tabs

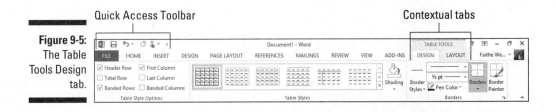

Figure 9-5:
The Table Tools Design tab.

The *Quick Access Toolbar* is the row of buttons above the Ribbon, which is visible in Figure 9-5. It contains shortcuts to a few commonly used commands, and you can add your own shortcuts to it as well. You can right-click any command on the Ribbon and choose Add to Quick Access Toolbar. One useful command that's only available on the Quick Access Toolbar is Undo, which reverses the last action performed. Its keyboard shortcut is Ctrl+Z in all Office applications.

The File menu

In each Office application, clicking the File tab opens the File menu (see Figure 9-6), also known as *Backstage view.* Backstage view provides access to commands that have to do with the data file you're working with — commands such as saving, opening, printing, mailing, and checking its properties. The File tab is a different color in each application. In Word, for example, it's blue. To leave Backstage view, press the Esc key or click the left-pointing arrow button in the upper-left corner. After opening the File menu, you can click a category on the left to see a different page of commands.

Categories

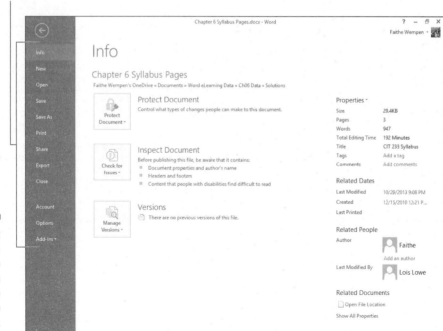

Figure 9-6: The File menu, also known as the Backstage view.

Moving around in an application

As you work in one of the Office applications, you may add so much content that you can't see it all onscreen at once. You might need to scroll through the document to view different parts of it. The simplest way to scroll through a document is by using the *scroll bars* with your mouse. See Figure 9-7.

Scrolling through a document with the scroll bars doesn't move the insertion point, so what you type or insert doesn't necessarily appear in the location that shows onscreen.

Scroll box

Figure 9-7:
Move
around your
document
with scroll
bars.

Scroll bars

Scroll arrows

You can also get around by moving the insertion point. When you do so, the document view scrolls automatically so you can see the newly selected location. You can move the insertion point either by clicking where you want it or by using keyboard shortcuts.

Here's a summary of how to move in a document using the scroll bar. These are geared toward Word, but it's similar in Excel and PowerPoint:

- Click a scroll arrow to scroll a small amount in that direction. In Excel, that's one row or column; in other applications, the exact amount varies per click.

- Hold down the left mouse button as you point to the scroll arrow to scroll continuously in that direction until you release the mouse button.

- Click above or below the scroll box to scroll one full screen in that direction if the document is tall/wide enough that there's undisplayed content in that direction.

- Drag the scroll box to scroll quickly in the direction you're dragging.

And, here's a summary of the ways you can move around in a document by using the keyboard:

- Press an arrow key to move the insertion point or cell cursor in the direction of the arrow. The exact amount of movement depends on the application; for example, in Excel, one arrow click moves the cursor by one cell. In Word, the up and down arrows move the cursor by one line, and the right and left arrows move it by one character.

- Press Page Up or Page Down to scroll one full screen in that direction.

- Press Home to move to the left side of the current row or line.

- Press End to move to the right side of the current row or line.

- Press Ctrl+Home to move to the upper-left corner of the document.

- Press Ctrl+End to move to the lower-right corner of the document.

Changing the zoom and the view

All Office applications have Zoom commands that can make the data appear larger or smaller onscreen. In addition, depending on what you're doing to the data in a particular application, you may find that changing the view is useful. Some applications have multiple viewing modes you can switch among; for example, PowerPoint's Normal view is suitable for slide editing, and its Slide Sorter view is suitable for rearranging the slides.

Zooming changes the magnification of the data shown on the screen. It doesn't change the magnification of the application window itself (for example, the Ribbon), and it doesn't change the size of the data on printouts. Zooming in increases the magnification, and zooming out decreases it.

Each application has its own views suited to working with the unique type of content it generates. You can choose a view from the View tab on the Ribbon, or you can click one of the View shortcut buttons near the lower right corner of the application window, as shown in Figure 9-8.

Figure 9-8:
Click a View
button to
switch to
a different
view.

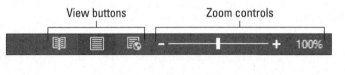

Creating a Document

In all the Office applications discussed in this book (except Outlook, which works somewhat differently), when you start the application, a Start screen appears, and if you press Esc from there, a new blank document appears. You can begin creating new content in this document and then save your work when you're finished editing. Alternatively, you can open an existing document or start a different type of document.

I use the term *document* generically to refer to a data file from Word, Excel, or PowerPoint. *Document* is actually the preferred term for a Word document. An Excel document is more commonly called a *workbook*, and a PowerPoint document is more commonly called a *presentation*.

After starting a new document, you type or insert content into it. Documents can contain text, graphic objects, or a combination of the two. You can use many types of graphic objects, such as photos, clip art, drawings, diagrams, and charts. You learn about these object types in later lessons.

Typing text

Because of the layout differences among Excel, Word, and PowerPoint, the process of entering text in each program differs. Excel stores text in *cells,* which are boxes at the intersections of rows and columns. Word stores text directly on the document page. PowerPoint places text in movable, resizable text boxes on slides.

To enter text, position the insertion point, using whatever method is appropriate for the application you are using, and then start typing. Use Backspace to erase the character to the left of the insertion point, or use Delete to erase the character to its right.

Inserting a picture

One of the most common types of graphic is what Office calls a *picture from file* (a picture that's saved as a separate file outside of Office). You can get pictures from the Internet, from friends, or from your own scanner or digital camera.

To insert a picture that you already have on your computer, click the Insert tab, and then click Pictures. An Insert Picture dialog box opens, from which you can choose the picture you want to use. See Figure 9-9. Click Insert to complete the insertion.

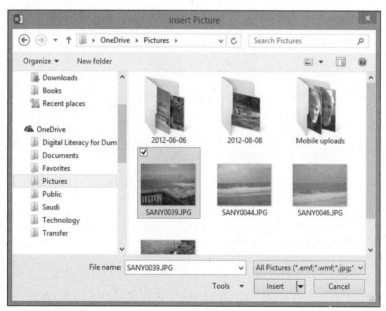

Figure 9-9: The Insert Picture dialog box.

Or, to find a picture on the Internet, click the Insert tab and then click Online Pictures. In the dialog box that appears, you can search for Office.com clip art (royalty-free artwork provided by Microsoft) or do a Bing image search to find pictures on the Internet.

You can the move and resize the picture as needed. You'll learn more about inserting pictures in Chapters 10 and 12, in Word and PowerPoint respectively.

If you find a picture using Bing Image Search, do not assume that you are free to use it without acknowledging or paying its creator. By default, the Bing image search in Office applications shows only pictures that are licensed under Creative Commons, but individual photographers and artists may have special rules for using their work.

Opening and Saving Files

In each Office application, you can create, open, and save data files. A data file stores your work in a particular application. If you don't save your work, whatever you've entered disappears when you close the application or turn off your computer.

Each Office 2013 application has its own data file format. For example:

- ✔ **Word:** Document files, `.docx`
- ✔ **Excel:** Workbook files, `.xlsx`
- ✔ **PowerPoint:** Presentation files, `.pptx`
- ✔ **Outlook:** Personal folders files, `.pst`

Word, Excel, and PowerPoint use a separate data file for each project you work on. Every time you use one of these programs, you open and save data files. Outlook uses just one data file for all your activities. This file is automatically saved and opened for you, so you usually don't have to think about data file management in Outlook.

The steps for saving and opening data files are almost exactly the same in Word, Excel, and PowerPoint, so mastering them in one program gives you a big head start in the other programs. In upcoming chapters, I will assume that you are able to save and open files in these applications, so pay close attention to the next few sections!

Saving your work for the first time

As you work in an application, the content you create is stored in the computer's memory. This memory is only temporary storage. When you exit the application or shut down the computer, whatever is stored in memory is flushed away forever — unless you save it.

The first time you save a file, the application prompts you to enter a name for it in the Save As dialog box, as shown in Figure 9-10. You can also choose a different save location and/or file type.

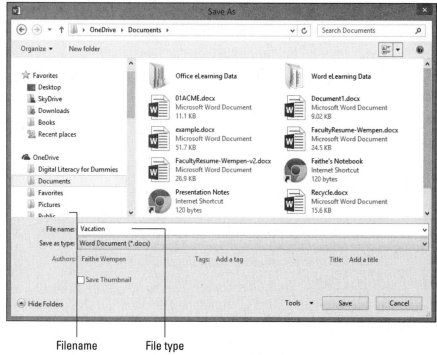

Filename   File type

Figure 9-10:
The Save As
dialog box.

When you resave a previously saved file, the Save As dialog box doesn't reappear; the file saves with the most recent settings. If you want to change the settings (such as the location or file type) or save under a different name, choose File➪Save As.

You can save your file in the default file format for that application (recommended unless you have a reason not to), or you can choose another file format. Each application has three important file format types to be aware of:

- ✔ **Default:** The default format in each application supports most Office 2007 and higher features except macros. The file extension ends in the letter *X* for each one: Word is `.docx`; Excel is `.xlsx`; PowerPoint is `.pptx`.

- ✔ **Macro-enabled:** This format supports most Office 2007 and higher features, including macros. The file extension ends in the letter *M* for each one: `.docm`, `.xlsm`, and `.pptm`.

Macros are recorded bits of code that can automate certain activities in a program, but they can also carry viruses. The default formats don't support macros for that reason. If you need to create a file that includes macros, you can save in a macro-enabled format.

✔ **97–2003:** Each application includes a file format for backward compatibility with earlier versions of the application (Office versions 97 through 2003). Some minor functionality may be lost when you save in this format. The file extensions are .doc, .xls, and .ppt.

Navigating in the Save As dialog box

Office 2013 uses the current Windows user's OneDrive as the default storage location. OneDrive is a cloud-based online storage area hosted by Microsoft. (You learned about clouds in Chapter 8.) Anyone who registers for the service, or who logs into Windows 8.1 with a Microsoft ID, is given a certain amount of free storage space, and can purchase more.

You can also save your files locally, where the default location is your Documents library, as it was with Office 2010. In Windows, each user has his own Documents folder (based on who is logged in to Windows at the moment).

New in Office 2013 applications, when you choose File⇨Save As, a dialog box doesn't open immediately. Instead, a Save As screen in Backstage view opens, prompting you to choose an overall save location, whether it's your OneDrive, your computer, or some custom location you might have set up. Only after you make that choice and click Browse does the Save As dialog box appear.

If you want the Save As dialog box to appear immediately when you choose File⇨Save As, open Backstage view and click Options. Then in the Options dialog box, click Save on the left and then mark the Don't Show the Backstage When Opening or Saving Files check box.

To understand how to change save locations, you should first understand the concept of a file path. (You got a bit of this in Chapter 4, but here's a refresher.)

Files are organized into folders, and you can have folders *inside* folders. For example, you might have

✔ A folder called *Work*

✔ Within that folder, another folder called *Job Search*

✔ Within that folder, a Word file called *Resume.docx*

The path for such a file would be

```
C:\Work\Job Search\Resume.docx
```

When you change the save location, you're changing to a different path for the file. You do that by navigating through the file system via the Save As dialog box. The Save As dialog box provides several ways of navigating, so you can pick the one you like best.

The bar at the left in the Save As dialog box is the *navigation pane*. It provides shortcuts for various places where you can save files. At the bottom of the navigation pane is a folder tree where the folders and drives on your computer can be chosen from a collapsible hierarchical tree-like structure. See Figure 9-11.

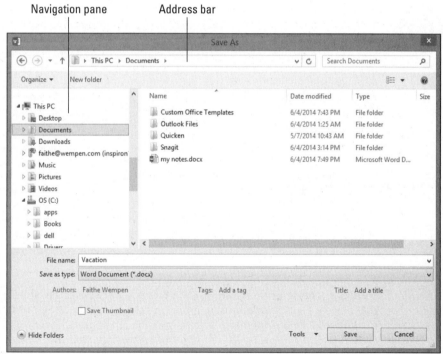

Figure 9-11: The navigation pane in the Save As dialog box.

The bar across the top is the *address bar*. It shows the current location. You can type a file path into the address bar manually if you know it.

Opening a document

When you open a file, you copy it from your hard drive (or other storage location) into the computer's memory, where Word can access it for viewing and modifying it.

The Open dialog box's navigation controls are almost exactly the same as those in the Save As dialog box, so you can browse to a different storage location if needed.

If you want to reopen a recently used file, there's an even quicker way than using the Open dialog box. Choose File⇨Open and then click the file's name on the Recent Files list.

Computers lock up occasionally, and applications sometimes crash in the middle of important projects. When that happens, any work that you haven't saved is gone. To minimize the pain of those situations, Word, Excel, and PowerPoint all have an AutoRecover feature that silently saves your drafts as you work, once every 10 minutes or at some other interval you specify. These drafts are saved in temporary hidden files that are deleted when you close the application successfully (that is, not abruptly due to a lockup, crash, or power outage). If the application crashes, those temporary saved files appear for your perusal when the program starts back up. You can choose to either keep or discard them.

Printing Files

You can print your work on paper to share with people who may not have computer access or to pass out as handouts at meetings and events. You can print the quick-and-easy way with the default settings or customize the settings to fit your needs.

To access the printing controls, click File and click Print. On the Print screen that appears, printing controls appear on the left and a preview of the print job appears on the right. The arrow buttons at the bottom of the screen enable you to page through the print preview if there is more than one page. See Figure 9-12.

Number of copies   Printer   Print preview

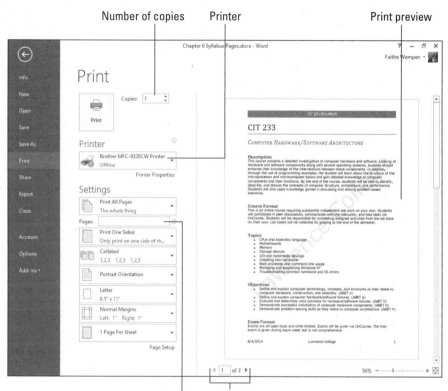

Figure 9-12:
The Print
screen.

Page range   Change the previewed page

Here are some settings you can adjust in Word. Excel and PowerPoint have some different settings specific to their content:

✔ **Copies:** One copy is the default. Enter a different number if desired.

✔ **Printer:** Choose which printer to use if you have more than one.

✔ **Page range:** In the Pages text box, you can enter the page numbers to print if you don't want to print everything. Separate individual numbers with commas, or specify a range with a dash like this: 1-3.

✔ **One-sided or two-sided:** Open the Print One Sided drop-down list and choose an option.

If you have a printer that only prints on one side at a time, you can use the Manually Print on Both Sides feature to print only every other page; you can reload the paper back into the printer to print the other side.

✔ **One-sided or two-sided:** Open the Print One Sided drop-down list and choose an option.

✔ **Collation:** If you are printing multiple copies of a multi-page document, you can choose to collate them (1, 2, 3, 1, 2, 3) or not (1, 1, 2, 2, 3, 3).

✔ **Orientation:** You can choose portrait (taller than it is wide) or landscape (wider than it is tall) page orientation.

✔ **Paper size:** You can choose a different paper size. (Don't forget to load the different paper into your printer.)

✔ **Margins:** You can adjust the page margins — that is, the amount of blank space on each side of the paper.

✔ **Pages per sheet:** You can shrink down your printout to fit multiple pages on a single piece of paper.

Chapter 10

Creating Personal Documents with Microsoft Word

- -

In This Chapter

▶ Using templates to create documents

▶ Editing and formatting text and paragraphs

▶ Applying styles

▶ Checking your work with proofing tools

▶ Creating and modifying tables

▶ Inserting and formatting pictures

▶ Discovering the benefits of desktop publishing software

- -

*M*icrosoft Word is the most popular of the Office applications because nearly everyone needs to create text documents of one type or another. With Word, you can create everything from brochures to school research papers to family holiday letters.

In this lesson, I explain how to create, edit, format, and share simple documents. By the end of this lesson, you'll have a good grasp of the entire process of document creation, from start to finish, including how to share your work with others via print or email.

Creating a New Document Using a Template

You can create a blank new document in Word, or you can base a new document on a template. Each Office application has some templates that are stored locally on your hard drive and many more that are available via the Internet. After starting a new document, you can adjust the paper size and orientation if needed.

A *template* is a special type of document that's designed to be a model for new documents. Templates have a different file extension (.dotx or .dotm) than regular documents (.docx or .doc). When you start a new document based on a template, the template file itself is unaffected, so it's always the same each time you use it.

Even when you start a blank document, you're still (technically) using a template. It's a template called Normal, and it specifies certain default settings for a new blank document, such as the default fonts (Calibri for body text and Cambria for headings), default font sizes (11 point for body text), and margins (1 inch on all sides).

To create a new document using a template, follow these steps:

1. **In Word, choose File⇨New.**

   Icons for creating new documents appear, as shown in Figure 10-1.

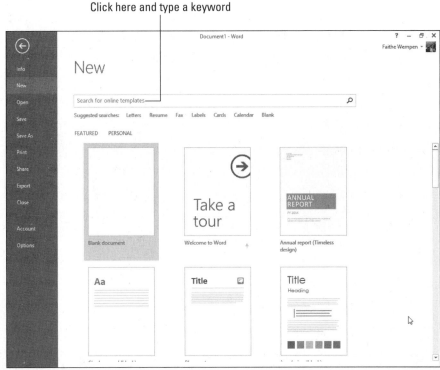

Figure 10-1: Create a new document in Word.

2. **Click in the Search for Online Templates box and type a word describing the type of template you are looking for (for example, Brochures). Then press Enter.**

   Word uses your Internet connection to retrieve a list of available brochure templates.

3. **If desired, narrow the results by clicking a category in the Category list at the right.**

   For example, you might choose Business.

   The list is filtered to show only templates that have business as a keyword.

4. **Narrow down the search further as desired. When you locate a suitable-looking template, click it to preview it, as shown in Figure 10-2.**

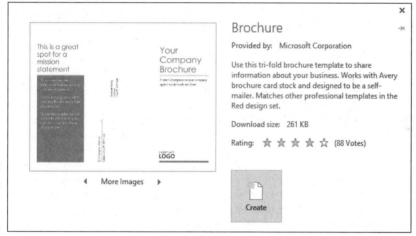

Figure 10-2:
A brochure
template.

5. **Click the Create button below the preview. The template is downloaded and a new document appears based on it.**

At this point you can add your own content to the template, save the document for later use, or just close it without saving it and try a different template.

When you create a new document by clicking the Blank Document icon or by pressing Ctrl+N, the resulting document is based on the Normal template. If you stick with the default values for the Normal template's definition, the Normal template doesn't exist as a separate file. It's built into Word itself. You won't find it if you search your hard drive for it. However, if you make a change to one or more of the Normal template's settings, Word saves them to a file called `Normal.dotm`. If Word at any point can't find `Normal.dotm`, it reverts to its internally stored copy and goes back to the default values. That's important to know because if you ever accidentally redefine the Normal template so that it produces documents with unwanted settings, or if it ever gets corrupted, all you have to do is find and delete `Normal.dotm` from your hard drive, and you go back to a fresh-from-the-factory version of the default settings for new blank documents. The template is stored in `C:\Users\`*user*`\AppData\Roaming\Microsoft\Templates`, where *user* is the logged-in username.

Adjusting Page Settings

A template might not always use the page settings for the work you want to create. You might want to change the page margins, orientation, or size, as described in the following sections.

Setting page margins

The *margins* are the amounts of blank space that Word reserves on each side of the paper. In most cases, you want them to be roughly the same on all sides, or at least the same at both the right/left, so the document looks symmetrical. In special cases, though, such as when you're going to bind the document on the left or at the top, you want to leave more blank space on one particular side.

Word provides several easy-to-use margin presets. You can also individually specify the margins for each side of the page if you prefer. To change the margins to one of the presets, choose Page Layout⮞Margins and make a selection from the Margins button's menu, as in Figure 10-3.

 One of the presets is called Mirrored. The Mirrored margin choice enables you to specify different margins for right and left, depending on whether the page number is odd or even. This option allows you to print pages for a two-sided booklet with the extra space on whichever side of the page will be in the binding.

If you have special margin needs that don't match any of the presets, you can use the Page Setup dialog box, as in the following steps.

1. Click the Margins button and then click Custom Margins.

The Page Setup dialog box opens.

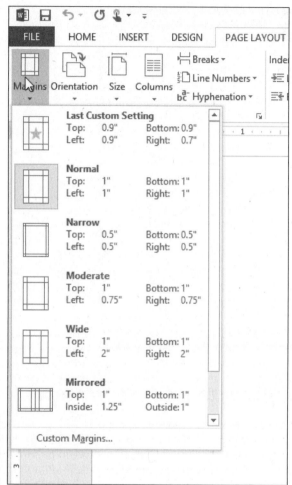

Figure 10-3:
Choose
margins.

2. **In the Top, Bottom, Right, and Left boxes, type the desired margin settings.**

   See Figure 10-4.

3. **Click OK. The margins change. You can tell the margins change because the text is positioned differently on the pages (that is, if you've typed any text, or if the template you chose provided any).**

   If there's no text in the document yet, you won't notice any change.

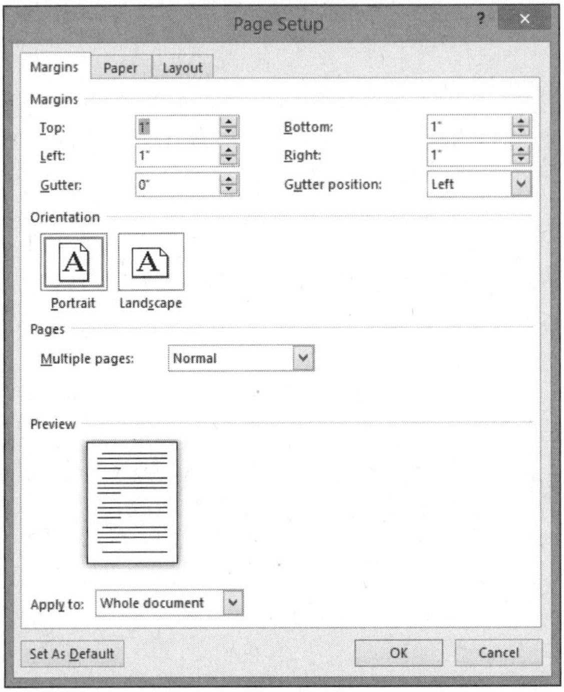

Page Setup

| Margins | Paper | Layout |

Margins

Top: 1"   Bottom: 1"
Left: 1"   Right: 1"
Gutter: 0"   Gutter position: Left

Orientation

Portrait   Landscape

Pages

Multiple pages: Normal

Preview

Apply to: Whole document

Set As Default   OK   Cancel

Figure 10-4:
Type in your desired margin settings.

Setting paper size and orientation

The standard paper size in the United States is 8.5 x 11 inches, also known as Letter. Most of the templates available through Word use this paper size, although some exceptions exist. For example, an envelope template might use a page size that matches a standard business envelope, or a legal brief template might use legal-size paper (8.5 x 14 inches).

To change the paper size, choose Page Layout⇨Size and select a paper size. See Figure 10-5. (Or, if you've got some really unusual paper size, click More Paper Sizes to set up the paper size in the Page Layout dialog box.)

Changing the paper size in Word doesn't change the paper size in your printer, of course, so if you print on a different size paper than you tell Word you're using, the printing may not be centered on the paper.

A document's *orientation* can be either portrait or landscape. *Portrait* is a standard page in which the tall part of the paper runs along the left and right sides. *Landscape* is a rotated page in which the tall part of the paper runs along the top and bottom. To set the page orientation, choose Page Layout⇨Orientation and choose Portrait or Landscape.

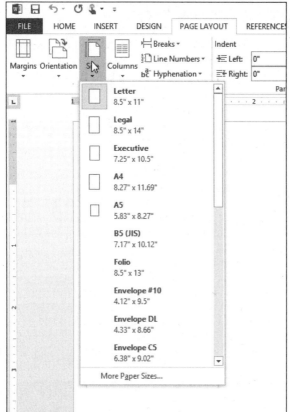

Figure 10-5:
Select a
paper size.

Editing and Selecting Text

After creating a document and settings its basic properties (such as margins, orientation, and page size), you're ready to start editing its content. Editing can include adding text, deleting text, modifying text, and moving and copying blocks of text from one location to another.

If you used a template to get started, you may already have some sample content in the document (text and/or graphics). You can edit this content, or you can delete it and start from scratch.

Filling text placeholders

Some templates include placeholders to guide you in creating content in a specific format. You aren't required to use the placeholders; you can delete them if you like. However, if you aren't sure how to get started with a particular type of document, the template's placeholders can be helpful guides.

Typing and editing text

Most documents don't contain text placeholders, so you're on your own in deciding what to type. Fortunately, it's easy to type and edit text in Word.

The text you type appears at the *insertion point*, a flashing vertical line that serves as a cursor. You can move the insertion point by clicking where you want it or by using the arrow keys to move it one space (to the right or left) or one line (up or down) per arrow key press.

To delete text, press Delete (to delete the character to the right of the insertion point) or Backspace (to delete the character to the left of the insertion point). To delete more than one character at once, select the block of text to delete and then press Delete or Backspace.

You can also select some text and then type over it. When you type after selecting text, the selected text is replaced by what you type.

Selecting text

Selecting blocks of text before you issue an editing or formatting command allows you to act on the entire block at once. For example, you can select multiple paragraphs before applying new line spacing or indentation settings, and those settings will apply to every paragraph in the selection.

You have many ways to select text:

- ✔ You can drag across the text with the mouse (with the left mouse button pressed) to select any amount of text.

- ✔ You can move the insertion point to the beginning of the text and then hold down the Shift key while you press the arrow keys to extend the selection.

✔ You can press the F8 key to turn on Extend mode, and then you can use the arrow keys to extend the selection.

✔ You can double-click a word to select it or triple-click within a paragraph to select it.

✔ You can press Ctrl+A to select the entire document.

✔ You can click to the left of a line to select that line.

Formatting Text

Text formatting can make a big difference in the readability of a document. By making certain text larger, boldface, or a different font, you can call attention to it and add interest for your readers.

The type of formatting covered in this section is commonly known as *character formatting* (formatting that can be applied to individual characters). Character formatting includes fonts, font sizes, text attributes (such as italics), character spacing (spacing between letters), and text color.

You can apply each type of character formatting individually, or you can use style sets or themes to apply multiple types of formatting at once.

Choosing text font, size, and color

The text in the document appears using a certain style of lettering, also called a *font* or a *typeface*. Office comes with dozens of typefaces, so you're sure to find one that meets the needs of whatever project you create. Choose a font from the Font drop-down list on the Home tab, as shown in Figure 10-6.

Each font is available in a wide variety of sizes. The sizes are measured in *points*, with each point being 1/72 of an inch on a printout. (The size it appears onscreen depends on the display zoom. You learn about zoom in Lesson 1.) Text sizes vary from very small (6 points) to very large (100 points or more). An average document uses body text that's between 10 and 12 points, and headings between 12 and 18 points. Chose a font size from the Font Size drop-down list (also on the Home tab). If the exact size you want doesn't appear on the list, you can type the exact size in the text box at the top of the list.

Font   Font Size

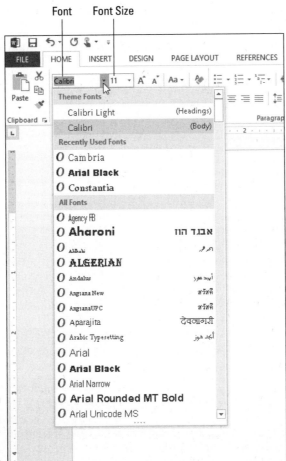

Figure 10-6:
Select a
font.

You can also color each font by using either a *standard color*, which doesn't change when you change document themes, or a *theme color*, which does change. Click the down arrow on the Font Color button to open the palette shown in Figure 10-7. The top row contains the theme colors, and the rows beneath that contain tints and shades of the theme colors. The bottom row contains the standard colors.

Applying text attributes and effects

You can modify text with a variety of *attributes*, such as bold, italics, underlining, and so on. You can apply some of these attributes from the Mini toolbar and/or the Font group on the Home tab. Others are available in the Font dialog box. Some of them also have keyboard shortcuts.

Tints and shades of theme colors

Theme colors

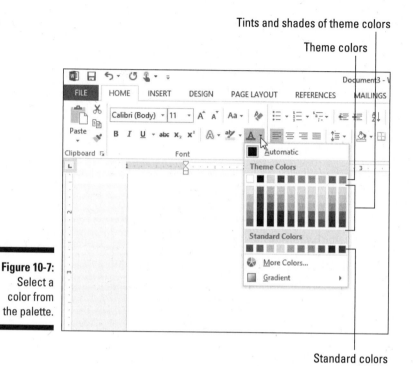

Figure 10-7:
Select a
color from
the palette.

Standard colors

To access the Font dialog box, from the Home tab, click the dialog box launcher for the Font group (the small symbol in the bottom right corner of the Font group). In the Font dialog box you can not only apply attributes, but you can also make all the other character formatting changes you've learned about so far in this chapter (font, size, and color). See Figure 10-8.

Bold   Dialog box launcher

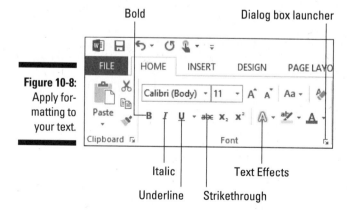

Figure 10-8:
Apply for-
matting to
your text.

Italic   Text Effects

Underline   Strikethrough

Figure 10-9 shows samples of some of these attributes. Table 10-1 summarizes the keyboard shortcuts for them.

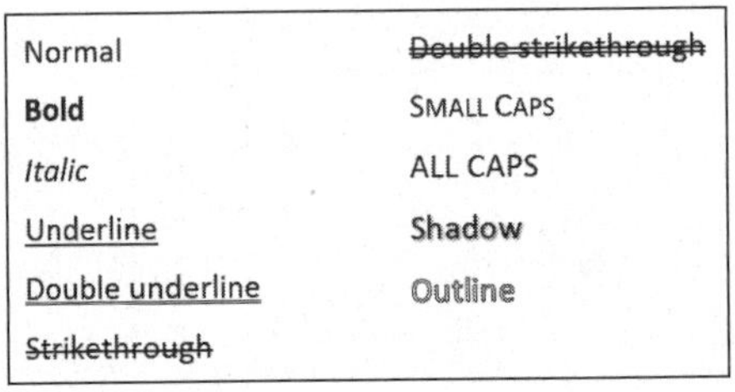

Figure 10-9:
Examples
of text
attributes.

Normal	~~Double strikethrough~~
Bold	SMALL CAPS
Italic	ALL CAPS
Underline	**Shadow**
Double underline	Outline
~~Strikethrough~~	

Table 10-1   Keyboard Shortcuts for Applying Text Attributes

Attribute	*Keyboard Shortcut*
Bold	Ctrl+B
Italic	Ctrl+I
Underline	Ctrl+U
Subscript	Ctrl+=
Superscript	Ctrl+Shift++ (plus sign)
Underline words but not space	Ctrl+Shift+W
Double underline text	Ctrl+Shift+D
Small caps	Ctrl+Shift+K
All caps	Ctrl+Shift+A

You can also apply *text effects*, also called *WordArt effects*. The available text effects include Outline, Shadow, Reflection, and Glow. Figure 10-9 shows examples of Shadow and Outline. Text effects are accessed from the Text Effects and Typography button's menu on the Home tab. See Figure 10-10. The Text Effects button's menu also includes a number of presets that combine color fills, outlines, and other effects in a single operation.

Working with themes

A *theme* is a file that contains settings for fonts (heading and body), colors, and object formatting effects (such as 3D effects for drawn shapes and SmartArt diagrams). Themes enable you to dramatically change the look of a document quickly.

Text Effects button

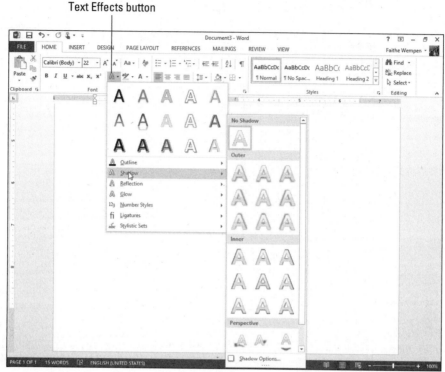

Figure 10-10:
Apply
effects to
your text.

All the Office applications use the same set of themes, so themes can help you standardize the look of your work across multiple applications. For example, you could make the fonts and colors on a brochure you create in Word similar to a presentation you create in PowerPoint.

In a Word document that contains only text, you won't notice the effect changes when you switch to a different theme, but the font and color changes will be apparent.

Themes affect only text that hasn't had manual formatting applied that overrides the defaults. For example, if you've specified a certain font or font color for some text, that text doesn't change when you change the theme. You can strip off manual formatting with the Clear Formatting button on the Home tab.

To choose a different theme, choose Design➪Themes and then choose a theme from the list. See Figure 10-11.

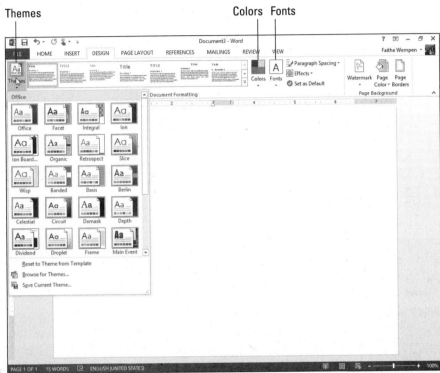

Themes   Colors Fonts

Figure 10-11:
Select a
theme.

You can also apply color themes, font themes, and/or effect themes separately. This ability is useful when none of the available themes exactly match what you want. After you make the selections you want to create the right combination of colors, fonts, and effects, you can save your choices as a new theme to use in other documents (including in Excel and PowerPoint as well as in Word). Use the Design⇨Colors command for colors, and the Design⇨Fonts command for fonts. To save a theme, choose Design⇨Themes⇨Save Current Theme.

Applying style sets

A *style set* is a preset combination of fonts, paragraph line spacing, character spacing, and indentation. Style sets enable you to quickly change the look of the document without manually reformatting each paragraph or changing themes. You can choose a style set from the Style Sets gallery on the Design tab. See Figure 10-12.

Style Sets gallery

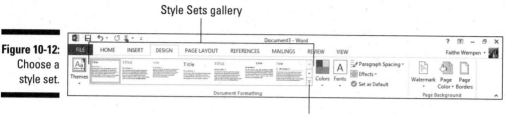

Figure 10-12:
Choose a
style set.

Click here to open the gallery

If you've manually applied specific fonts, you won't see a change when you apply a different style set. If you don't get the results you expect with a style set, select the entire document (Ctrl+A) and then clear the formatting by clicking the Clear Formatting button on the Home tab or by pressing Ctrl+spacebar.

Formatting Paragraphs

Paragraph formatting is formatting that affects whole paragraphs and cannot be applied to individual characters. For example, line spacing is a type of paragraph formatting, along with indentation and alignment. Paragraph formatting is applied from the Paragraph group on the Home tab.

If you apply paragraph formatting when no text is selected, the formatting applies to the paragraph in which the insertion point is currently located.

If you apply paragraph formatting when text is selected, the formatting applies to whatever paragraphs are included in that selection, even if only one character of the paragraph is included. Being able to format paragraphs this way is useful because you can select multiple paragraphs at once and then format them as a group.

To set the paragraph formatting for the entire document at once, press Ctrl+A to select the entire document and then issue the paragraph formatting commands.

Applying horizontal alignment

Horizontal alignment refers to the positioning of the paragraph between the right and left margins. The horizontal alignment choices are Align Text Left, Center, Align Text Right, and Justify. Figure 10-13 shows an example of each of the alignment types. It also points out the horizontal alignment buttons on the Home tab.

Align Text Right

Align Text Left   Center | Justify

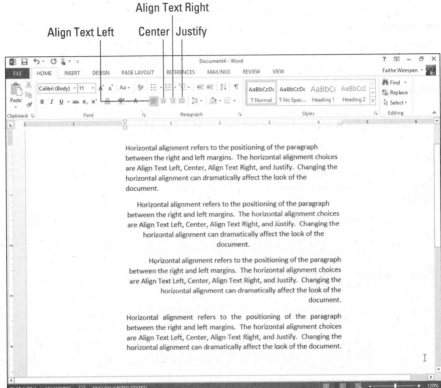

Figure 10-13:
Select
alignment
from the
Home tab.

Each of those is pretty self-evident except the last one. *Justify* aligns both the left and right sides of the paragraph with the margins, stretching out or compressing the text in each line as needed to make it fit. The final line in the paragraph is exempt and appears left-aligned.

If you apply Justify alignment to a paragraph that contains only one line, it looks like it is left-aligned. However, if you then type more text into the paragraph so it wraps to additional lines, the Justify alignment becomes apparent.

Indenting a paragraph

The *indentation* of a paragraph refers to how its left and/or right sides are inset. When a paragraph has no indentation, it's allowed to take up the full range of space between the left and right margins. When you set indentation for a paragraph, its left and/or right sides are inset by the amount you specify. Many people like to indent quotations to set them apart from the rest of the text for emphasis, for example.

In addition to a left and right indent value, each paragraph can optionally have a special indent for the first line. If the first line is indented more than the rest of the paragraph, it's known as a *first-line indent*. (Clever name.) If the first line is indented less than the rest of the paragraph, it's called a *hanging indent*.

First-line indents are sometimes used in reports and books to help the reader's eye catch the beginning of a paragraph. In layouts where there is vertical space between paragraphs, first-line indents are less useful because it's easy to see where a new paragraph begins without that help.

Hanging indents are typically used to create listings. In a bulleted or numbered list, the bullet or number hangs off the left edge of the paragraph, in a hanging indent. However, in Word, when you create bulleted or numbered lists (covered later in this lesson), Word adjusts the paragraph's hanging indent automatically, so you don't have to think about it.

If you want to indent all the lines on the left, you can use the Increase Indent button on the Home tab. (There's a Decrease Indent button too, for reversing the indentation.) If you want any other kind of indent, though, you have to open the Paragraph dialog box.

Follow these steps to adjust indentation in the Paragraph dialog box.

1. **Select the paragraphs to affect.**

2. **Click the dialog box launcher in the Paragraph group to open the Paragraph dialog box.**

   See Figure 10-14.

3. **Do either or both of the following as desired:**

   • Under Indentation, adjust the amounts for Left and/or Right indents. The numbers are in inches.

   • Open the Special drop-down list and choose either First Line or Hanging, and then enter an amount in the By box.

4. **Click OK.**

You can also create a first-line indent by positioning the insertion point at the beginning of a paragraph and pressing the Tab key. Normally this would place a 0.5-inch tab at the beginning of the paragraph, but the Word AutoCorrect feature immediately converts it to a real first-line indent for you.

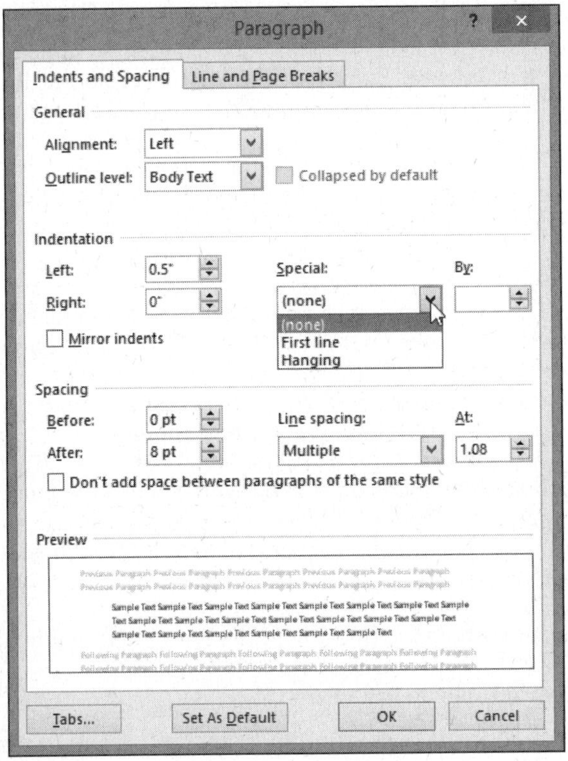

Figure 10-14:
The
Paragraph
dialog box.

Changing vertical spacing

Vertical spacing refers to the amount of space (also known as the leading) between each line. A paragraph has three values you can set for its spacing:

- ✔ **Line spacing:** The space between the lines within a multi-line paragraph
- ✔ **Before:** Extra spacing added above the first line of the paragraph
- ✔ **After:** Extra spacing added below the last line of the paragraph

You can set line spacing of a paragraph to any of several presets, such as Single, Double, and 1.5 Lines, or to an exact value, measured in points. Space before and after a paragraph is specified in points, too.

If you specify an exact amount of space per line and you change the font size, the text may not look right anymore. For example, if you change the font size to a larger size than the exact spacing is set for, the lines might overlap vertically. If you aren't sure what font sizes you need, don't use exact spacing.

To choose a preset for line spacing, you can click the Line Spacing button on the Home tab and choose from a menu, as in Figure 10-15. Notice that you can also add or remove space before or after a paragraph from this menu.

Line Spacing

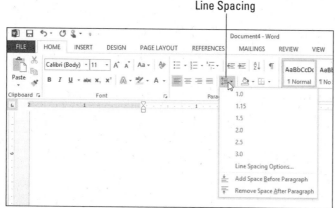

Figure 10-15:
Choose a preset line spacing.

For a broader array of options, you can open the Paragraph dialog box. Follow these steps:

1. **Select the paragraphs to affect.**

2. **Click the Line Spacing button to open its menu (Figure 10-15) and then choose Line Spacing Options.**

   The Paragraph dialog box opens. (It's the one in Figure 10-14.)

   You can click the dialog box launcher for the Paragraph group to open the Paragraph dialog box if you prefer that method.

3. **Set the desired spacing before and after the paragraph, in points, in the Before and After boxes.**

4. **Open the Line spacing drop-down list and choose a line spacing value.**

   Some of the choices here are absolutes, like Single, 1.5 Lines, or Double. Others require you to enter a setting in the At box, such as Exactly, At Least, or Multiple.

5. **Click OK to accept the new setting.**

Creating bulleted and numbered lists

Word makes it easy to create bulleted and numbered lists in your documents. You can create a list from existing paragraphs, or you can turn on the list feature and type the list as you go. Either way, you're working with the Bullets button or the Numbering button on the Home tab.

Use a *bulleted list* for lists where the order of items isn't significant, and the same "bullet" character (such as • or ➪) is used in front of each item. You might use a bulleted list for a packing list for a trip, for example, or a go-forward list.

Use a *numbered list* for lists where the order of items *is* significant and a where sequential step number is used to indicate order. A numbered list might contain the steps for a recipe or a meeting agenda.

To create a basic bulleted or numbered list, select the paragraphs to affect and then click the Bullets or Numbering button on the Home tab. Each of those buttons also has a drop-down list associated with it, for more bullet and numbering style choices. Figure 10-16 shows the one for numbered lists.

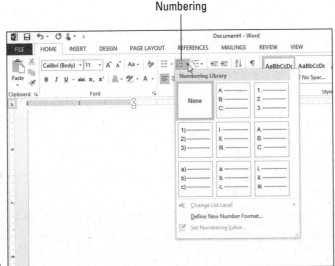

Figure 10-16:
Create a
bulleted or
numbered
list.

Working with Styles

A *style* is a named set of formatting specifications. Using a style makes it easy to apply consistent formatting throughout a document. For example, you might apply the Heading 1 style to all headings in the document and the Normal style to all the regular body text. Here are the advantages of this approach:

✔ **Ease:** Applying a style is easier than manually applying formatting. And changing a style's formatting is a snap. If you want the headings to look different, for example, you can modify the Heading 1 style to change them all at once.

✔ **Consistency:** You don't have to worry about all the headings being formatted consistently; because they're all using the same style, they're automatically all the same.

By default, each paragraph is assigned a Normal style. The template in use determines the styles available and how they're defined.

In Word 2013 in documents that use the default blank (Normal) template, the Normal style uses Calibri 11-point font and left-aligns the text, with no indentation.

You can redefine the styles in a document, and you can even create your own new styles.

Applying a style

In the Styles group on the Home tab is a Styles gallery. The first row appears on the Ribbon itself, and you can see the rest of it by clicking the More button to open the full gallery, shown in Figure 10-17.

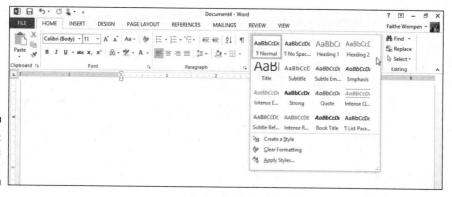

Figure 10-17:
The Styles
gallery.

Not all styles appear in the Styles gallery — only the ones that are designated to appear there in their definition. The rest of them appear only in the Styles pane. To open the Styles pane, click the dialog box launcher on the Styles group. See Figure 10-18.

To apply a style, select the paragraph(s) that you want to affect or move the insertion point into the paragraph. Then click the style you want to apply, either in the Styles gallery or in the Styles pane. Some styles also have keyboard shortcuts assigned to them for quick applying.

The dialog box launcher opens the Styles pane   Styles pane

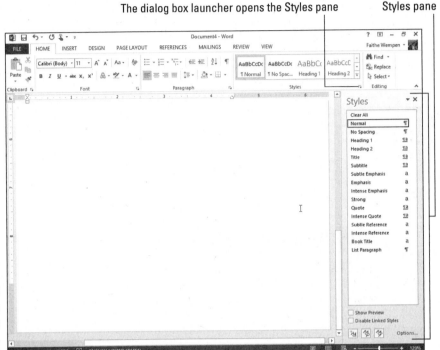

Figure 10-18:
The Styles
pane.

Modifying a style

To modify a style, first apply the style to a paragraph. Then reformat the paragraph the way you want the style to be, and then in the Styles pane, right-click the style and choose Update *style* to Match Selection (where *style* is the style name). See Figure 10-19.

Creating a new style

You can also create your own styles. This is especially useful if you want to build a template that you can give to other people to make sure that everyone formats documents the same way, such as in a group where each person assembles a different section of a report.

When you create your own styles, you can name them anything you like. Most people like to name styles based on their purposes, to make it easier to choose which style to apply. For example, *Figure Caption* would be a good name; *Style13* would not.

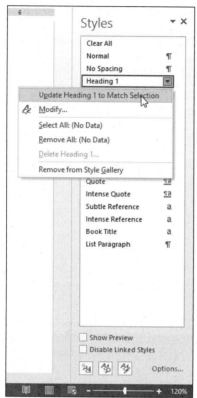

Figure 10-19:
Update
a style to
match your
selection.

To create a style, format a paragraph the way you want the new style to be, and then at the bottom of the Styles pane, click the New Style button. In the dialog box that appears (see Figure 10-20), type a name for the style in the Name text box and click OK. That's all there is to it!

Copying formatting with Format Painter

When many different blocks of text need to be formatted the same way, it can be tedious to select and format each block. As a shortcut, Word offers the *Format Painter* feature. Format Painter picks up the formatting from one block of text and applies it to another.

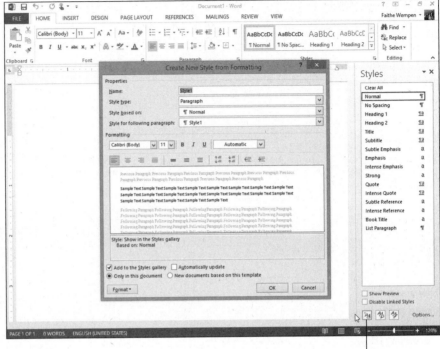

Figure 10-20:
The Create
New
Style from
Formatting
dialog box.

New Style

To use Format Painter, follow these steps:

1. **Select some text that is already formatted the way you want.**

2. **Click the Format Painter button on the Home tab. It's the button that looks like a paintbrush in the Clipboard group.**

3. **Select the text that should receive the copied formatting.**

After that last step, Format Painter turns itself off automatically. If you want it to stay on so you can copy that same formatting to other text too, double-click instead of clicking the button in Step 2.

Checking Spelling and Grammar

Spelling and grammar errors in your documents can leave a bad impression with your audience, and can be the cause of lost customers, jobs, and opportunities. Fortunately, Word can help save you from the consequences of such errors, whether they're errors due to carelessness or errors due to lack of knowledge of spelling and grammar.

Word automatically checks your spelling and grammar as you type. Wavy red underlines indicate possible spelling errors, and wavy blue underlines indicate possible grammar errors. To correct one of these errors on the fly, right-click the underlined text and choose a quick correction from the shortcut menu. See Figure 10-21.

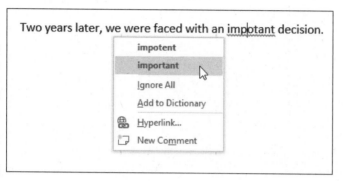

Figure 10-21:
Choose
a correct
spelling
from the
shortcut
menu.

You can also run the full-blown Spelling and Grammar utility within Word to check the entire document at once. Word has a more robust and powerful Spelling and Grammar checker than the other Office applications do, but they all have similar functionality. One by one, each potential error appears in a task pane, and you click buttons to decide how to deal with each one. To do that, choose Review➪Spelling & Grammar. Figure 10-22 shows the checker in action.

One of the choices when dealing with a potentially misspelled word is to add the word to the dictionary so that it isn't flagged as misspelled in any future spell-check in any document. The dictionary file is common to all the Office applications, so any word you add to the dictionary in Word will also no longer be flagged as misspelled in Excel, PowerPoint, or Outlook.

Creating a Table

A table is a grid of rows and columns, somewhat like a spreadsheet. Tables are useful for displaying information in multicolumn layouts, such as address lists and schedules. You may be surprised at all the uses you can find for tables in your documents!

When inserting a new table, you can specify a number of rows and columns to create a blank grid and then fill in the grid by typing. Press the Tab key to move to the next cell. When you reach the end of the last row, you can press Tab to add a row to the table.

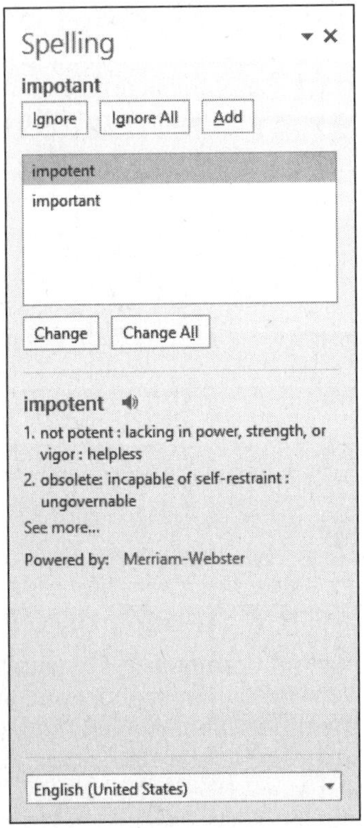

Spelling

impotant

| Ignore | Ignore All | Add |

| impotent |
| important |

| Change | Change All |

impotent 🔊

1. not potent : lacking in power, strength, or vigor : helpless
2. obsolete: incapable of self-restraint : ungovernable

See more...

Powered by: Merriam-Webster

English (United States)

Figure 10-22:
Check your
grammar
and spelling.

To create a new table, choose Insert⇨Table and, in the menu that appears with a grid, drag across the grid to select the desired number of rows and three columns, as shown in Figure 10-23. Then release the mouse button to create the table.

To type in a table, click in the cell in which you want to enter text and start typing. You can press Tab to move to the next cell or Shift+Tab to move to the previous cell.

Selecting rows and columns

Working with a table often involves selecting one or more cells, rows, or columns. Here are the many ways to do this:

- Drag across the cells you want to select.
- Click in the upper-left cell you want to select and then hold down the Shift key and press arrow keys to extend the selection.
- Click outside of the table on the left side to select an entire row.

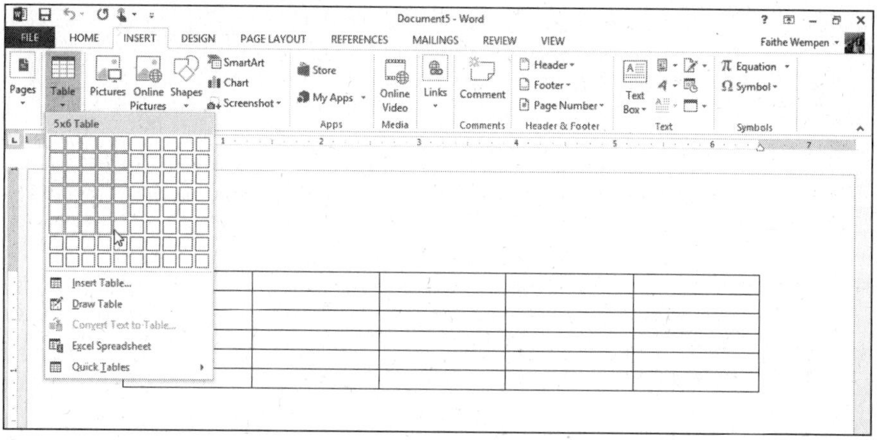

Figure 10-23:
Create a
basic table.

- ✔ Click outside of the table above the table to select an entire column.

- ✔ Click the table selector icon (the four-headed arrow in a box; see Figure 10-24) in the upper-left corner of the table to select the entire table.

- ✔ On the Table Tools Layout tab, click the Select button and then choose what you want to select from the menu that appears.

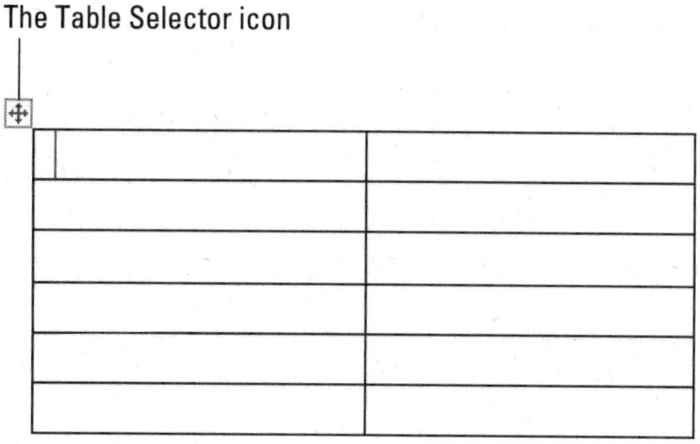

The Table Selector icon

Figure 10-24:
The four-
headed
arrow is the
table selec-
tor icon.

Resizing rows and columns

Word handles row height automatically for you, so you usually don't have to think about it. The row height changes as needed to accommodate the font size of the text in the cells of that row. Text in a cell wraps automatically to the next line when it runs out of room horizontally, so you can expect your table rows to expand in height as you type more text into them.

If you manually resize a row's height, the ability to auto-resize to fit content is turned off for that row. Therefore, if you add more text to that row later, Word doesn't automatically expand that row's height to accommodate it, and some text may be truncated.

In contrast, column width remains fixed until you change it, regardless of the cell's content. If you want the width of a column to change, you must change it yourself.

To auto-resize a column width to fit the longest entry, double-click the divider between that column and the one to its right. Alternatively, you can select the columns to resize and then choose Table Tools Layout⇨AutoFit⇨AutoFit Contents.

You can also drag the column divider to resize the column manually.

If you select certain cells before resizing a column, only the rows containing those cells will be affected by the resize operation, and you'll be left with a table with uneven columns. (Maybe that's what you want, maybe not.)

Those same techniques work for resizing row height too: You can double-click a divider to autofit, or you can drag the divider manually.

Formatting table borders

First, let's get some terminology straight. *Gridlines* are the dividers that separate a table's rows and columns. A *border* is formatting applied to a gridline that makes it appear when printed. Got it? Good.

Gridlines can be displayed or hidden onscreen (via Table Tools Layout⇨View Gridlines). Gridlines do not print, and when displayed onscreen, they appear as thin blue or gray dashed lines. You probably won't see the gridlines in most tables because they're covered by borders. By default, table gridlines have a plain black ½ point.

You can change the borders to different colors, styles (such as dotted or dashed), and thicknesses, or remove the borders altogether.

The most basic way of formatting borders is to use the Borders button on the Table Tools Design tab. Open the button's drop-down list and choose the type of border to apply to the selected cells. See Figure 10-25.

To change the line weight, line style (for example, dotted or dashed), and/or line color, use their respective drop-down list in the Borders group on the Table Tools Design tab. After you make those selections, you may need to reapply the border using the Borders button again.

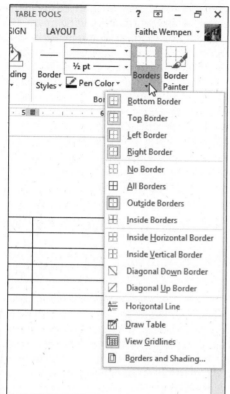

Figure 10-25:
Choose a
border to
apply.

Working with Pictures

Pictures can liven up even the most boring document. In the following sections, you'll learn several ways of inserting pictures into Word documents and placing them where you want them.

Inserting pictures from the web

Clip art is generic artwork. In the days before most businesses had computers, companies that needed stock artwork would buy large books of line drawings, and when they needed an image, they would clip it out of the book with scissors and glue it to a paste-up layout. That's where the name comes from. Today, *clip art* refers to line-based drawings such as the ones you can get from Office.com.

When you buy any of the Office applications, you get free access to a large online library of clip art maintained by Microsoft at Office.com. Each of the main Office applications has an Online Pictures command that opens a dialog box in which you can search this library and insert images from it into your documents. This image library contains not only clip art but also royalty-free stock photography.

Office.com is only one of the possible sources of online images you can explore. You can also retrieve files via a Bing Image Search on the web. Bing (`www.bing.com`) is a search engine sponsored by Microsoft, and the Bing Image Search feature in Office applications enables you to easily locate images from all over the Internet.

Understanding vector and raster graphics

There are two types of computer graphics: vector and raster. They're very different from one another, and each is best suited for a different purpose.

Clip art is a type of vector graphic. A *vector graphic* is created behind the scenes by using math formulas; if you've taken a geometry class where you plotted a function on graph paper, you get the idea. Computerized clip art builds images by layering and combining individual lines and shapes, each one constructed via a math formula. As a result, the clips can be resized without losing any quality because resizing simply changes the math formula. Clip art files are also very small compared with raster graphics. The main drawback of clip art is that the images don't look real — they look like drawings.

Photos from digital cameras are examples of *raster* graphics. A raster graphic is a densely packed collection of colored dots that together form an image. If you zoom in on a photo on a computer, you can see these dots individually. In a raster graphic, each dot is called a *pixel*, and its color is represented by a numeric code (usually 24 or 32 binary digits in length per pixel). Raster graphics can be photorealistic, but because so much data is required to define each pixel, the file sizes tend to be large.

Microsoft Office uses the terms *image*, *picture*, and *graphic* interchangeably in its documentation and help system, and so does this book. All three refer generically to any picture, regardless of its type or source. The term photograph refers specifically to raster images, and the terms *clip art* and *illustration* refer specifically to vector images.

To insert a clip art image, follow these steps:

1. **Position the insertion point where you want the picture to appear.**

2. **Choose Insert⇨Online Pictures. The Insert Pictures dialog box opens.**

3. **Click in the Office.com Clip Art search box, type a word that describes what you are looking for, and press Enter.**

   A selection of pictures that have that word as a keyword appear in the task pane. See Figure 10-26.

Online Pictures

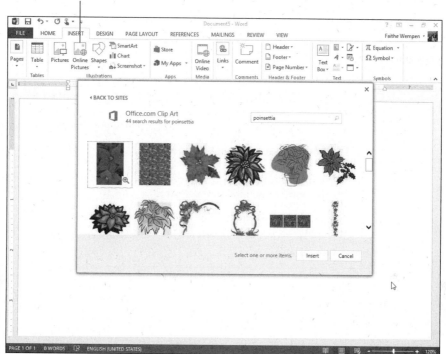

Figure 10-26:
Choose a
piece of
clip art.

4. **Scroll through the resulting clips. Notice that the results are a mixture of line drawings and photographs.**

5. **Click one of the clips and then click the Insert button to insert it. The clip appears in the document.**

Notice that the clip is placed in the document as an inline image. An inline image is treated like a really large character of text. The height of the image makes the first line of the paragraph extra tall, as you can see in Figure 10-27. Later in this chapter, in the section, "Changing the text wrap setting for a picture," you learn how to make text wrap more gracefully around a picture.

Inline image is treated like a character of text

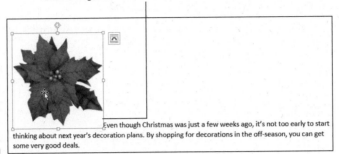

Even though Christmas was just a few weeks ago, it's not too early to start thinking about next year's decoration plans. By shopping for decorations in the off-season, you can get some very good deals.

Figure 10-27: Wrap text around an image.

To insert an image using Bing image search, follow these steps:

1. **Position the insertion point where you want the picture to appear.**

2. **Choose Insert⇨Online Pictures. The Insert Pictures dialog box opens.**

3. **Click in the Bing Image Search box, type a word that describes the image you want, and press Enter.**

   A selection of pictures that have that word as a keyword appear in the task pane. See Figure 10-28.

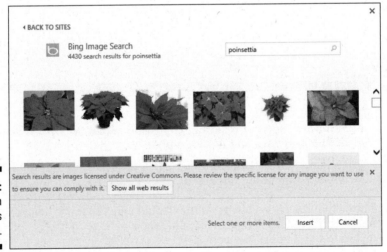

Figure 10-28: Search for photos online.

These images come from the web rather than from Microsoft. Notice the information that appears across the bottom of the dialog box indicating that the images shown are licensed under Creative Commons. This filter helps you avoid violating someone's copyright by using a found image. You can turn off this filter by clicking Show All Web Results if desired.

4. **Click one of the pictures and then click the Insert button to insert it.**

The image appears in the document. Depending on the picture you chose, the image may be small, or may take up the entire page width.

Inserting photos from files

The clips available online are generic. Sometimes, you might want to insert a more personal picture, such as a digital photo you took or a picture that a friend or co-worker sent you via email.

To insert a picture that you already have, follow these steps:

1. **Position the insertion point where you want the picture to appear.**

2. **Choose Insert ⇨Pictures.**

The Insert Picture dialog box opens.

3. **Navigate to the folder containing the picture you want and select the picture.**

4. **Click the Insert button. The picture is inserted in the document.**

Changing the text wrap setting for a picture

After you insert a graphic in a document, you may decide you want to change how the text around it interacts with it. For example, you might want the text to wrap around the graphic or even run on top of it.

By default, as I mention earlier, a picture is inserted as an inline image, which means it's treated like a text character. That's not usually the best way for an image to interact with the text, though. More often you want the text to flow around the image so that, if the text moves (due to editing), the graphic stays where you put it. You can change a picture's *text wrap* setting to control this.

To change the text wrap setting, select the picture, so that the Picture Tools Format tab becomes available. Then choose Picture Tools Format⇨Wrap Text to open a menu of text wrap settings. See Figure 10-29. Select the desired wrap setting. For example, Square wraps the text around the picture with rectangular edges, and Tight wraps the text tightly around the image itself.

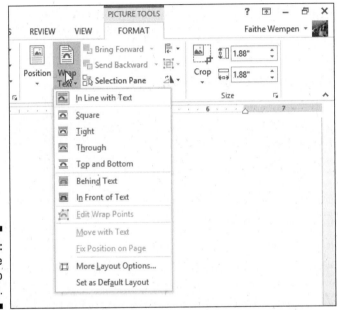

Figure 10-29: Change the text wrap setting.

Figure 10-30 shows examples of some of the different settings: Square, Tight, Behind Text, and In Front of Text.

Notice the icon next to the selected picture that looks like an arch? You can click that button to open a floating version of the Wrap Text button's menu, as an alternative to clicking the Text Wrap button on the Ribbon.

Moving a picture

You can move a picture by dragging it where you want it to go. Position the mouse pointer over the image (anywhere except over a selection handle) and drag.

The way a picture moves when you drag it varies depending on the text wrap setting you've chosen for the picture. If the default setting of In Line with Text is in effect, you can drag a picture only to a spot where you can also drag text: either within existing paragraphs or before or after existing paragraphs. You can't place a picture outside of the document margins or below the end-of-document marker.

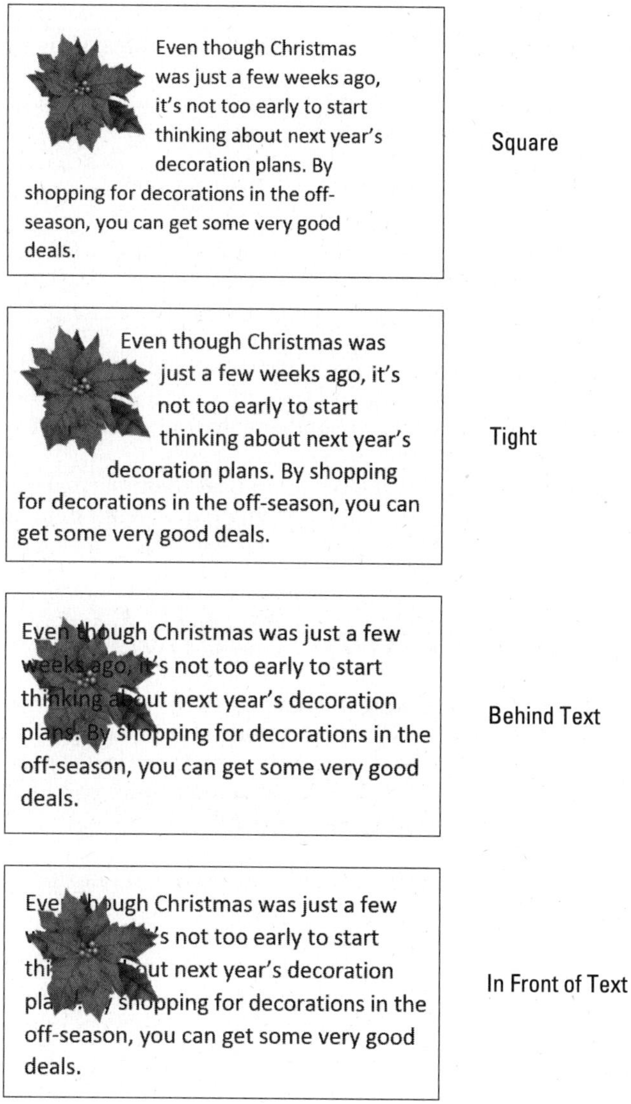

Even though Christmas was just a few weeks ago, it's not too early to start thinking about next year's decoration plans. By shopping for decorations in the off-season, you can get some very good deals.

Square

Even though Christmas was just a few weeks ago, it's not too early to start thinking about next year's decoration plans. By shopping for decorations in the off-season, you can get some very good deals.

Tight

Even though Christmas was just a few weeks ago, it's not too early to start thinking about next year's decoration plans. By shopping for decorations in the off-season, you can get some very good deals.

Behind Text

Even though Christmas was just a few weeks ago, it's not too early to start thinking about next year's decoration plans. By shopping for decorations in the off-season, you can get some very good deals.

In Front of Text

Figure 10-30: Examples of different text wrap settings.

If any other text wrapping setting is in effect, you can drag a picture anywhere on the page. So, if you're having trouble dragging a picture where you want it, change the Text Wrap setting to Square or Tight and the problem will disappear.

Resizing a picture

You can resize a picture by dragging its selection handles or by specifying an exact height and width for the picture in the Height and Width boxes on the Picture Tools Format tab. The selection handles are the small squares around the outside border of the picture when it is selected.

When you resize a picture, its *aspect ratio* can change. The aspect ratio is the proportion of width to height. A photo may not look right if you don't maintain the aspect ratio; clip art is less likely to suffer from small differences in the ratio. When you drag a corner selection handle, the aspect ratio is maintained; when you drag a side selection handle, it is not.

Most image types maintain the aspect ratio automatically if you drag a corner selection handle. If the aspect ratio doesn't stay constant when you drag a corner selection handle, hold down Shift as you drag to force it to do so.

Raster images look fuzzy if you enlarge them past their original size. That's one advantage of vector images: They remain crisp and sharp at any size.

Understanding Desktop Publishing

Word creates professional-looking documents such as reports, memos, and flyers, but there may be times when you need an application that offers more control over the document layout. For example, if you are laying out the pages of a magazine or creating a professional brochure, you might find it difficult to achieve the desired layout in Word.

A desktop publishing application can provide the layout flexibility needed for such projects.

The main difference between desktop publishing and word processing is that desktop publishing places all the content in frames rather than directly on the page background. Each frame is individually resizable and movable, so it can be placed exactly where you want it. A desktop publishing application will also have more typography control features and can create files that you can send to professional printing companies, including color separations.

There are many desktop publishing applications available, at a variety of prices and feature sets. At the low end, you might consider Microsoft Publisher, a consumer-level application that shares many of the same user interface features as Office applications. (Publisher is even included in some editions of Office.) Figure 10-31 shows Microsoft Publisher. For professional use, applications such as Adobe InDesign and QuarkXPress offer a full feature set for maximum document control.

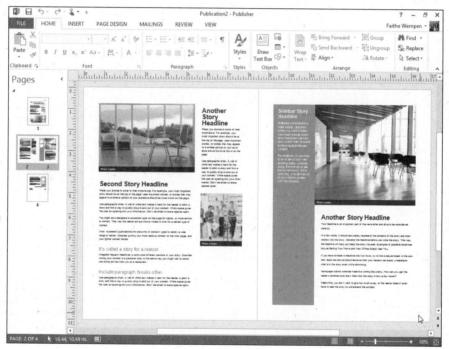

Figure 10-31:
Microsoft Publisher is a basic desktop publishing program.

Chapter 11

Managing and Calculating Data with Microsoft Excel

*E*xcel has many practical uses. You can use its orderly row-and-column worksheet structure to organize multicolumn lists, create business forms, and much more. Excel provides more than just data organization, however; it enables you to write formulas that perform calculations on your data. This feature makes Excel an ideal tool for storing financial information, such as checkbook register and investment portfolio data.

In this chapter, I explain how to create Excel worksheets that include data, calculations, and formatting, and how to create charts from that data and print your work. After completing this chapter, you will understand how to use Excel for your own tasks.

Understanding the Excel Interface

Excel is very much like Word and other Office applications. Excel has a File tab that opens a Backstage view, a Ribbon with multiple tabs that contain commands you can click to execute, a Quick Access toolbar, a status bar, scroll bars, and a Zoom slider. Figure 11-1 provides a quick overview.

Quick Access toolbar

Tabs

Ribbon

Figure 11-1:
The basics
of the Excel
interface.

Scroll bars

Active cell

Zoom slider

Name box shows active cell's address

Starting out with some basic terminology is a good idea. A *worksheet* is a grid composed of rows and columns. At the intersection of each row and column is a *cell*. You can type text, numbers, and formulas into cells to build your worksheet. In Excel, worksheets are dubbed *worksheets* or just *sheets*. Worksheets are stored in data files, or *workbooks*, and each workbook can contain multiple worksheets. *Worksheet tabs* at the bottom of a workbook window enable you to switch quickly between worksheets.

Notice that each row in Figure 11-1 has a unique number, and each column has a unique letter. The combination of a letter and a number forms a *cell address*. The letter comes first. For example, the cell in the upper-left corner is A1. When you type something in Excel, your typing is entered into the *active cell*, which features the *cell cursor*, or a thick green outline. The active cell's name appears in the *Name box*.

Moving the cell cursor

To type in a cell, you must first make it active by moving the cell cursor there. The *cell cursor* is a thick outline that indicates the active cell. In Figure 11-1, it is on cell C5. You can move the cell cursor by pressing the arrow keys on the keyboard, by clicking the desired cell, or by using one of the Excel keyboard shortcuts. Table 11-1 provides some of the most common keyboard shortcuts for moving the cell cursor.

Table 11-1	Movement Shortcuts
Press This . . .	*To Move . . .*
Arrow keys	One cell in the direction of the arrow
Tab	One cell to the right
Shift+Tab	One cell to the left
Ctrl+arrow key	To the edge of the current data region (the first or last cell that isn't empty) in the direction of the arrow
End	To the cell in the lower-right corner of the window*
Ctrl+End	To the last cell in the worksheet, in the lowest used row of the rightmost used column
Home	To the beginning of the row containing the active cell
Ctrl+Home	To the beginning of the worksheet (cell A1)
Page Down	One screen down
Alt+Page Down	One screen to the right
Ctrl+Page Down	To the next sheet in the workbook
Page Up	One screen up
Alt+Page Up	One screen to the left
Ctrl+Page Up	To the previous sheet in the workbook

* This works only when the Scroll Lock key has been pressed on your keyboard to turn on the Scroll Lock function.

Selecting ranges

You might sometimes want to select a multi-cell *range* before you issue a command. For example, if you want to format all the text in a range a certain way, select that range and then issue the formatting command. Technically, a range can consist of a single cell; however, a range most commonly consists of multiple cells.

Range names are written with the upper-left cell address, a colon, and the lower-right cell address, as in the example A1:F3. Here A1:F3 means the range that begins in the upper-left corner with A1 and ends in the lower-right corner with F3.

A range is usually *contiguous,* or all the cells are in a single rectangular block, but they don't have to be. You can also select *noncontiguous* cells in a range by holding down the Ctrl key while you select additional cells. Figure 11-2 shows a non-contiguous range that consists of A1:F3 plus D6:F7. (D6 does not appear shaded along with the others because it is the active cell.)

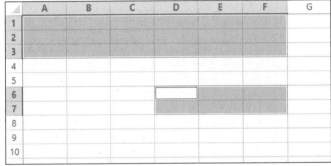

Figure 11-2:
A noncon-
tiguous
range of
cells.

When a range contains noncontiguous cells, the pieces are separated by commas, like this: A1:F3,D6:F7. The range name tells Excel to select the range from A1 through F3, plus the range from D6 through F7.

You can select a range by using either the keyboard or the mouse. Table 11-2 provides some of the most common range selection shortcuts.

Table 11-2	Range Selection Shortcuts
Press This . . .	*To Extend the Selection To . . .*
Ctrl+Shift+arrow key	The last nonblank cell in the same column or row as the active cell; or if the next cell is blank, to the next nonblank cell
Ctrl+Shift+End	The last used cell on the worksheet (lower-right corner of the range containing data)
Ctrl+Shift+Home	The beginning of the worksheet (cell A1)
Ctrl+spacebar	The entire column where the active cell is located
Shift+spacebar	The entire row where the active cell is located
Ctrl+A	The entire worksheet

Typing and Editing Cell Content

To type in a cell, simply select the cell and begin typing. When you finish typing, you can leave the cell in any of these ways:

- ✔ **Press Enter:** Moves you to the next cell down
- ✔ **Press Tab:** Moves you to the next cell to the right
- ✔ **Press Shift+Tab:** Moves you to the next cell to the left
- ✔ **Press an arrow key:** Moves you in the direction of the arrow
- ✔ **Click in another cell:** Moves you to that cell

If you make a mistake when editing, you can press the Esc key to cancel the edit before you leave the cell. If you need to undo an edit after you leave the cell, press Ctrl+Z or click the Undo button on the Quick Access toolbar.

The *formula bar* is the text area immediately above the worksheet grid, to the right of the Name box. This bar shows the active cell's contents. When the content is text or a number, what appears in the cell and what appears in the Formula bar are identical. When the content is a formula or function, the Formula bar shows the actual formula/function, and the cell itself shows the result of it. In Figure 11-3, cell B2 is selected and its content appears in the Formula bar.

Formula bar shows contents of active cell

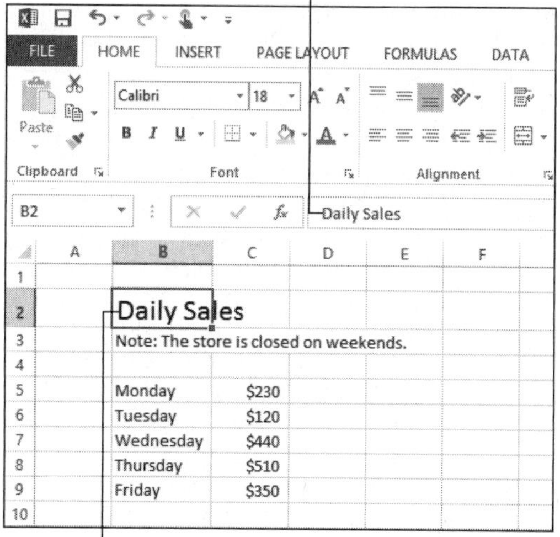

Figure 11-3: The content of a selected cell appears in the Formula bar.

Active cell (B2) is the cell with the cell cursor around it

Editing data in cells

If you need to edit the content in a cell, you can

✔ Click the cell to select it, and then click the cell again to move the insertion point into it. Edit just as you would in any text program.

✔ Click the cell to select it and then type a new entry to replace the old one.

If you decide you don't want the text you typed in a particular cell, you can get rid of it in several ways:

✔ Select the cell; then right-click the cell and choose Clear Contents from the menu that appears.

✔ Select the cell; then choose Home⇨Clear⇨Clear Contents.

✔ Select the cell, press the spacebar, and then press Enter. This technically doesn't clear the cell's content, but it replaces it with a space.

✔ Select the cell and press the Delete key.

Don't confuse the Delete key on the keyboard (which issues the Clear command) with the Delete command on the Ribbon. The Delete command doesn't *clear* the cell content; instead, it *removes* the entire cell. You find out more about deleting cells in the upcoming section, "Changing the Worksheet Structure."

And while I'm on the subject, don't confuse Clear with Cut, either. The Cut command works in conjunction with the Clipboard. Cut moves the content to the Clipboard, and you can then paste it somewhere else. Excel, however, differs from other applications in the way this command works: Using Cut doesn't immediately remove the content. Instead, Excel puts a flashing dotted box around the content and waits for you to reposition the cell cursor and issue the Paste command. If you do something else in the interim, the cut-and-paste operation is canceled, and the content that you cut remains in its original location. You learn more about cutting and pasting in the section "Copy and move data between cells" later in this lesson.

Copying and moving data between cells

When you're creating a worksheet, it's common not to get everything in the right cells on your first try. Fortunately, moving content between cells is easy.

Here are the two methods you can use to move content:

- ✔ **Mouse method:** Point at the dark outline around the selected range and then drag to the new location. If you want to copy rather than move, hold down the Ctrl key while you drag.

- ✔ **Clipboard method:** Choose Home⇨Cut or press Ctrl+X. (If you want to copy rather than simply move, choose Home⇨Copy rather than Cut or press Ctrl+C.) Then click the destination cell and choose Home⇨Paste or press Ctrl+V.

If you're moving or copying a multi-cell range with the Clipboard method, you can either select the same size and shape of range for the destination, or you can select a single cell, in which case the paste occurs with the selected cell in the upper-left corner.

Using AutoFill to fill cell content

When you have a lot of data to enter and that data consists of some type of repeatable pattern or sequence, you can save time by using AutoFill. To use AutoFill, you select the cell or cells that already contain an example of what you want to fill and then drag the fill handle. The *fill handle* is the little black square in the lower-right corner of the selected cell or range. See Figure 11-4.

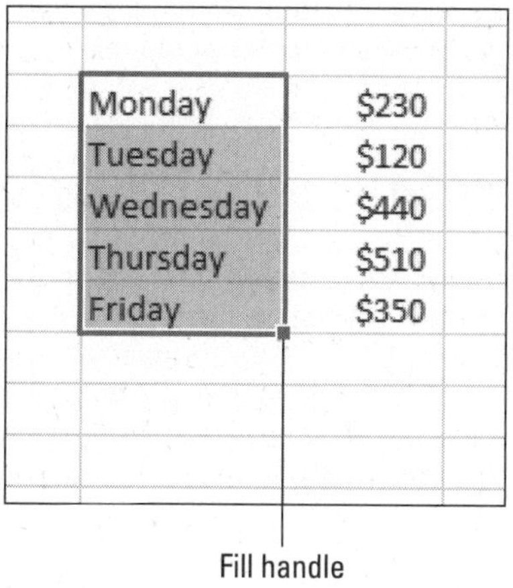

Monday	$230
Tuesday	$120
Wednesday	$440
Thursday	$510
Friday	$350

Figure 11-4: Drag the fill handle to AutoFill.

Fill handle

Depending on how you use it, AutoFill can either fill the same value into every cell in the target area, or it can fill in a sequence (such as days of the month, days of the week, or a numeric sequence such as 2, 4, 6, 8). Here are the general rules for how it works:

✔ When AutoFill recognizes the selected text as a member of one of its preset lists, such as days of the week or months of the year, it automatically increments those. For example, if the selected cell contains August, AutoFill places September in the next adjacent cell.

✔ When AutoFill doesn't recognize the selected text, it fills the chosen cell with a duplicate of the selected text.

✔ When AutoFill is used on a single cell containing a number, it fills with a duplicate of the number.

✔ When Auto Fill is used on a range of two or more cells containing numbers, AutoFill attempts to determine the interval between them and continues filling using that same pattern. For example, if the two selected cells contain 2 and 4, the next adjacent cell would be filled with 6.

Changing the Worksheet Structure

Even if you're a careful planner, you'll likely decide that you want to change your worksheet's structure. Maybe you want data in a different column, or certain rows turn out to be unnecessary. Excel makes it easy to insert and delete rows and columns to deal with these kinds of changes.

Inserting and deleting rows and columns

When you insert a new row or column, the existing ones move to make room for it. Select an existing row or column (by clicking its row or column header) and then choose Home⇨Insert.

You can insert multiple rows or columns at once by selecting multiple ones before issuing the Insert command. There's no limit on the number you can insert at once.

Similarly, you can delete multiple rows or columns by selecting them and then choosing Home⇨Delete.

Inserting and deleting cells and ranges

You can also insert and delete individual cells or even ranges that don't neatly correspond to entire rows or columns. You use the same Home⇨Insert and Home⇨Delete commands as with rows and columns, but this time you select individual cells first.

When you insert or delete individual cells, the surrounding cells shift. In the case of an insertion, cells move down or to the right of the area where the new cells are being inserted. In the case of a deletion, cells move up or to the left to fill in the voided space.

Deleting a cell is different from clearing a cell's content, and this becomes apparent when you start working with individual cells and ranges. When you clear the content, the cell itself remains. When you delete the cell itself, the adjacent cells shift.

When shifting cells, Excel is smart enough that it tries to guess which direction you want existing content to move when you insert or delete cells. If you have content immediately to the right of a deleted cell, for example, Excel shifts it left. If you have content immediately below the deleted cell, Excel shifts it up.

If you want the cells to shift a certain way, open the Insert or Delete button's drop-down list and then choose Insert Cells (or Delete Cells). In the dialog box that appears, choose how you want the shift to occur. Figure 11-5 shows the dialog box for inserting.

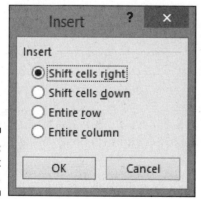

Figure 11-5:
The Insert
dialog box.

Calculating with Formulas

A *formula* is a math calculation, like 2+2 or 3(4+1). In Excel, a formula can perform calculations with fixed numbers or cell contents. Formulas are different from regular text in two ways:

- ✓ Formulas begin with an equal sign, like this: =2+2.
- ✓ Formulas don't contain alphabetic characters (except for function names and cell references). They contain only symbols that are allowed in math formulas, such as parentheses, commas, and decimal points.

Excel formulas can do everything that a basic calculator can do, so if you're in a hurry and don't want to pull up the Windows Calculator application, you can enter a formula in Excel to get a quick result. Experimenting with this type of formula is a great way to get accustomed to formulas in general.

Excel also has an advantage over some basic calculators (including the one in Windows): It easily does exponentiation. For example, if you want to calculate 5 to the 8th power, you would write it in Excel as =5^8.

Just as in basic math, formulas are calculated by an order of precedence. Table 11-3 lists the order.

Table 11-3	Order of Precedence in a Formula	
Order	*Item*	*Example*
1	Anything in parentheses	=2*(2+1)
2	Exponentiation	=2^3
3	Multiplication and division	=1+2*2
4	Addition and subtraction	=10−4

One of Excel's best features is that it can reference cells in formulas. When a cell is referenced in a formula, whatever value it contains is used in the formula. When the value changes, the result of the formula changes too.

For example, if you want to repeat the value from one cell in another cell, enter an equals sign and then that cell's address. For example, to repeat whatever is in cell C3, you can use =C3.

You can combine math operators with cell references to perform math on the contents of cells. For example, to multiply the values in C3 and C4, use this: =C3*C4.

When referring to a range of cells, you must type each cell's address individually in a formula. (It's different in a function, as you'll see later in this chapter.) For example, to sum all the values in B3, B4, B5, and B6 in a formula, you would type =B3+B4+B5+B6.

Moving and copying formulas

Earlier in this chapter you learned how to move and copy text and numbers between cells, but when it comes to copying formulas, beware of a few gotchas.

When you move or copy a formula, Excel automatically changes the cell references to work with the new location. That's because, by default, cell references in formulas are relative references. A *relative reference* is a cell reference that changes if copied to another cell.

For example, in Figure 11-6, suppose you wanted to copy the formula from B5 into C5. The new formula in C5 should refer to values in column C, not to column B; otherwise the formula wouldn't make much sense. So, when B5's formula is copied to C5, it becomes =C3+C4 there.

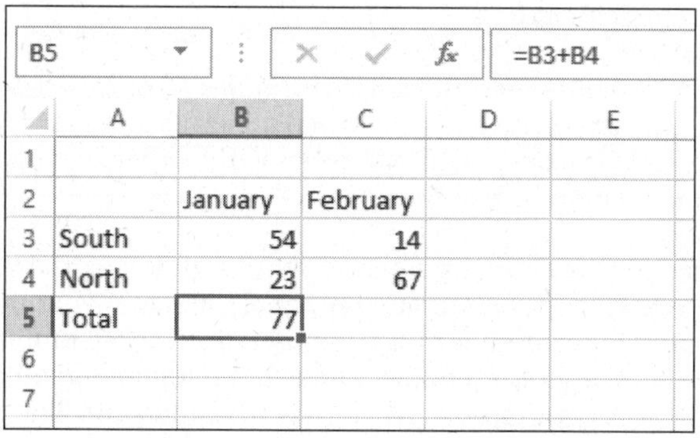

Figure 11-6: Formulas update when they're copied.

You might not always want the cell references in a formula to change when you move or copy it. In other words, you want an absolute reference to that cell. An *absolute reference* is a cell reference that doesn't change when copied to another cell. To make a reference absolute, you add dollar signs before the column letter and before the row number. So, for example, an absolute reference to cell C1 would be =C1.

If you want to lock down only one dimension of the cell reference, you can place a dollar sign before only the column or only the row. For example, =$C1 would make only the column letter fixed, and =C$1 would make only the row number fixed. That's called a *mixed reference.*

Introducing functions

Sometimes it's awkward or lengthy to write a formula to perform a calculation. For example, suppose you want to sum the values in cells A1 through A10. To express that as a formula, you'd have to write each cell reference individually, like this:

```
=A1+A2+A3+A4+A5+A6+A7+A8+A9+A10
```

In Excel, a *function* refers to a certain math calculation. Functions can greatly reduce the amount of typing you have to do to create a particular result. For example, instead of using the =A1+A2+A3+A4+A5+A6+A7+A8+A9+A10 formula, you could use the SUM function like this: =SUM(A1:A10).

With a function, you can represent a range with the upper-left corner's cell reference, a colon, and the lower-right corner's cell reference. In the case of A1:A10, there is only one column, so the upper-left corner is cell A1, and the lower-right corner is cell A10.

Range references cannot be used in simple formulas — only in functions. For example, =A6:A9 would be invalid as a formula because no math operation is specified in it. You can't insert math operators within a range. To use ranges in a calculation, you must use a function.

Each function has one or more arguments, along with its own rules about how many required and optional arguments there are and what they represent. An *argument* is a placeholder for a number, text string, or cell reference. For example, the SUM function requires at least one argument: a range of cells. So, in the preceding example, A1:A10 is the argument. The arguments for a function are enclosed in a set of parentheses.

You don't have to memorize the sequence of arguments for each function; Excel asks you for them. Excel can even suggest a function to use for a certain situation if you aren't sure what you need. A formula's *syntax* is the sequence and rules for the arguments of a function. When there are multiple arguments in the syntax, they are separated by commas.

Using the SUM function

The SUM function is by far the most popular function; it sums (that is, adds) a data range consisting of one or more cells, like this:

```
=SUM(D12:D15)
```

You don't *have* to use a range in a SUM function; you can specify the individual cell addresses if you want. Separate them by commas, like this:

```
=SUM(D12, D13, D14, D15)
```

If the data range is not a contiguous block, you need to specify the individual cells that are outside the block. The main block is one argument, and each individual other cell is an additional argument, like this:

```
=SUM(D12:D15, E22)
```

Inserting a function

Typing a function and its arguments directly into a cell works fine if you happen to know the function you want and its arguments. Many times, though, you may not know these details. In those cases, the Insert Function feature can help you.

Insert Function enables you to pick a function from a list based on descriptive keywords. After you make your selection, it provides fill-in-the-blank prompts for the arguments. Click the Insert Function button on the Formula bar (looks like *fx)* to open the Insert Function dialog box. This dialog box helps you find the function you need, even if you don't know its name. Type what you want to do in the Search for a function box, and Excel will suggest a function that may serve your purpose. If you select a function, a description of it appears below the list. See Figure 11-7.

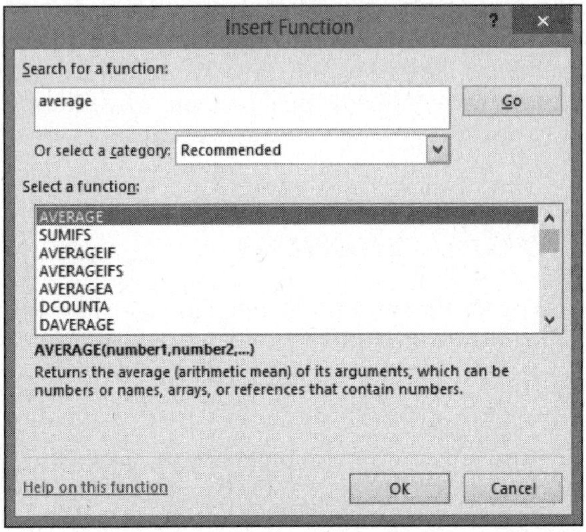

Figure 11-7:
The Insert
Function
dialog box.

After you select a function and click OK, a Function Arguments dialog box appears. It has a text box for each argument. The argument name appears bold if it's required, and not-bold if it's optional. In Figure 11-8, the Average function's arguments appear. When you click OK, the function is placed in the active cell.

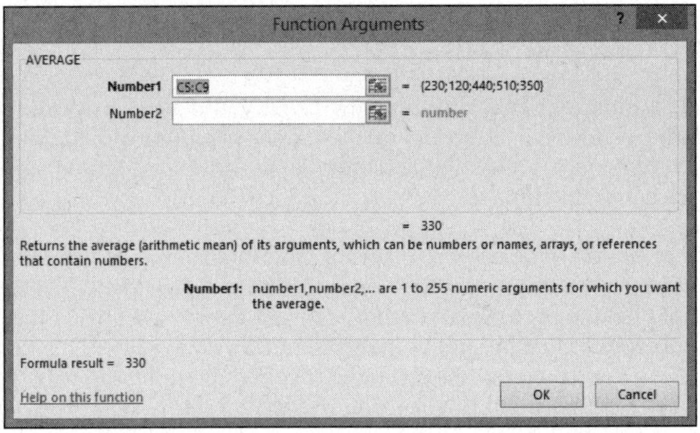

Figure 11-8:
The
Function
Arguments
dialog box.

Touring some basic functions

Excel has hundreds of functions, but most of them are very specialized. The basic set that the average user works with is much more manageable.

Start with the simplest functions of them all — those without arguments. Two prime examples are

- ✔ NOW: Reports the current date and time.

- ✔ TODAY: Reports the current date.

Even though neither uses any arguments, you still have to include the parentheses, so they look like this:

```
=NOW( )
=TODAY( )
```

Another basic kind of function performs a single, simple math operation and has a single argument that specifies what cell or range it operates on. Table 11-4 summarizes some important functions that work this way.

Table 11-4	Simple One-Argument Functions	
Function	*What It Does*	*Example*
SUM	Sums the values in a range of cells	=SUM(A1:A10)
AVERAGE	Averages the values in a range of cells	=AVERAGE(A1:A10)
MIN	Provides the smallest number in a range of cells	=MIN(A1:A10)
MAX	Provides the largest number in a range of cells	=MAX(A1:A10)
COUNT	Counts the number of cells that contain numeric values in the range	=COUNT(A1:A10)
COUNTA	Counts the number of non-empty cells in the range	=COUNTA(A1:A10)
COUNTBLANK	Counts the number of empty cells in the range	=COUNTBLANK(A1:A10)

Formatting a Worksheet

Face it: Plain worksheets aren't that much to look at. A worksheet packed full of rows and columns of numbers is enough to make anyone's eyes glaze over. However, formatting can dramatically improve a worksheet's readability, which in turn enables the reader to understand its meaning much more easily.

You can apply formatting at the whole-worksheet level or at the individual-cell level. Formatting individual cells is much the same as formatting in Word: use the Font group on the Home tab to apply the settings. In the following sections, you'll learn some formatting techniques that are specific to Excel.

Adjusting rows and columns

Each column in a worksheet starts with the same width, which is 8.43 characters (based on the default font and font size) unless you've changed the default setting. That's approximately seven digits and either one large symbol (such as $) or two small ones (such as decimal points and commas).

You can define the default width setting for new worksheets: Choose Home➪Format➪Default Width and then fill in the desired default width.

As you enter data into cells, those column widths may no longer be optimal. Data may overflow out of a cell if the width is too narrow, or there may be excess blank space in a column if its width is too wide. (Blank space is not always a bad thing, but if you're trying to fit all the data on one page, for example, it can be a hindrance.)

In some cases, Excel makes an adjustment for you automatically, as follows:

- ✔ **For column widths:** When you enter numbers in a cell, Excel widens a column as needed to accommodate the longest number in that column, provided you haven't manually set a column width for it.

- ✔ **For row heights:** Generally, a row adjusts automatically to fit the largest font used in it. You don't have to adjust row heights manually to allow text to fit. You can change the row height if you want, though, to create special effects, such as extra blank space in the layout.

After you manually resize a row's height or a column's width, it won't change its size automatically for you anymore. That's because manual settings override automatic ones.

The units of measurement are different for rows versus columns, by the way. Column width is measured in characters of the default font size. Row height is measured in points. A point is 1/72 of an inch.

You can resize rows and columns in several ways:

- ✔ **AutoFit:** Double-click the dividing line between two row or column headings to automatically adjust the row above the line or column to the left of the line to fit its content.

✔ **Drag:** Drag-and-drop the dividing line between two row or column headings to manually change the row height or column width.

✔ **Dialog box:** Select the row or column to adjust and then choose Home⇨Format⇨Row Height or Home⇨Format⇨Column Width to open a dialog box in which you can specify an exact value.

When content overruns a cell's width, different results occur depending on the type of data and whether the cell's column width has been adjusted manually.

With text, when the adjacent cell is empty, the content bleeds into that cell. When the adjacent cell is not empty, the content appears truncated. (It's not really truncated, though, and if you widen the column, you'll see the full entry.)

With numeric data, if an exact setting has not been specified for the column, the column widens as needed to accommodate a long number. If the column width is fixed, but no number format has been assigned to the cell (from the Number group on the General tab), Excel displays the number in scientific format, which is a very compact number format, like this: 2.3E+10. If the column width is fixed and a specific number format has been applied, Excel displays hash marks (###) in place of the number.

Applying a workbook theme

Themes are standard across most Office applications (including Word, Excel, and PowerPoint), so you can standardize your formatting across all the documents you create. To apply a theme, choose one from the Themes drop-down list on the Page Layout tab. The choice of theme affects the fonts, colors, and effects used in the workbook, the same as in a Word document. However, with mostly numeric data, you will probably mostly notice the font change.

Printing Worksheets

You can print your work in Excel on paper to share with people who may not have computer access or to pass out as handouts at meetings and events. You can print the quick-and-easy way with the default settings or customize the settings to fit your needs.

For a quick printout of the active worksheet, choose File⇨Print and click the Print button.

For more control, after choosing File⇨Print, make some changes to the settings you find there.

In Excel 2013, Print Preview is built into Backstage view, so you see a preview of the printout at the same place where you change the print settings.

By default, when you print Excel prints the entire active worksheet — that is, whichever worksheet is displayed or selected at the moment. But Excel also gives you other printing options:

- ✔ **Print multiple worksheets:** If more than one worksheet is selected (for example, if you have more than one worksheet tab selected at the bottom of the Excel window), all selected worksheets are included in the printed version. As an alternative, you can print all the worksheets in the workbook. To select more than one worksheet, hold down the Ctrl key as you click the tabs of the sheets you want.

- ✔ **Print selected cells or ranges:** You can choose to print only selected cells, or you can define a print range and print only that range (regardless of what cells happen to be selected).

As shown in Figure 11-9, you can also select a different number of copies and a different printer if desired.

There are many additional controls available on the Print page of Backstage view. These settings are one-time-only settings; they don't carry over to the document in general. For example, if you change the orientation to Landscape here, the default Portrait orientation does not change except for this printing instance.

If the worksheet almost fits on a certain number of pages but not quite, you might choose to use *scaling*, one of the choices on the Print page in Backstage view. Scaling shrinks the printout enough so that it fits on the specified number of pages.

Creating Charts

Is a picture really worth a thousand words? Just ask anyone who has been faced with a worksheet full of numbers to analyze. Creating charts that summarize data is a quick way to make sense of data — or to present data to someone else.

Excel offers various chart types, each suited for a different type of data analysis: Pie charts show how parts contribute to a whole, line and column charts compare values over time, stock charts show daily pricing information, and so on. As you become more familiar with charts, you'll learn which ones work best to convey the message you want to put forth.

Click here to print   Copies   Printer   Print preview

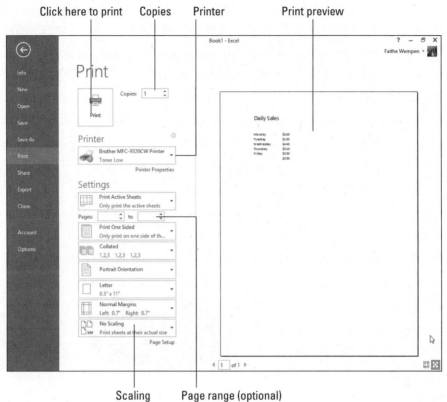

Figure 11-9:
The Print
window.

Scaling   Page range (optional)

Creating a pie chart

A *pie chart* shows a circle divided into slices. The relative size of each slice represents a data point's contribution to the whole. Each pie chart shows one *data series* — that is, only one related set of numeric values.

Pie charts are good for situations in which the relationship among the values being charted is the most significant thing. For example, suppose Vick sold 15 cars, Dave sold 8, and Tom sold 7. If the important thing is that Vick sold 50 percent of all the cars, a pie chart is ideal. Pie charts are limited in that they can handle only one data series. For example, you couldn't use a single pie chart to show Vick, Dave, and Tom's sales for several different periods; you'd have to do a separate pie chart for each period.

To create a pie chart, select the data for the chart (a single row or column of labels, and a single row or column of data). Then on the Insert tab, click the Insert Pie or Doughnut Chart button in the Charts group, as shown in Figure 11-10. On the menu that appears, click the type of pie you want. It appears on the worksheet as a floating object that you can resize and move as needed.

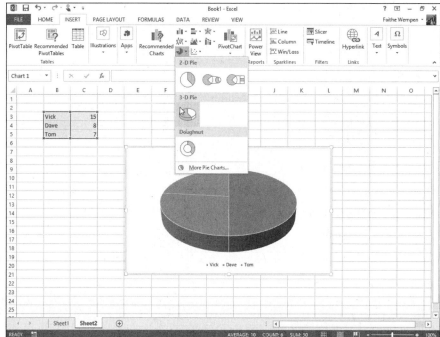

Figure 11-10: A basic chart in Excel.

Creating a column or bar chart

Bar charts and column charts are the same thing, except on a column chart the bars run vertically and on a bar chart the bars run horizontally.

A column or bar chart is good for showing multiple data series on a two-axis grid. For example, in Figure 11-11, notice that each editor has different values for each month. Depending on how you plot the data, each month could be a data series or each editor could be a data series. (See the next section to learn how to switch.)

To create a column chart, select the cells and then on the Insert tab, in the Charts group, click the Insert Column Chart button. Choose the desired chart subtype from the list, and the chart appears. See Figure 11-12. A bar chart is just the same except you use the Insert Bar Chart button instead.

	A	B	C	D	E
1	Number of Projects Per Editor				
2					
3					
4	Editors	January	February	March	
5	Sandy	5	3	2	
6	Mchael	3	2	2	
7	Lorna	4	2	1	
8	Kelly	1	2	1	
9	Ruth	4	2	1	
10	Bill	3	3	2	
11					

Figure 11-11: A basic table with data.

Switching rows and columns

Numbers don't lie, but presenting the numbers in different ways can make your audience think about the numbers differently. For example, in Figure 11-12, this column chart invites the audience to consider each editor separately. If you wanted the audience to compare the different months with one another for each month, you could switch the rows and columns so that the series become the categories rather than the months.

To switch between rows and columns, go to the Chart Tools Design tab and click the Switch Row/Column button.

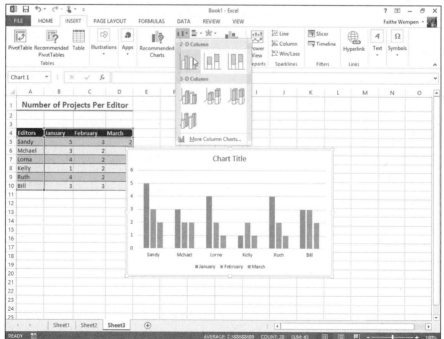

Figure 11-12: A column chart in Excel.

Understanding the elements of a chart

Each chart has many elements— and you can customize each element separately. Learning the names for the elements of a chart helps you understand what's going on later in the chapter, in "Adding and positioning chart elements." Figure 11-13 points out some key elements of a chart, and Table 11-5 describes them.

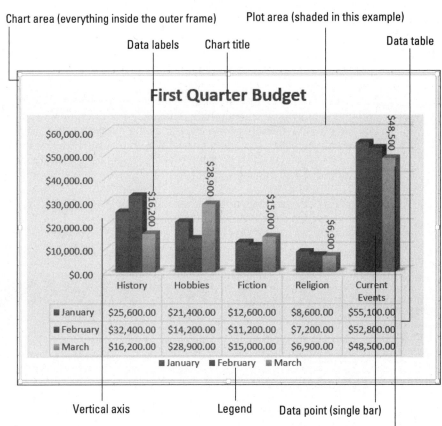

Table 11-5	The Elements of a Chart	
Element	*What It Is*	*Usage*
Chart area	The entire contents of the chart frame	Everything in Figure 11-13 is considered part of the chart area.
Chart title	A title that identifies the chart	Use if it's not already obvious what the chart represents.
Data point	A single bar, line, column, pie slice, and so on	Each column is a data point in Figure 11-13.
Data series	All the bars (lines, columns, and so on) of a common color	All the blue columns are a data series in Figure 11-13.
Data table	An optional table that appears below the chart, showing the data that comprises it	Used mostly when a chart is on a separate tab from the data.
Floor	On a 3-D chart, the area that the 3-D bars rest on	A floor can give a 3-D chart an additional appearance of being three-dimensional.
Horizontal axis	The axis that runs side to side	In Figure 11-13, the horizontal axis shows the book types.
Legend	The key that tells what each data series represents	The legend can appear at the bottom (as in Figure 11-13) or in any other position around the plot area. When the data table duplicates the legend, as in Figure 11-13, the legend can be omitted.
Plot area	The area of the chart that contains the data, the axes, and the data table (if present)	In Figure 11-13, the plot area is shaded to distinguish it from the chart area.
Vertical axis	The axis that runs up and down	In Figure 11-13, vertical axis shows the numeric values.
Vertical axis title	A text label that explains what the vertical axis represents	Figure 11-13 does not use a vertical axis title, but if it did, it might be Budgeted Amount.
Wall	The area directly behind the data	In Figure 11-13, the wall is shaded light gray to distinguish it from the plot area.
Data labels	Numeric values on or adjacent to a data point	In Figure 11-13, the green series of bars has data labels.

Editing the chart data range

You can decide after initially creating a chart that you want a different data range to be plotted in it. For example, you might want to add or remove a data series or exclude certain data points.

To edit the data range, select the chart and then on the Chart Tools Design tab, click Select Data. The Select Data Source dialog box opens, and the current data selection appears in the worksheet with a moving dashed outline around it. See Figure 11-14. Make any changes in the dialog box as needed and click OK.

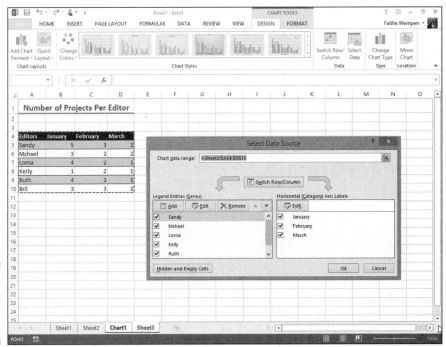

Figure 11-14:
The Select
Data Source
dialog box.

Changing the chart type

Rather than completely re-creating a chart if you decide you didn't choose the right type initially, you can change the chart's type. In fact, it's so easy to change the chart type that you might want to experiment with several chart types before you make the final decision on which one to use.

To change the chart type, select the chart, and then on the Chart Tools Design tab, click Change Chart Type. In the Change Chart Type dialog box, choose a different type and click OK. See Figure 11-15.

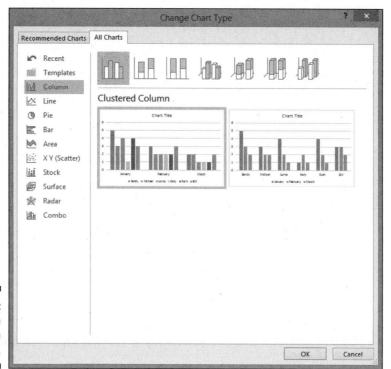

Figure 11-15:
The Change
Chart Type
dialog box.

Resizing a chart

You can resize a chart by dragging a selection handle on the border of its frame in any direction. Selection handles are marked with small dots; the side selection handles are in the center of each side, and the corner selection handles are in each corner. You can also specify an exact size for a chart's frame using the Height and Width text boxes on the Chart Tools Format tab.

Moving a chart to its own worksheet

On a crowded worksheet, you may not have much room for a chart, and as a result, the chart might need to be resized down to a size where it's not as easy to read as it might otherwise be. To solve this problem, you might want to move a chart to its own sheet.

To move a chart, right-click the chart and choose Move Chart. (If you don't see Move Chart on the menu, try right-clicking in a different place on the chart, such as near the chart's outer border.) In the Move Chart dialog box, choose New Sheet. See Figure 11-16. Change the name of the sheet in the New Sheet text box if desired. (The name will appear on the sheet's tab.) Then click OK to move the chart.

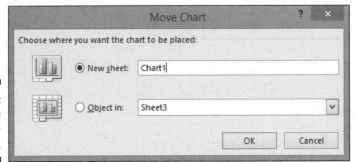

Figure 11-16: The Move Chart dialog box.

When a chart is on its own sheet, a data table is sometimes useful to remind the reader what data the chart represents.

Adding and positioning chart elements

As I hint earlier in the lesson, when reviewing the elements of a chart (refer to Figure 11-13), each element is individually customizable. You can turn elements on and off, change their positions, and so on.

There are two ways to get at the controls for chart elements. One is to click the Chart Elements button in the upper right corner of the chart frame, opening a menu of choices. You can mark or clear a check box to enable or disable a certain chart element. Each of those chart elements also has a submenu with more choices. See Figure 11-17.

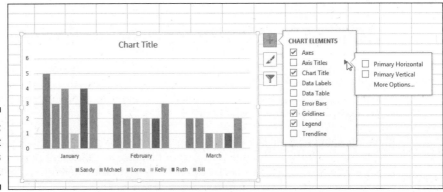

Figure 11-17: The Chart Elements menu.

The other way is to click the Add Chart Element button on the Chart Tools Design tab. This opens a similar menu, but with a few additional options on some of the submenus.

If none of the menus and submenus for chart elements has what you want on it, use the Options command at the bottom of a menu to open a dialog box or task pane that provides more choices. The name of the command depends on the chart element; for example, for data tables, the option is More Data Table Options.

Formatting a chart

Chart formatting can make a big difference in a chart's attractiveness and readability. Depending on the look you're after, you may prefer to make blanket formatting changes to the entire chart by applying a chart style, or to select and make changes to individual elements. For each individual part of the chart, you can change its fill color, its outline, and its text (including font, size, color, attributes, alignment, and so on).

Chart styles are collections of formatting presets that you can apply to the entire chart at once. Each chart style can be applied in a variety of color combinations, all based on the theme colors for the workbook. You can apply chart styles from the Chart Styles group on the Chart Tools Design tab.

When you resize a chart, some of the text in it resizes also. If you want certain text to be larger or smaller in relation to the chart size, though, you can manually change its font size. You can also change the font's color, typeface, and attributes. This works just the same as in Word; select the element you want to change and then use the buttons in the Font group on the Home tab to make changes.

When formatting a chart, you'll likely want to increase the legend's text size because by default, Excel's legends are a bit small.

Each element of a chart can be recolored individually. This includes the data points and series, the chart's walls, its plot area, the entire chart area, the legend, and all the text used for every purpose.

It's common to change the colors of one or more of the data series in a bar chart, or to change one or more pie slice colors in a pie chart. To change the color of an element, select it and then use the controls on the Chart Tools Format tab, in the Shape Styles group.

Usually when you change the color of a data bar (or other data-related object), you want to change the color for the entire series, not just for one individual data point. If you have a legend that shows what each color means and then you change the color of the whole series, the legend updates automatically. However, if you change the color of only one data point, the legend still shows the color for the other bars in the series, and that one data point does not match up with anything in the legend.

Chapter 12

Creating Presentations with Microsoft PowerPoint

*P*owerPoint is the most popular presentation software in the world. Presentation software creates support materials for people who give speeches. You can project PowerPoint slides on a big screen behind you as you speak, create handouts to distribute to the audience, and print note pages for your own reference.

Although PowerPoint is best known for creating business presentations — slide shows, if you will — it's actually a much more versatile tool than that. PowerPoint is a great tool for almost any situation where you need to convey a visual message. For example, an overview of an organization or club for new members, posters and signs with large lettering, such as *Please Help Yourself* or *Sign In Here,* a photo tribute for an anniversary celebration or memorial service, lyrics for a group sing-along, or information about meeting rooms and activities at a seminar.

In this chapter, you discover how to use PowerPoint to create simple, attractive presentations that can meet a variety of needs. You learn how to use layouts and themes, how to enter text and graphics, how to incorporate multimedia clips, and how to print and distribute your work.

Exploring the PowerPoint Interface

In PowerPoint, you work with slides and presentations rather than pages and documents (as in Word) or worksheets and workbooks (as in Excel). A *slide* is an individual page of the presentation. The term *page* isn't a perfect descriptor, though, because PowerPoint slides are designed to be displayed on a computer screen or with a projector rather than printed. A *presentation* is a collection of one or more slides saved in a single data file.

At a big-picture level, the PowerPoint interface is very similar to that in Word and Excel: It has a Ribbon, a File tab, and a status bar. The default view of the presentation, called Normal view, consists of three panes, as shown in Figure 12-1. (You may or may not see the rulers onscreen, depending on your settings.)

Slides pane (thumbnail images)   Slide pane (edit slides here)

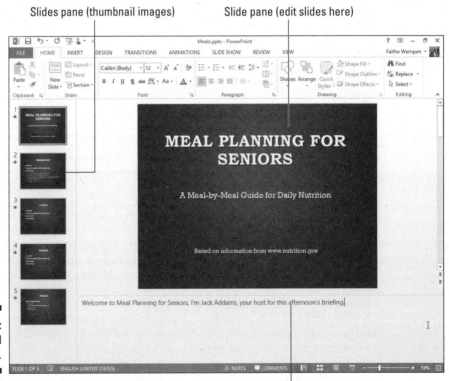

Figure 12-1:
Normal
view.

Notes pane

✔ **The Slides pane** is the bar along the left side. Thumbnail images of the slides appear here. It is sometimes called the *thumbnail pane*.

✔ **The Slide pane** (that's singular, not plural) in the middle shows the active slide in a large, editable pane. Here's where you do most of your work on each slide. It is sometimes called the editing pane.

✔ **The Notes pane** runs along the bottom of the screen. Here you can type any notes to yourself about the active slide. These notes don't show onscreen when you display the presentation, and they don't print (unless you explicitly choose to print them).

Moving around in a presentation

You can navigate a presentation in many of the same ways you moved through other applications' content. The Page Up and Page Down keys scroll one full screen at a time, and you can drag the scroll bars to scroll as well. You can also select slides from the Slides pane by clicking their thumbnail image.

Understanding PowerPoint views

PowerPoint provides several views for you to work with. Each view is useful for a different set of activities. Normal view (refer to Figure 12-1), the default, is the most commonly used view. You can switch to one of the other views in either of these ways:

✔ Click one of the View buttons in the bottom-right corner of the PowerPoint window. (Not all the views are represented there.)

✔ On the View tab, click a button for the view you want.

Figure 12-2 shows Slide Sorter view. You can switch views in two places: on the View tab and on the status bar. Slide Sorter view is best for rearranging slides and viewing the entire presentation at a glance.

Other views include Notes Page, which gives you more space to create speaker notes than other views do, and Outline, which is just like Normal view except it has a text outline pane instead of the Slides pane.

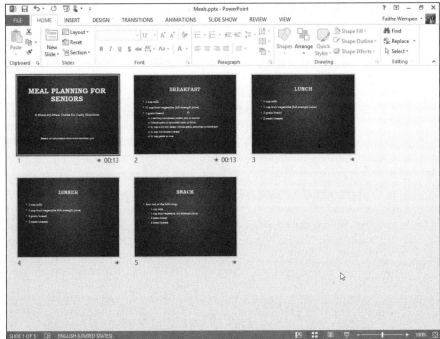

Creating a New Presentation

When you start PowerPoint and then press Esc or click the Blank Presentation template, a new blank presentation appears, containing a single slide. The fastest and simplest way to create a new presentation is to start with a blank one. You can then add text to the presentation, including additional slides. You can also press Ctrl+N at any time to create a new blank presentation.

PowerPoint templates give you a jump start to creating complete presentations. Each template employs one or more themes. A *theme* is a collection of settings including colors, fonts, background graphics, bullet graphics, margins, and placement. To use a template, choose File➪New and then select a template, like you learned to do for Word in Chapter 10.

Creating new slides

Each new blank presentation begins with one slide in it: a title slide. You can easily add more slides to the presentation by using the default layout (Title and Content) or any other layout you prefer.

Several methods are available for creating new slides, and each one is best suited for a particular situation.

The most straightforward way to create a new slide is with the Home⇨New Slide command. You can click the button face to choose the default layout or you can open the button's drop-down list to select a specific layout, as shown in Figure 12-3. (You'll learn more about layouts shortly.)

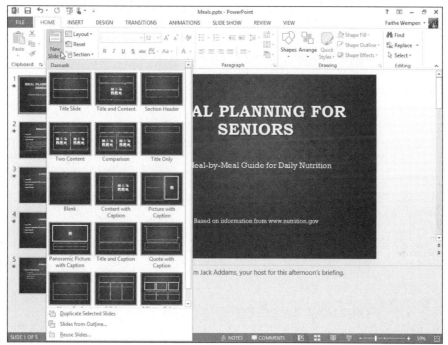

In the Slides pane in Normal view, you can click to place a horizontal insertion point between two existing slides or at the bottom of the list of slides and then press Enter.

In Outline view, you click to place a text insertion point at the beginning of the title of an existing slide in the Outline pane, and then you press Enter to create a new title (and a new slide).

Duplicating a slide

If you need to create a series of very similar slides, you might find it easier to copy or duplicate a slide and then make the small modifications to each copy.

Copying and duplicating are two separate commands in PowerPoint, but they have essentially the same result. When you copy a slide (or multiple slides), you place a copy of it on the Clipboard, and then you paste it from the Clipboard into the presentation. You can paste anywhere in the presentation or into a different presentation (or, for that matter, a different document altogether). To copy and paste a slide, use the Clipboard, as you learned in Chapter 9.

When you duplicate a slide (or multiple slides), go to the Home tab, click the New Slide button, and choose Duplicate Selected Slides. You don't have to paste because that command accomplishes both a copy and a paste operation at the same time. However, you also don't get to choose where they're pasted; they're pasted directly below the original selection.

Deleting a slide

Deleting a slide removes it from the presentation. You can delete a slide either by pressing the Delete key or by right-clicking the slide in the Slides pane at the left and choosing Delete Slide from the shortcut menu.

There's no Recycle Bin for slides; you can't get them back after you delete them. However, you can undo your last action(s) with the Undo button on the Quick Access toolbar, and that includes undoing deletions. If you haven't saved your work since you made the deletion, you can also get a deleted slide back by closing the file without saving changes and then reopening it.

Adding text to a slide

Each slide layout (except Blank) contains one or more placeholders for text or other content. Adding text to a slide is as easy as clicking in a placeholder box and typing. You can also type text on the Outline pane in Outline view or create your own text boxes in addition to the placeholders.

Typing in a slide placeholder

A *slide layout* is a combination of one or more content placeholders. For example, the default slide layout — Title and Content — has two boxes: a text box at the top for the slide's title, and one multipurpose content placeholder in the middle that can be used for text, a graphic, or any of several other content types. See Figure 12-4.

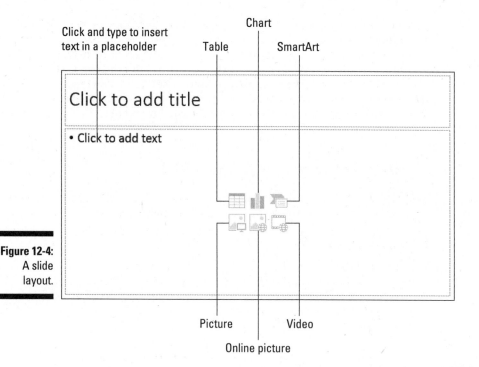

Figure 12-4:
A slide
layout.

Some placeholders are specifically for text. For example, the placeholder for each slide's title is text-only. Click such a placeholder and type the text you want. A content placeholder, such as the large placeholder on the default layout, can hold any *one* type of content: text, table, chart, SmartArt graphic, picture, clip art, or media clip (video or sound).

You can type either on the slide itself or in the Outline pane in Outline view. Either way, the text is placed in the slide's placeholders. Text you type at the highest outline level on the outline is placed in the slide's Title placeholder, and text you type at subordinate outline levels is placed in the Content placeholder.

Manually placing text on a slide

Whenever possible, you should use the layout placeholders to insert slide content. However, sometimes you might not be able to find a layout that's exactly what you want. For example, maybe you want to add a caption or note next to a picture, or you want to create a collage of text snippets arranged artistically on a slide.

The text in such a text box doesn't appear in the outline, so use this type of text box sparingly if having a comprehensive outline is important to you.

When you place a text box manually (Insert tab⇨Text Box), you can use two possible techniques: You can drag to draw the width of the box you want, or you can click the slide and start typing. The resulting text boxes have different properties based on the method you use. If you drag to draw the box you want, it will be a fixed width and any text you type in it will wrap to the next line as needed. If you click and start typing, the box widens as needed to hold the text and you must manually make your own line breaks.

Manipulating slide content

Each placeholder box and each manually created text box or other item is a separate object that you can move around and resize freely.

Resizing a slide object

To resize an object, select it and then drag a selection handle. A *selection handle* is a circle or square on the border of an object. Each box has eight selection handles: one in each corner and one on each side. (The additional circle arrow handle at the top of the selected box is a rotation handle; it rotates it when dragged.) See Figure 12-5.

Figure 12-5:
A selection
handle.

To maintain the height-width proportion for the box — its *aspect ratio* — hold down the Shift key while you drag one of the corner selection handles.

Moving a slide object

To move a text box, position the mouse pointer over the border of the box but not over a selection handle. The mouse pointer changes to a four-headed arrow. Click and drag the box to a new location. It works the same when you're moving nontext objects such as pictures, except that you don't have to be so fussy about pointing at the border when you drag a nontext object; you can point anywhere in the center of the object instead if you like.

If you want to move or resize a certain placeholder on every slide in your presentation, do so from Slide Master view. That way, you can make the change to the layout's template, and the change is applied automatically to every slide that uses that layout. To open Slide Master view, choose View⇨Slide Master.

Deleting a slide object

Deleting a slide object is a lot like deleting a slide except that you select the object first rather than selecting an entire slide. The easiest way to get rid of an object is to select it and press the Delete key. You can also right-click the object's border, choose Cut to cut it to the Clipboard, and then just not paste it anywhere.

Formatting a Presentation

Formatting can dramatically increase a presentation's effectiveness and impact. In PowerPoint, you can use themes to apply preset formatting to the entire presentation at once, or you can format individual elements. You can apply text formatting just as you do in other Office applications, from the Home tab, and you can apply background fills and borders to text boxes as well.

Applying themes

A *theme* is a design set that you apply to a data file to change several elements at once. In PowerPoint, the theme affects the background, color scheme, fonts, and the positions of the placeholders on the various layouts. Word and Excel also use themes, but in PowerPoint, the theme feature is exceptionally strong and full featured.

All presentations have a theme, but the default theme — simply named *Blank* — is so plain that it's almost like it's not there at all. Blank uses a white background, black Calibri text, and no background or design graphics.

You can switch to a different theme from the Design tab. Click the More button in the Themes group to open the Themes gallery and make your selection.

Some themes offer variations on the main design, called *variants*. Variants may have different colored background images. Themes designed for earlier versions of PowerPoint do not have variants. If available, variants are found in the Variants group on the Design tab.

Besides applying a different variant, you can also change the *color theme* for a presentation. A color theme redefines the colors used for the color placeholders in the presentation, resulting in a different set of colors being applied to any objects that are formatted using theme colors. Unlike variants, themes are available in all presentations regardless of the design used for them. Choose a color theme by opening the gallery in the Variants group on the Design tab and then choosing Colors from the menu that appears. See Figure 12-6.

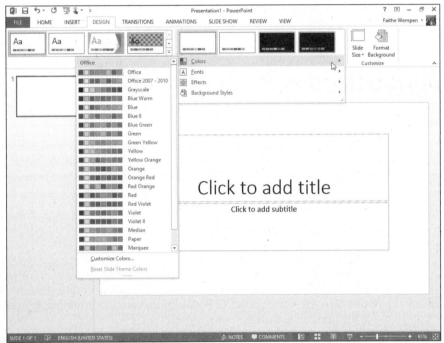

Figure 12-6:
The color
gallery.

Each theme has a set of two fonts that it uses: one designated for headings and one for body text. You can use the fonts from any other theme available if you don't like the ones that your chosen theme provides. Choose fonts from the same place you choose colors, as shown in Figure 12-6. Open the gallery in the Variants group and click Fonts.

Applying shape styles

The easiest way to apply formatting to an object is with the Shape Styles command. *Shape styles* are formatting presets that use the theme colors and effects in the presentation to format objects in multiple ways at once.

Depending on the style you choose, a shape style can include a border, a fill color, and special effects that make the shape look shiny, matte, or raised. Although from the name you might expect shape styles to apply only to graphical shapes, they still work with text boxes because PowerPoint considers a text box to be a shape (a rectangle).

To apply a shape style, select an object (such as a text box) and on the drawing Tools Format tab, open the gallery in the Shape Styles group and make your selection. See Figure 12-7.

Figure 12-7:
The gallery
in the Shape
Styles group.

Shape Styles group

Applying a background fill

A text box, by default, has no background fill. Whatever is behind it shows through. You can apply a number of different background fills to a text box to make it opaque. You can choose solid colors, of course, from either the theme colors or the standard colors. You can also choose to apply gradients, textures, patterns, or even pictures as background fills.

To apply a background fill to an object, use the Drawing Tools Format tab. Open the Shape Fill drop-down list and choose the desired fill. See Figure 12-8.

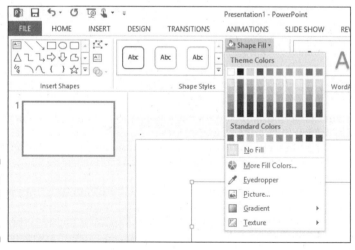

Figure 12-8:
The Shape
Fill drop-
down list.

Applying and removing borders

A *border* is a line around the outside of an object. When you first create them, text boxes don't have borders, so they blend in with the slide background. You can add a border to any object, choosing a line style (solid, dashed, and so on), line color, and line weight (thickness). You can also remove the border from a text box at any time.

Use the Shape Outline button on the Drawing Tools Format tab to apply and remove borders. Notice in Figure 12-9 that this menu has Weight, Dashes, and Arrows submenus so you can define not only the color of the outline but its properties.

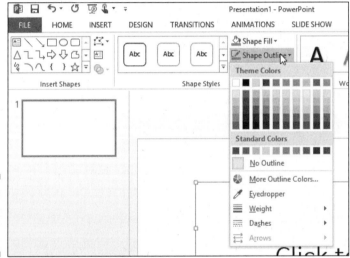

Figure 12-9:
The Shape
Outline
menu.

Applying shape effects

Shape effects are enhancements like shadow, reflection, glow, and bevel that you can optionally apply to shapes (including text boxes) to dress them up. Some of the shape styles (covered earlier in the lesson) apply some of these effects, and you can also apply the effects separately.

To apply shape effects, use the Shape Effects button on the Drawing Tools Format tab, as shown in Figure 12-10. Each command there has a submenu from which you can select a variety of presets.

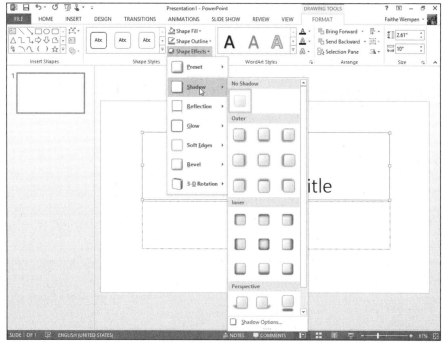

Figure 12-10:
The Shape
Effects
button.

Turning text Autofit on or off

If you type more text than will fit in that text box (which is especially common for a slide title, for example), the text automatically shrinks itself as much as is needed to allow it to fit. This feature, called *Autofit*, is turned on by default in text placeholders. Autofit is very useful because it prevents text from being truncated.

In manually placed text boxes, a different Autofit behavior occurs by default: The text box itself gets larger as needed to accommodate the text.

Both of those behaviors can be very useful, but you may sometimes need to change the Autofit setting for one or more text boxes to achieve certain effects. For example, you may not want a manually placed text box to shrink if you delete some text from it, or it might be unacceptable to you for the font size used in the title of one slide to be different from that of another.

To control a text box's AutoFit setting, right-click the border of the text box and click Size and Position. The Format Shape task pane opens. Expand the Text Box heading in the task pane to see its controls, and then select a different AutoFit setting. See Figure 12-11.

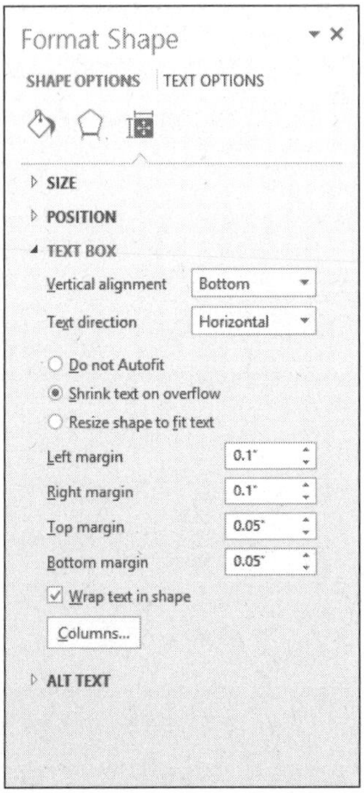

Figure 12-11:
The Format
Shape task
pane.

Inserting Graphics

You learned about inserting graphics in Word in Lesson 10, and inserting them in PowerPoint is similar. The commands on the Insert tab in both applications include buttons for inserting a graphic from a file and also for inserting online images such as clip art.

However, PowerPoint has one big difference: placeholders. You have two ways of inserting graphics in PowerPoint: via the Insert tab (as in Word) and via the icons in a content placeholder. Depending on which method you choose, the graphic behaves differently.

The placeholder method offers several advantages. If you insert a graphic using one of the content placeholders, the graphic integrates more seamlessly with the other content on the slide, and if you change to a layout that positions that placeholder differently, or a theme that arranges the placeholders differently, the graphic moves automatically to the new position. In contrast, if you insert a graphic using the Insert tab's commands, it becomes a fixed, manually placed object on the slide, and it doesn't automatically shift when the layout shifts.

Inserting an online image from Office.com

In PowerPoint 2013, you access Microsoft's artwork collection via Office.com from within PowerPoint itself. This artwork collection includes both *clip art* illustrations (line drawings) and *digital photographs*.

To insert an image from the Internet in a placeholder, click the Online Pictures icon in the empty content placeholder box (second icon in the bottom row of the placeholder icons), or choose Insert➪Online Pictures.

In the Insert Pictures dialog box, you have a choice of searching Offic.com Clip Art or Bing Image Search. The Office.com collection contains royalty-free images from Microsoft; the Bing Image Search looks for pictures on the entire Internet. (However, it restricts itself by default to images that are licensed under Creative Commons for public use.) See Figure 12-12.

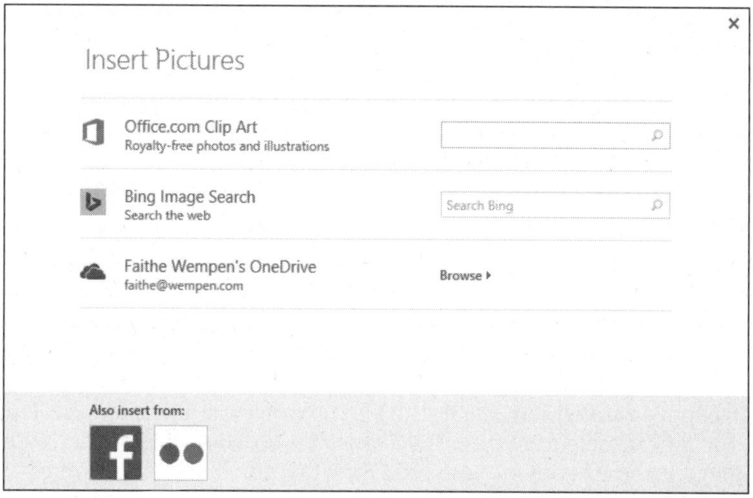

Figure 12-12:
The Insert Pictures dialog box.

After the search has located some images, click the one you want in the results window and click Insert to insert it in the presentation.

Inserting your own pictures

You can also insert pictures you've acquired yourself, either from someone else or from your own digital camera or scanner. These pictures are stored as separate files on your hard drive or other media. PowerPoint supports many different picture formats, including `.tif`, `.jpg`, `.gif`, `.bmp`, and `.png`.

To insert one of your own pictures, click the Pictures icon in a content place-holder or choose Insert⇨Pictures. In the dialog box that appears, select the picture you want and click Insert to add it to the presentation.

Adding Slide Transition Effects

Transitions are movements from one slide to another. The default transition effect is None, which means the slide simply goes away and the next one appears. Some of the alternatives include Fade, Push, Wipe, Split, and Cut, to name only a few. You can apply transitions from the Transitions tab.

Some of the transition effects have effect options that determine the direction of the action. For example, a Wipe transition might wipe from the left, right, top, or bottom, or from one of the corners. Other effects have no such options because they can happen only one way. If options are available, you can click the Transitions tab and choose them from the Effect Options button's menu.

You can also set several other properties for a transition. You can assign a sound to it, for example, and you can control its duration (speed). You can choose when the transition should occur:

- ✔ On mouse click
- ✔ Automatically after a certain amount of time has passed

Each transition has default settings, so you can apply a basic transition effect with just a few clicks. You can then optionally fine-tune those settings later.

To apply a transition, select the slide to affect and then on the Transitions tab, make a selection from the Transition to This Slide gallery. If the effect you choose has any options, the Effect Options button becomes available to apply them. To apply the same transition to all slides in the presentation, click Apply to All. See Figure 12-13.

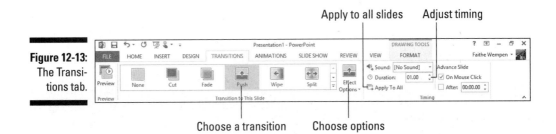

Figure 12-13: The Transitions tab.

Apply to all slides   Adjust timing

Choose a transition   Choose options

Using Apply to All is much faster and easier than applying the same transition effect manually to multiple slides. If you don't want it to affect certain slides, you can remove the transition from those slides later by choosing None as the transition effect for them.

Setting Slides to Advance Manually or Automatically

Slides advance on mouse click by default. That means that no matter how long you leave a slide onscreen, PowerPoint won't try to advance to the next slide until you give the signal. (That signal can be an actual mouse click, or it can be the press of a key, such as Enter, spacebar, or the right-arrow key.)

If you want certain (or all) slides to advance automatically after a certain amount of time, you can specify this advancement on the Transitions tab. You can specify an automatic transition instead of or in addition to the default On Click behavior. See Figure 12-13.

Inserting Sounds and Videos

One way to make a presentation more interesting is to include multimedia content such as sounds and video clips. You can place clips directly on a slide and set them up to play either automatically or on click.

Inserting a sound clip on a slide

When you place a sound clip (sometimes called an audio clip) on a slide, a speaker icon appears to represent it. Playback controls appear beneath the icon, so you can control the clip during the show. You can set the clip to playback on click or automatically.

You can control whether or not the playback controls appear by marking or clearing the Show Media Controls check box on the Slide Show tab.

To insert a sound clip, choose Insert⇨Audio⇨Audio on My PC. Navigate to the location of the sound clip, select it, and click Insert. A speaker icon appears in the center of the slide, with playback controls beneath it. See Figure 12-14.

Figure 12-14:
A speaker
icon with
playback
controls.

If you want to specify any options for the sound, use the Audio Tools Playback controls, as shown in Figure 12-15. For example, you could mark the Play Across Slides check box to let the sound continue when you move to the next slide during the presentation.

Figure 12-15:
The Audio
Tools
Playback
controls.

Play Across Slides

Inserting a video clip on a slide

PowerPoint 2013 accepts video clips in a variety of formats, including Windows Media, Windows Video, QuickTime, MP4, and Flash. You can place a video clip on a slide either within a content placeholder or as a standalone item. You can also apply formatting to a video clip, such as a video style that governs the shape and appearance of the clip's frame.

Using a placeholder means that the clip will be resized or shifted as needed if you change layouts or themes; inserting a clip manually makes it stay as-is regardless of the layout or theme. To insert a video clip, click the Insert tab and then the Video button.

To insert a video clip, choose Insert⇨Video⇨Video on My PC. Browse and select the video clip and click Insert.

If you want to specify options for the video, use the Video Tools Playback tab, as shown in Figure 12-16. For example, you can change the clip's volume, change when it starts, and choose to show it full-screen.

Figure 12-16:
The Video
Tools Play-
back tab.

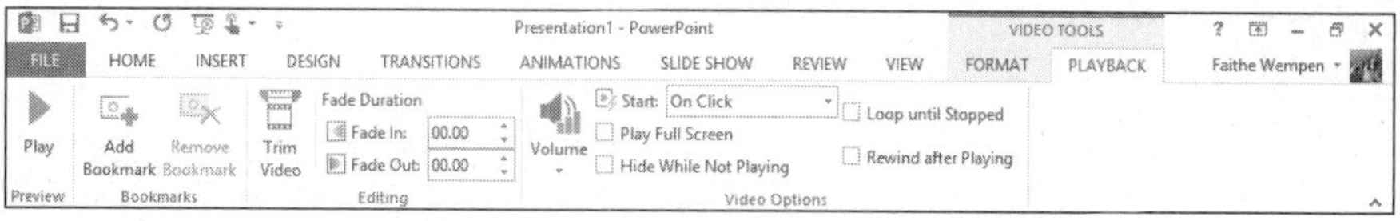

Presenting a Slide Show

PowerPoint 2013 gives you various methods for delivering your presentation: You can deliver a presentation live in a meeting room, broadcast it on the Internet, package it on a writeable CD, or send it out via email, just to name a few. This section focuses on the most popular delivery method: delivering a live show to an audience in person.

To give an onscreen show, switch to Slide Show view. Slide Show view isn't one of the views on the View tab; you choose it from the Slide Show tab instead, by either clicking From Beginning or From Current Slide. See Figure 12-17.

Figure 12-17:
The Slide
Show tab.

Slide Show view displays each slide full-screen, one at a time. For larger audiences, you may want to hook up a projector to your computer so the audience can see the slides more easily. (The Windows key + P shortcut easily connects a notebook PC to a projector or a second screen.)

Moving between slides

To move from one slide to the next or to trigger the next on-click animation on a slide, click the left mouse button. That's all you need to know at the most basic level. You can also get much fancier than that about moving around. You can use shortcut keys to move to specific locations, and you can right-click and use the shortcut menu that appears to move around.

Right-click and choose Help in Slide Show view to get a list of the shortcut keys available.

You can also use the buttons in the lower-left corner of the screen in Slide Show view. They're very faint at first, but if you move the mouse pointer over one, it become solid. Click a button to open a menu, as in Figure 12-18, or click the right- or left-arrow buttons there to move forward and back in the presentation.

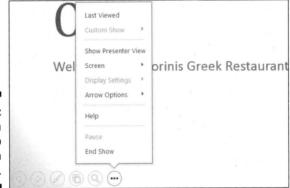

Figure 12-18:
Click a
button to
open a
menu.

Ending the slide show

To end the slide show early (before you get to the last slide), press the Esc key on the keyboard, or right-click and choose End Show.

Printing Handouts and Notes

Handouts are paper copies of your presentation that you give to the audience. They give your audience something tangible to refer to, and to take home with them. They can also write on the handouts to make their own notes. (Some handout layouts even include lines for writing.)

To print your presentation, choose File➪Print. You will recognize many of the options on the Print screen from Word and Excel, such as the controls for page range, number of copies, and printer. See Figure 12-19.

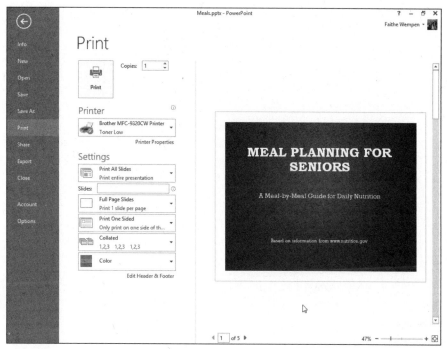

When you print in PowerPoint, you have a choice of the type of printout you want. (Technically you can use any of these printout types as handouts, although the Handouts type is obviously custom-made for that purpose.) Click the Full Page Slides button (the default setting) and choose one of these menu options, as shown in Figure 12-20.

- ✔ **Full Page Slides:** A full-page copy of one slide per sheet.
- ✔ **Notes Pages:** One slide per page, but with the slide occupying only the top half of the page. The bottom half is devoted to any speaker notes you typed into PowerPoint.
- ✔ **Outline View:** A text-only version of the presentation, structured as an outline, with the slide titles as the top-level outline items.
- ✔ **Handouts:** Multiple slides per page (two to nine, depending on your choice of settings), suitable for giving to the audience to take home.

Different numbers of slides per page have different layouts. For example, if you choose three slides per page, the layout has lines next to each slide so the audience can take notes.

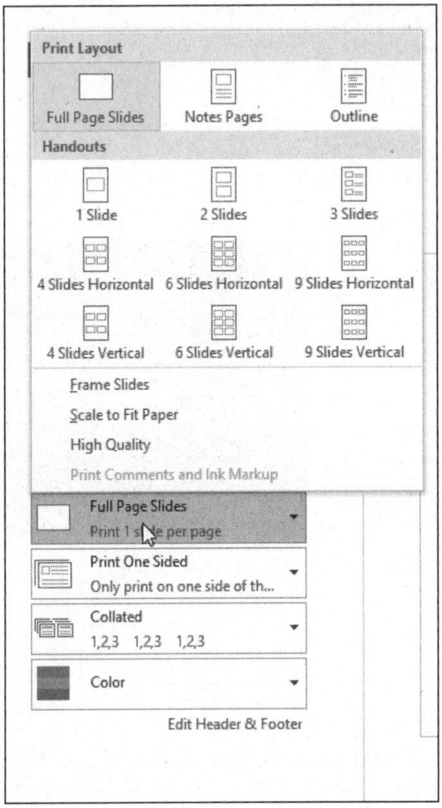

Figure 12-20: Choose a menu option.

Chapter 13

Storing and Retrieving Data with Microsoft Access

In This Chapter

▶ Discovering the basic concepts of a database

▶ Creating a database

▶ Entering and editing database records

▶ Creating queries

▶ Creating reports

A database is a collection of structured data — that is, data in a consistent format. For example, an address book is a database, as is a catalog of items for sale, because the same facts are stored about each instance.

You can store structured data in Excel, but in many cases, the size and complexity of a database make Excel an impractical tool for it. Microsoft Access is a better choice when you have multiple tables of data and when you need to sort and manipulate that data in several different ways.

In this chapter, you discover some basics about databases, and you find out how to use Microsoft Access to create and store a simple database.

Understanding Database and Access Basics

Access is a popular application for creating and managing small to medium databases. This type of application is called a *database management system (DBMS)*.

TIP

Large databases, such as the inventory for a large online retailer, are not stored in consumer-level applications like Access. Instead they are stored in powerful, multi-user systems produced by companies like Citrix and Oracle. Managing these large databases is a professional job, and database administrators make a career of this work.

Database data is stored in one or more tables. At its most basic level, a *table* is a collection of fields into which users can input records. A *record* is an instance of something. For example, in an address book, each person is a record, and in an inventory, each product is a record. The information stored about each record are the *fields*. For example, for a person, First Name is a field.

In Access, a table can be displayed in *Datasheet view*, which makes its data appear in a two-dimensional grid that looks a lot like an Excel worksheet. See Figure 13-1. The field names appear across the tops of the columns and the data records appear in rows beneath those column headings.

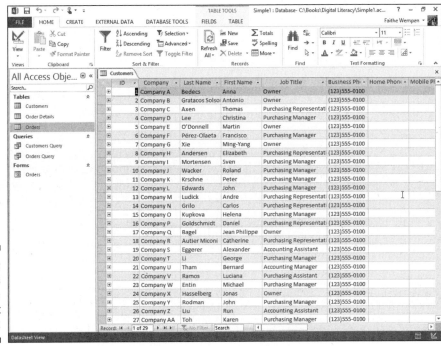

Figure 13-1:
An Access
table in
Datasheet
view.

You can enter new data into the first empty row at the bottom of a table data-sheet, as you would enter it in an Excel worksheet. There is another option, however; in Access, you can create forms for data entry. A *form* makes the process of data entry more user-friendly by displaying only one record at a time, as shown in Figure 13-2. The form itself contains no data; it merely funnels data into the table(s) with which it is associated.

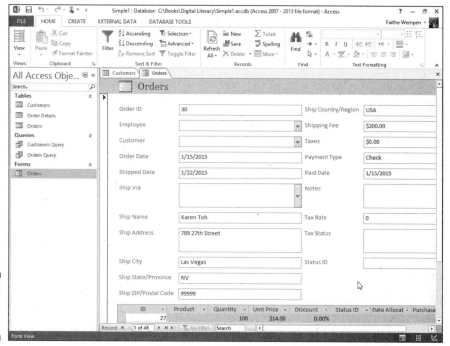

Figure 13-2:
A form in
Access.

One of the benefits of using Access is that you can have two (or more) tables in the same data file, and you can create a relationship between the tables. For example, you could have Customers and Orders tables for your business. In the Customers table, you could store the full contact information for each customer, and in the Orders table, you could store information about each order placed. The Orders table could have a Customer ID field that has a relationship to the Customer ID field in the Customers table, so that each order is tied to a particular customer's record. You could also have a table called

Order Details that contains each line-item of each order, with an Order ID field that is related to the Order ID field in the Orders table. Figure 13-3 shows these tables and relationships. Creating relationships between tables is very useful, and it's one of the main benefits of using Access rather than Excel.

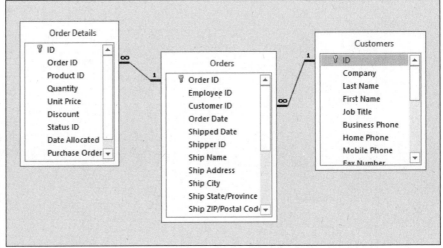

Figure 13-3:
Create
relation-
ships
between
tables.

To sort and filter the data from one or more tables, you can create a query, which is a set of saved specifications for sorting, filtering, and other data manipulation. A query's results display in a datasheet, like a table does, but may include a subset of the fields and/or records from the table on which it is based. A query can also be used to combine the data from multiple related tables. For example, looking back at the relationships in Figure 13-3, you could create a query that shows a record for each order placed on a certain date and the postal code to which it was shipped. The order date would come from the Orders table, and the postal code would come from the Customers table.

A query can help you find key information quickly, such as in the preceding example, but the results it generates will be presented in a plain-looking data-sheet. When you want to present data in a more attractive format, you can generate a report. A *report* takes data from a table or query and lays it out for printing with a title and page headers/footers. Reports can also option-ally summarize data rather than presenting the full set of records. Figure 13-4 shows a sample report.

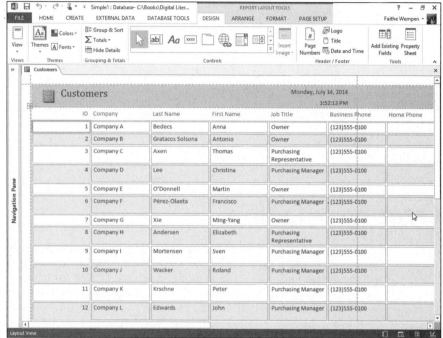

Figure 13-4:
A report in
Access.

Creating a New Database

When you start Microsoft Access 2013, a Start screen appears. Click Blank desktop database to get started with a new, basic database that you can use to practice in this chapter. You can later explore the templates that Access provides on your own.

The first thing Access does is prompt you for a file name for your new database. That's because Access works a little differently from other applications; when you enter records into a table, it saves those records automatically; you don't have to save your work unless you are modifying the database's structure. Because of that, you have to save the database file upfront, before you start working on it. Type a name in the prompt that appears, as in Figure 13-5, and click Create.

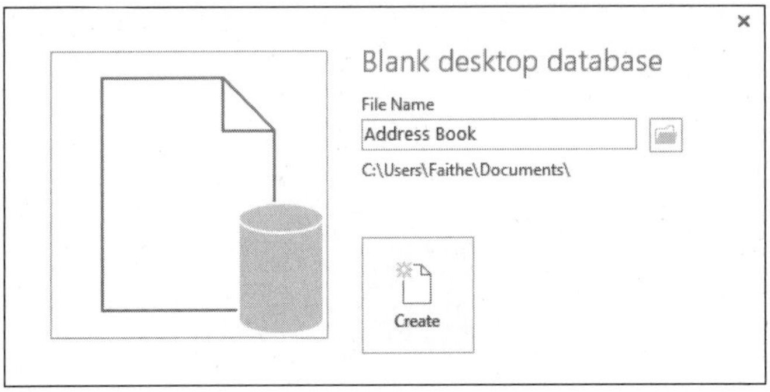

Figure 13-5:
A new database in Access.

Creating a Table

When you create a new database, Access creates a new table for you automatically and opens it up in Datasheet view. The table appears on the right, and on the left you see a navigation pane, which contains a list of all of the database objects. (There's only one right now, Table1, as shown in Figure 13-6.) A database file starts with a table because a table is the only database object that can hold data, so you must construct your tables before you can do any data entry or create any other objects.

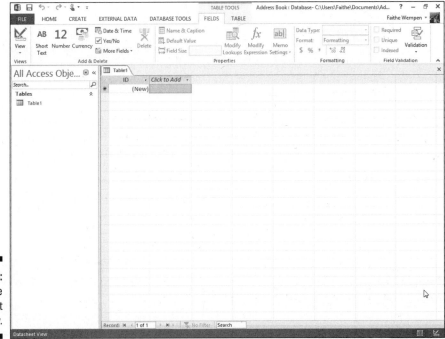

Figure 13-6:
A new table in Datasheet view.

Because a table is open in Figure 13-6, the Table Tools contextual tabs appear: Fields and Table. These tabs contain commands for working with the table. Other contextual tab sets may appear when you are working with other object types.

In Figure 13-6, note that the fields are in columns and the records are in rows. There aren't any records yet, and only one field: ID. The ID field is automatically generated; it will contain a unique value for each record. This field is the *primary key field.* The primary key field is the field that positively defines each record because each record has a unique value for it. The primary key field in a table is usually an ID field, but it could be some other field in some circumstances, such as a Product ID field for an inventory or a Social Security Number field for a database of taxpayers.

You can create a table in Datasheet view, or for more control over the table's structure, you can switch to Design view and work with it there. To switch between views, use the View buttons on the status bar or click the down arrow under the View button on the Ribbon (Table Tools Fields tab) and choose the desired view.

To create more fields, click the Click to Add heading. On the drop-down list of field types, select the desired type, as shown in Figure 13-7. (Text is most common.) A generic name appears in the column heading, with the name highlighted, ready to be changed. Type the new field name and press Enter. Repeat that process to create all the fields you need in your table.

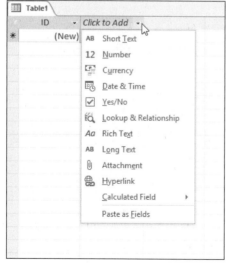

Figure 13-7: Choose a field type.

If you switch over to Design view, you have more options available. Click the View button on the Table Tools Fields tab to do so. If it's a new table, you'll be prompted to give it a name. Give it a name that describes its contents and click OK.

In Design view, shown in Figure 13-8, you can do any of the following:

Figure 13-8:
Design view.

✔ Rearrange the fields by dragging them up or down on the list.

✔ Set a field's properties by selecting it and then working in the Field Properties area at the bottom of the screen.

✔ Rename a field by changing its name.

✔ Change the field type by changing its setting in the Data Type column.

✔ Delete a field by selecting it and pressing the Delete key on the keyboard or clicking Delete Rows on the Table Tools Design tab.

✔ Make a different field the primary key by selecting the field and clicking the Primary Key button on the Table Tools Design tab.

When you are done modifying the table, save your work. Because modifying a table is a structural change, Access doesn't save the changes automatically as it does when working with records.

If you want to create an additional table, on the Create tab you can either click Table to start another new table in Datasheet view, or click Table Design to start a new table in Design view.

Creating Relationships Between Tables

Relationships can be tricky, both in real life and in Access databases. Many beginners make the mistake of creating relationships willy-nilly, without thinking about the appropriate match-ups. Bad relationships are worse than none at all — again, both in life and in databases.

The most common type of relationship is a *one-to-many relationship*. (Here's where the real-life relationships metaphor breaks down.) A one-to-many relationship in Access connects the primary key field in one table (that's the "one" side) with a field in another table that stores the exact same type of data but isn't unique to each record (that's the "many" side, also called the *foreign key field*). For example, the ID field in the Customers table might have a relationship to the Customer ID field in the Orders table. Look back at Figure 13-3, which shows relationships between an Orders table and two other tables.

The purpose of a relationship is to connect the data between the tables. With the aforementioned relationship, the Orders table can reference people from the Customers table easily and efficiently. A relationship can optionally have *referential integrity* enforced. That means that Access won't allow entries in the field on the "many" side that don't have corresponding entries on the "one" side. In the aforementioned example, if referential integrity were enforced, you wouldn't be able to create orders in the Orders table for nonexistent customers (that is, people who don't appear in the Customers table).

Referential integrity has two options: Cascade Update and Cascade Delete. Cascade Update changes the entry in the foreign key table when the entry in the primary key table changes. For example, if a customer's ID number changes in the Customers table, her ID will be automatically updated for each of her records in the Orders table.

Cascade Delete deletes the entry in the foreign key table when the entry in the primary key table is deleted. For example, suppose a customer is removed from the Customers table for some reason (for example, the customer dies, or asks to be removed). If Cascade Delete is enabled, all records in the Orders table from previous orders that customer placed would be deleted.

Follow these steps to create a relationship:

1. **Ensure that the fields to be related have the same data type.**

   Check the data types for each field in each table in Table Design view if needed. For this evaluation, you can consider AutoNumber to be the Number data type. (Automatically numbered fields such as ID have an AutoNumber type.)

2. **Click Database Tools⇨Relationships.**

   The Relationships window opens.

3. **If the table(s) you want to work with do not appear, click Show Table on the Relationship Tools tab. Click the table to show and click Add. Close the dialog box when you're done.**

4. **Drag-and-drop the primary key field from one table onto the foreign key field in the related table. The Edit Relationships dialog box opens. See Figure 13-9.**

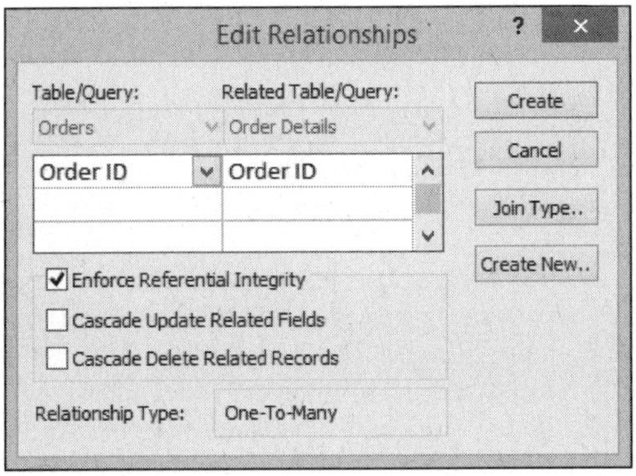

Figure 13-9: The Edit Relationships dialog box.

5. **(Recommended but optional.) Select the Enforce Referential Integrity check box.**

6. **(Optional) Mark the Cascade Update and/or Cascade Delete check boxes if appropriate.**

7. **Click Create to create the relationship.**

8. **When you're done creating relationships, choose Relationship Tools Design⇨Close and save your changes when prompted.**

Entering and Editing Records

It is a good idea not to enter any data until you have finalized the tables and their relationships because changing a table's fields and properties may change the rules for what data a field will accept. For example, if you change a field's type from Text to Number, text-based data in that field will become invalid.

You can enter data directly into a table in Datasheet view. Click in the first cell in the first blank row of the datasheet (scroll down if needed), and start typing. Press Tab to move to the next field, or press Shift+Tab to go back to the previous field. When you reach the final cell in the row, pressing Tab moves to the beginning of the next row and starts a new record. If you don't want to tab all the way to the end of the row, just click the mouse to move the insertion point outside of that row, or click the Save button in the Records group on the Home tab. Records are saved automatically when you navigate away from them; you don't have to click the Save button after each one to save it.

There are several ways to delete a record. Select it (by clicking the selection box, which is the gray blank box to the left of the record), and then do any of the following:

✓ Press the Delete key.

✓ Right-click the record and choose Delete Record.

✓ Choose Home⇨Delete.

Creating Queries

A *query* is a view of a table that shows it in a different way. A query can hide certain fields, hide certain records, show records sorted in a certain order, and more. Queries are useful for cutting out the unimportant data to find an answer to a question, and for extracting data that helps make sense of a situation. For example, a query could answer the question, "What orders did customer X place in January?" or "What were the top ten best-selling products in the Northeast region?" A query can also be used to make the data from two or more related tables appear together in a single datasheet. That query can then be used as the basis for a report, allowing you to create reports using data that spans multiple tables.

You can create a query using the Query Wizard, which walks you step-by-step through the process of creating a query, or you can use Design view. This chapter briefly explains both.

Creating a query with the Simple Query Wizard

The Simple Query Wizard is a good place to start for your first query because it makes the process very, well, simple. The Simple Query Wizard enables you to create a query that includes fields from one or more related tables, and that includes only certain fields. It can either show all the records (a *detail query*) or show a summary of them (a *summary query*).

The drawback to the Simple Query Wizard is that it does not allow you to filter the records. In other words, it shows all the records (or a summary of all the records). You could not, for example, show only one customer, or only one date range of orders.

To create a query with the Simple Query Wizard, follow these steps:

1. **Choose Create➪Query Wizard.**

   The New Query dialog box opens.

2. **Click Simple Query Wizard and click OK.**

   The Simple Query Wizard runs.

3. **Open the Tables/Queries list and choose the table from which to pull fields.**

4. **In the Available Fields list, click a field you want to include and click the > button to add it to the Selected Fields list.**

   Do this for each field to include. See Figure 13-10. Or, to add all the fields from the table, click the >> button.

5. **If you want another table's fields to be included, repeat Steps 3 and 4. Otherwise click Next to continue.**

6. **If you included one or more fields that can be calculated, such as a Number of Currency field, a screen appears asking if you want a detail or summary query. Choose Detail and then click Next.**

7. **If desired, change the default name of the query in the What Title Do You Want for Your Query? text box.**

8. **Click Finish.**

   The query results appear in Datasheet view. The query's name appears in the navigation pane. The query results show the chosen fields in a datasheet.

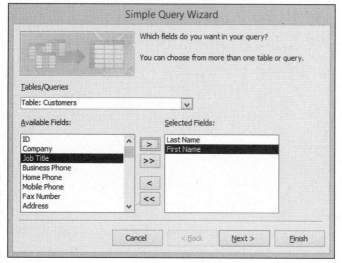

Figure 13-10:
The Simple
Query
Wizard.

Creating a query in Query Design View

When you create a query in Design view, you have full control over the query. You can filter out certain fields, and also certain records by the criteria you specify.

In Query Design view, the top section shows the fields from the tables that you add to the grid. The bottom section is the Query By Example (QBE) grid; you drag individual fields here and then set properties to configure how they will appear in the query results. For example, in Figure 13-11, four fields are included: Company (from the Customers table), Order Date (from the Orders table), and Quantity and Unit Price (from the Order Details table). The query is sorted first by Company and then by Order Date, and filtered to show only orders with a date between 3/1/2015 and 3/31/2015.

For a query that just selects data, like the ones you create in this chapter, switching to Datasheet view and clicking the Run button do the same thing. For other types of queries that you might create, though, the buttons serve differently: Run executes the instructions in the query to actually modify the data, whereas switching to Datasheet view does not.

Follow these steps to create a query in Design view:

1. **Choose Create➪Query Design. A blank QBE grid opens, and the Show Table dialog box opens.**

2. **Click a table from which you want to use fields, and click Add. Repeat for each additional table you also want to use fields from, and then click Close to close the dialog box.**

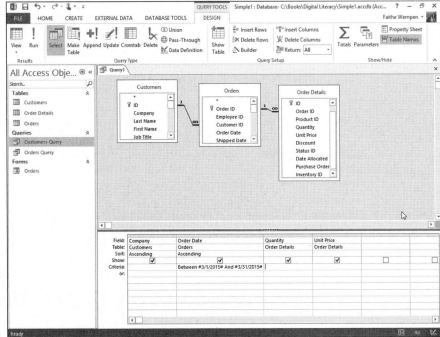

Figure 13-11:
Query
Design view.

3. **Drag a field from a table to the QBE grid at the bottom of the screen. Do this for each field you want to include, as shown in Figure 13-11, in the order they should appear in the query results.**

If you make a mistake in the order, you can drag a field to reposition it. Select it by clicking the thin gray bar above the field name in the QBE grid, so that the column for that field turns black, and then drag to the left or right.

4. **To sort by a certain field, click in the Sort line for that field, so that a drop-down list arrow appears. Open the drop-down list and choose Ascending or Descending.**

If more than one field has sorting enabled, data will be sorted from left to right; the leftmost field marked for sorting will be the primary sort.

5. **To filter by a certain field, enter the criteria in the Criteria line for that field. Table 13-1 summarizes the way to enter different types of data. In Figure 13-11, the query filters by the Order Date field, for example.**

6. **(Optional) If you want to hide a certain field from the results, clear the check box in its Show line.**

   You might filter by a certain field but then hide that field from the results, for example.

7. **Click the Run button on the Query Tools Design tab to see the query results, or switch to Datasheet view.**

Table 13-1	Writing Criteria in the QBE Grid	
Data Type	*Instructions*	*Example*
Text	Place in quotation marks	"Chicago" Finds only records that contain exactly that value.
	Exclude values with NOT	NOT "Chicago" Finds records that do not contain exactly that value.
	Begin with the specified string with Like	Like "Chi*" Finds records that begin with that string (Chicago, China).
	Exclude beginning with a specified string with Not Like	Not Like "Chi*" Excludes records that begin with that string.
	Include the specified string with Like and a wildcard character *	Like "*Chicago*" Finds records that have that string anywhere in that field (Old Chicago, Chicago Heights).
	Use OR to include any of a short list of values	"Chicago" OR "New York" Finds records that have one or the other of those two values.
	Use IN to include any of a longer list of values	In ("Chicago", "New York", "Philadelphia", "Seattle") Finds records that have any of the listed values.
Empty or Non-Empty Fields	Use Is Null to find empty fields or Is Not Null to find non-empty fields	Is Null finds empty fields. Is Not Null finds non-empty fields.

(continued)

Table 13-1 *(continued)*

Data Type	Instructions	Example
Number or Currency Fields	Use the numbers without any special characters	12 Finds records that have an exact value of 12.
	Use NOT to exclude a value	NOT 12 Finds records that do not have an exact value of 12.
	Use > and < for greater-than and less-than Use >= for greater than or equal to Use <= for less than or equal to	>6 Finds records where the value is greater than 6.
	Use Between to specify a range	Between 0 and 12 Finds records where the values are greater than 0 and less than 12.
	Use IN to include any of a longer list of values	IN ($5, $10, $15, $20) Finds records that contain one of the listed values.
Date and Time Fields	Use # around an exact date	#12/21/2014# Finds records that contain exactly that date.
	Use > and < for greater than and less than Use >= for greater than or equal to Use <= for less than or equal to	>#12/21/2014# Finds records where the date is after the specified date. >#2/1/2014# and <#2/28/2014# Finds values that fall within the specified date range. <#2/1/2014# or >#2/28/2014# Finds values that fall outside of the specified date range.

Creating Reports

Whereas most of the other objects in a database are designed to be used onscreen, reports are designed to be printed. Reports have two different views for creating and editing them: Layout and Design Use Layout for simple edits that a beginner can make, and Design for precise control.

To create a report, use the Report button in the Report group on the Create tab to create a default-styled report with all the fields from the selected table or query, or try out the Report Wizard for a few more choices.

For reports, a Report view and a Print Preview view are both available. Report view is designed for reading the report onscreen, whereas Print Preview view is designed for seeing how the report will look when printed, but they are similar.

Creating a quick report is very simple. In the navigation pane, select the table or query on which to base the report. Then choose Create➪Report. A report opens in Layout view using default settings. You can then adjust it in Layout view as needed. Figure 13-12 shows a report in Layout view.

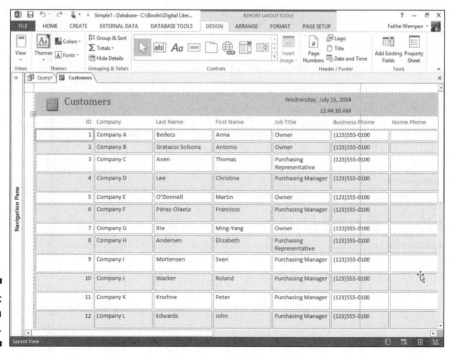

Figure 13-12:
A report in
Layout view.

In Layout view, you can use the Report Layout Tools tabs to make many different changes to a report. The tabs available on the Ribbon are

- ✔ **Design:** Here you can insert page numbers, add fields, apply themes, and add grouping and sorting to the report.

- ✔ **Arrange:** On this tab you can insert and delete rows and columns, changing the report layout (for example, Stacked vs. Table), and merge and split cells, as well as adjust the margins and padding around each item on the report.

- ✔ **Format:** This tab contains controls for changing text fonts, sizes, and attributes, changing number formatting, applying conditional formatting, and using a background image.

- ✔ **Page Setup:** This is where you set the paper size, orientation, and margins.

To preview a report before you print it, choose File➪Print and then click Print Preview.

To print a report, choose File➪Print and then click Print. Adjust the settings as needed in the Print dialog box (Figure 13-13) and then click OK.

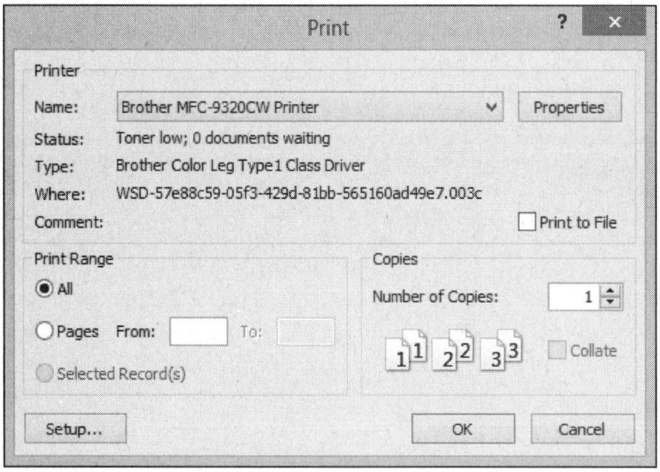

Figure 13-13: The Print dialog box.

Part IV
Digital Security and Privacy

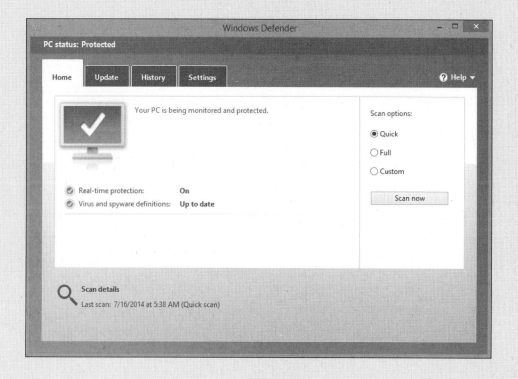

Check out www.dummies.com/extras/digitalliteracy for information about proxy services and how they affect security.

In this part . . .

- Find out how to protect your computer and its data from many kinds of harm, including accidents, viruses, and criminals.

- Discover how to protect your online privacy and how to shield children from online predators and inappropriate computer content.

Chapter 14

Protecting Your Computer and Data from Harm

In This Chapter

▶ Finding out about the different types of computer security risks and threats

▶ Discovering how to protect against natural risks

▶ Learning how to protect against human-created threats

▶ Increasing security through web and mail settings

▶ Learning best practices for staying safe on the web

*W*orst case scenario here: What would you lose if your computer's hard drive stopped working right now, never to run again? Maybe it died in a flood (computers *hate* water), or of natural causes such as a hardware failure, or maybe a virus wiped it clean. At any rate, everything you had on it is gone and never coming back: the operating system, the applications, all your writings, your family photos, and your entire music collection.

The scary thing is, that's not just a horror story I made up to frighten you — it happens to people all the time. People who, like you, thought it could never happen to them.

In this chapter, I clue you in on the major security threats and risks to be aware of in computing — both natural threats and those caused by malicious human behavior. You learn about some of the security settings you can adjust in Windows to beef up your protection, and about some third-party applications that can help too.

Understanding the Risks

Before we get started here, I want to define a few of terms. This chapter deals with *computer security*. Security has three components to it, as summarized in Figure 14-1:

✔ **Confidentiality:** You should be able to restrict access to only those you choose to give access to.

✔ **Integrity:** Your computer and its data and applications should be uncorrupted and intact. The data that you store *stays* stored, and your hardware continues to work correctly.

✔ **Availability:** Your data and applications should be available when you want them, including after a mishap or disaster.

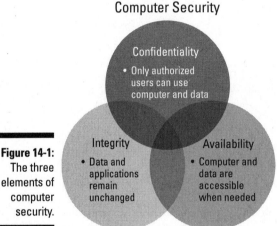

Figure 14-1:
The three elements of computer security.

In contrast, *computer privacy* refers to preventing unauthorized people from getting ahold of computer -stored or -transmitted information that they shouldn't have. It's an offshoot of confidentiality, but it takes on its own life too because there are so many computer-related ways for privacy to be violated. For example, if someone guesses your password and logs into your Facebook account, or tricks you with a phony website into revealing your credit card data, that's a privacy issue. This chapter deals mainly with the security side of things; I address privacy in Chapter 15.

Risks

Computing comes with security risks and threats. A *risk* is a generic potential for a problem to occur. For example, if you place your computer on the edge of a table, there's a risk of accidentally bumping it and knocking it onto the floor. If you don't back up your data, you risk losing access to it if your computer breaks down. Risks are generally physical and environmental. They are not usually network or Internet-based. Some common risks of computing include

✔ **Data loss:** All computer users live with an ongoing risk of data loss. If you don't have a backup of an important file, and the file gets destroyed (for whatever reason), you are out of luck. Some data files for businesses are worth millions of dollars and would take thousands of hours of effort to reconstruct.

✔ **Hardware failure:** Sometimes components of a computer just die for no apparent reason. Hard disk drives are particularly prone to premature death because of their many mechanical parts.

✔ **Trauma:** Falling off of tables or getting knocked, hit, or kicked.

✔ **Water:** Even a very small amount of water can short-circuit almost any computer component, often ruining it permanently. That's because water is a very good electrical conductor, and the electricity, if given a choice, will take a path through the water rather than the path it is supposed to take.

✔ **Cold:** When a computer runs in a very cold environment, the heat from the computer running melts the frost on the components, forming water. (See previous bullet.)

✔ **Heat:** When a computer operates in a hot environment, it is harder to adequately cool the CPU and other components that generate heat as they operate. The most common result of extreme heat is the computer shutting down, and failing to start up again until it cools off. Extreme heat can also permanently damage components.

✔ **Static electricity:** Computer circuit boards are extremely sensitive to static electricity (also known as electrostatic discharge, or ESD), and it's possible to ruin a circuit board just by touching it, delivering a static electricity jolt to the component that the person doesn't even feel. This isn't an issue when handling a computer from the outside — only when working on its innards.

✔ **Electrical spikes:** If the AC power delivered by your wall outlet isn't consistent, brief, sudden increases in the voltage level can occur, called *spikes*. This is most common when there is a lightning strike near the building. Electrical spikes can ruin any computer components that are plugged in at the time.

Threats

A *threat* is an active, human-caused potential for harm. For example, if you don't run antivirus software, your computer is vulnerable to attacks from malware. Here are some important terms to know regarding threats:

✔ **Malware:** A generic term for any software that was written specifically to cause a problem on a computer. The problem it creates, known as its *payload*, can be anything from displaying annoying onscreen ads to deleting important operating system files.

- **Virus:** Executable code that attaches itself to a program file, so that the code runs when the program runs. The virus's code might destroy files, steal data, display onscreen messages, or perform other types of harm or inconvenience.

- **Worm:** Executable code that spreads via web pages, network connections, and email. A worm might distribute itself to everyone in your email address book, for example. A worm's code, in addition to spreading itself, might install malware.

- **Spyware:** A type of malware that spies on the usage of the computer on which it is installed and relays information back to the spyware's creator. The information gathered can include credit card numbers, passwords, and usage habits.

- **Adware:** A type of malware that pops up unwanted ads on the computer on which it is installed.

- **Exploit:** A type of malware that uses a vulnerability (such as a bug or a programming error) in an operating system's code to perform some harmful action.

- **Trojan horse:** A type of malware that appears to be doing something useful, in order to trick the user into running it, but actually performs some harmful action.

- **Keg logger:** A spyware program that logs every keystroke to collect passwords, user IDs, credit card information, and other sensitive data.

- **Ransomware**: A type of malware that displays some kind of threatening message onscreen, trying to bully you into making a payment to make the problem go away. It could say that your computer has a virus and you must pay for an antivirus program to remove it, or that you have been accused of a computer crime and you must pay a fine.

Protecting Against Natural Risks

Natural risks, as you learned in the previous section, are risks of computer or data loss that occur naturally — in other words, "that's life!" situations. They can include devices failing due to manufacturing defects or wearing out, overheating, accidents such as liquid spills and items being knocked off tables . . . just about anything that isn't done intentionally.

Creating a computer-friendly workspace

You can't prevent all computer malfunctions and breakdowns, of course, but you can minimize the potential for accidents and malfunctions. A computer-friendly workspace is one that is

✔ **Safe:** Put your computer where it can't be easily kicked or knocked off a table.

✔ **Cool:** Computers like cool environments — cooler than most humans prefer. The cooler the room, the less hard the computer's cooling devices have to work to keep the computer from overheating. If your computer has been shutting down unexpectedly, overheating may be the cause. Check all the fans inside the computer to make sure they are still spinning when the power is on, and clean out any clumps of dust inside the case that might block airflow.

✔ **Not cramped:** Don't shut a desktop computer up in a small cabinet, drawer, or cubbyhole with no airflow around it. Part of keeping cool is having a steady supply of room-temperature air circulating into and out of the case.

✔ **Dry:** Computers hate liquids of all kind, because liquid, especially water, causes short-circuiting. If you have to have a beverage near your computer (and I don't recommend it), position it so that if it were to spill, it would not get any liquid on any of the computer parts, or use a cup with a lid and a straw. If you have to clean a component, use a very small amount of alcohol, not water, and make sure it's completely dry before you turn the computer back on again.

✔ **Static-free:** Try to keep the environment as free from static electricity as you can. Tile and linoleum floors are better than carpet for this; and rubber-soled or leather shoes, or bare feet, are better than stocking feet. Natural-fiber clothing (like cotton) is better than artificial (polyester, rayon) because it generates less static electricity. High humidity (50 percent or so) is better than low humidity.

✔ **Surge-protected:** Plug all your devices into surge-protected power strips, not directly into a wall outlet, to protect against damage from power surges.

Making data backups

When a computer component fails, you may be able to replace it. If the computer is under warranty, all the better — depending on the warranty, you might even get someone to come to your house and fix it. What you probably won't be able to replace, though, is any data that was lost if it was a data-containing component that failed.

The best defense against lost data is a recent backup. You can back up in many different ways:

- ✔ You can copy all your important files to a removable disc periodically, such as a writeable DVD or an external hard drive. This backup is only as good as the media it's on, though; if the external hard drive is next to the computer and your house burns down, that backup didn't do you any good.

- ✔ You can back up to an online backup service, or to your own cloud storage area, such as OneDrive. (See Chapter 8 for more about cloud storage.)

- ✔ You can back up to another computer on your network. This is the way big business does it; the computer that holds the backups is located somewhere other than where the computers being backed up are, eliminating the "building burning down" risk of data loss.

When backing up, you can copy the files as-is, or you can use backup software that compressed and archives the backed up files so that they take up less space. The drawback there is that you can't browse the archives like regular storage; you have to use the same backup software to do a restore operation in the event that you need the files again.

Don't back up any files that are replaceable, such as the operating system and applications. You can reinstall those from their original sources any time you need to. Focus your backup efforts on your data files, personal photos, and anything else that you can't get back otherwise.

Protecting Against Human-Created Threats

You can't protect yourself 100 percent from all human-created computer threats, but you can make it a lot harder for a would-be criminal to strike your system. The following sections provide some suggestions.

Strong passwords

It's very important to use strong passwords, both for your user account in the operating system and for each of the websites that you register with. A *strong password* is one that is difficult for an unauthorized person to guess. It should contain a mix of uppercase and lowercase letters, numbers, and special characters such as @ or #, and be difficult or impossible for other people to guess. An example of a weak password might be "manchester." You could easily strengthen the password, however, by changing out some of the letters for other characters, like this: "M@nch35Ter." You should, of course, create a password that you can remember, and also change the password on a regular basis.

Although it may be tempting to use the same password on every website, it can also cause problems. If that website's security is compromised and your user account and password are stolen, the thief can try that username/password combination on other popular websites, and possibly gain access to your other accounts as well. If you have to write down your passwords to remember all of them, do so offline (on a piece of paper), and hide that piece of paper somewhere safe. Storing your passwords on the computer means that if someone breaks into your computer, they have access to every aspect of your computing life. Although someone might steal the piece of paper, they would have to break into your house to do it, and that's less likely than someone breaking into your computer over the Internet.

If you are worried about the security of writing down your passwords somewhere, try encoding them using a technique that you come up with on your own. For example, you could write every password backwards on your hint sheet, or write every number or letter as one higher than the actual one. For example, the password Beach123 would become Cfbdi234.

Operating system updates

Operating systems such as Windows and Mac OS X update themselves automatically if you allow them to do so. In most cases, it is a very good idea to allow it. Keeping OS files updated can protect against some exploits that target security flaws in the OS's code.

In businesses with IT departments, however, sometimes the IT department will decide not to allow each user to individually download and install OS updates. It may be more efficient for the IT department to download the update once and then roll it out to all user PCs at the same time. If your computer operates in such a situation, automatic updates may be disabled on your PC.

To check your automatic update settings, open the Control Panel in Windows and choose System and Security, and then click Windows Update. Figure 14-2 shows that the computer has been configured to automatically download and install automatic updates. Notice, however, that there are optional updates available too, and these are not automatically installed. If you see that indicator, you can click it (it's a hyperlink) to see a list of updates. From there, you can mark or clear the check boxes for each individual update and then click OK to install them, as in Figure 14-3.

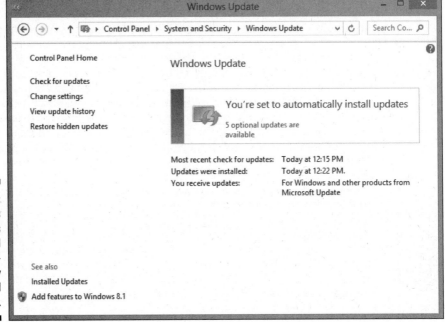

Figure 14-2:
Windows Update is configured to automatically download updates.

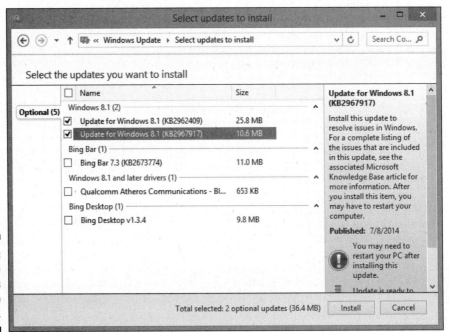

Figure 14-3:
Select the updates you want to install.

Virus and malware protection

Viruses and other malware try to infect computers in many different ways — through unauthorized downloads on websites users visit, through email attachments, and through executable files transferred between computers on discs. The first and best line of defense from all these different threat types is a utility (or a group of utilities) that provides protection. Such programs are typically called *antivirus programs*, but in reality they protect against many other types of threats besides viruses. They are more accurately called *anti-malware programs*.

Symantec and McAfee are two major brands of third-party malware utilities, and each company sells a variety of different products aimed at different audiences and their needs, from home users to large corporations. Most of their products are suites that include not only antivirus protection but also enhanced firewall features and junk email filtering. For large businesses, for example, Symantec offers an advanced protection suite called Endpoint Protection, shown in Figure 14-4, that covers virus and spyware protection, firewall service, and more.

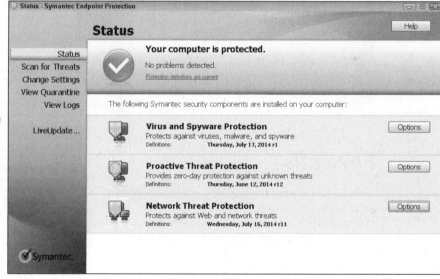

Figure 14-4: Symantec Endpoint Protection provides advanced protection for big businesses.

Although these third-party tools provide excellent protection, most people don't need them because Windows itself provides basic protection in most areas. For example, Windows Defender (shown in Figure 14-5), which comes free with Windows 7 and higher, includes a broad range of anti-malware features, including antivirus protection. You find it in Windows 8 on the Start screen's Apps list, in the Windows System category.

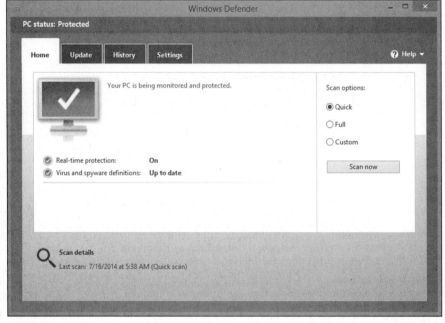

Figure 14-5: Windows Defender comes free with Windows 7 and later editions.

Firewalls

A *firewall* is a security barrier on your computer or network that controls what traffic is allowed into and out of your computer or network. The barrier is designed to separate your computer or network, which you trust, from an external network, which you might not.

To understand firewalls, you need to know that network communications take place on various channels called *ports*. For example, email is often received via port 110 and sent via port 25. That's how your computer knows to direct one packet of data to your browser and another to your email program. In addition to the common ports that your computer uses a lot, there are many unused ports. One way that hackers get into another computer remotely on a network is by taking advantage of these unused ports to slip in unnoticed.

A firewall monitors port usage and prevents ports from being used that are not assigned to a legitimate application. It looks at every packet of data that attempts to travel through the firewall in either direction and decides whether to allow it or block it. Most firewalls come with a set of default rules, but they can be adjusted, enabling you to configure yours to allow or deny whatever traffic you choose. If you play computer games, for example, you may need to configure the firewalls on your router and your computer to allow the gaming traffic through.

Windows includes a free firewall application called Windows Firewall. It is enabled by default, so you don't have to do anything with it unless you're having a problem with it. You can check out its settings in the Control Panel in Windows, as shown in Figure 14-6. From the Control Panel's main screen, choose System and Security, and then click Windows Firewall.

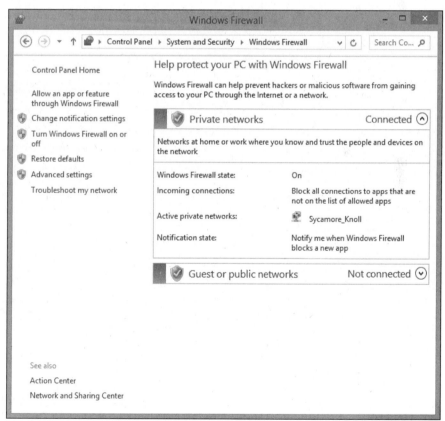

Figure 14-6:
Configure the Windows Firewall settings here.

Adjusting Settings to Increase Security

In addition to using utility programs to increase your computer's security, as you learned about in the previous section, you can also change some of the settings in ordinary programs that you use every day to help make your computer more secure. The following sections explain some of the security options in Internet Explorer and email programs.

Web browser security settings

Each web browser has its own ways of managing security settings. This chapter focuses on Internet Explorer 11, the browser in Windows 8.1.

The browser assigns a website certain permissions to do certain things, such as run ActiveX controls (a type of mini-application embedded in a website), run JavaScript scripts, open new windows, and so on. Internet Explorer categorizes sites into one of four categories:

- **Internet:** All sites that are not categorized otherwise fit into this category.
- **Local intranet:** Sites that are a part of your company's own network are here. These sites typically have the lowest security settings.
- **Trusted sites:** Sites that you have chosen to trust more than the norm.
- **Restricted sites:** Sites that you have chosen to trust less than the norm.

When you configure security settings, you first choose a zone, and then you choose settings to apply to that zone. You can choose a preset collection of settings (such as Medium or Medium-High), or you can customize the settings.

Follow these steps to adjust security settings for a zone:

1. **Open the desktop version of Internet Explorer and click the Tools icon (the cog) in the upper-right corner.**

2. **On the menu that appears, click Internet Options.**

   The Internet Options dialog box opens.

3. **Click the Security tab.**

   The icons across the top of the dialog box, as shown in Figure 14-7, represent different zones.

Figure 14-7:
Configure
security
settings on
the Security
tab.

4. **If it is not already selected, click the Internet icon to work with the Internet zone.**

5. **If you don't see the vertical slider bar shown in Figure 14-7, click the Default Level button.**

6. **Drag the slider up or down to adjust the setting. Medium-High, the default, is appropriate for most computers.**

   Medium may expose you to more threats, and High may impede some pages' ability to show content.

7. **(Optional.) Click the Custom Level button to open a dialog box of settings and adjust specific settings if desired. Click OK to return to the Internet Options dialog box when finished.**

8. **(Optional.) Choose a different zone and repeat Steps 5–7 if you want to change the setting for a different zone.**

9. **(Optional.) If you want to specify the sites that belong in a certain zone (other than Internet), select the zone's icon and then click the Sites button. In the dialog box that appears, enter a URL and click Add to add it to the list. If you mark the Require Server Verification check box, only secure (https://) addresses will be allowed; clear the check box to add a URL that is not secure. See Figure 14-8. Then click Close to return to the Internet Options dialog box.**

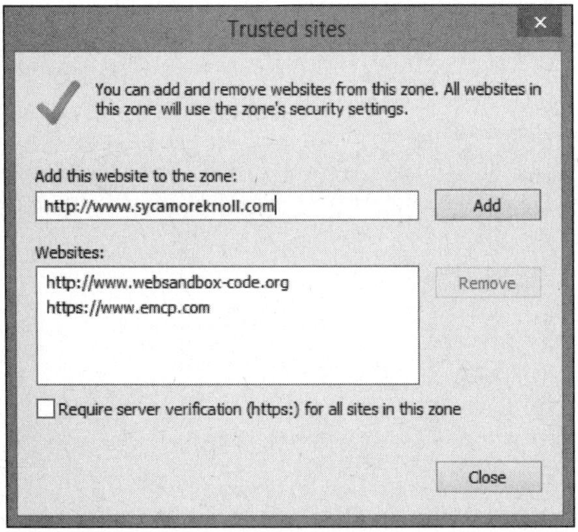

Figure 14-8:
Indicate the sites you trust here.

10. **Click OK to apply the setting changes for the zones you modified and close the dialog box.**

Email security settings

Email isn't a particularly secure technology for sending and receiving information. On most servers, messages are sent and received without any encryption, so it's possible for a computer expert with the right software to intercept copies of the data packets being exchanged and make some sense of the information it contains. Furthermore, because the mail is stored on a server while it is waiting for the user to pick it up, the email is only as secure as the server itself. If a hacker breaks into the server, every email waiting on that server for delivery can be read and its contents exploited. That's why people recommend that you don't send credit card information via email.

To solve one of those problems — the unencrypted nature of email delivery — some mail servers allow users to connect using an encrypted connection. An encrypted email connection is similar to a secure website; both use the same basic technology. Ask your email provider about how to set up your email account for encryption. The process may involve changing the port numbers for incoming and outgoing email in the advanced account settings in your email program.

Bottom line, if you have something to say that is so private that you would be seriously inconvenienced or embarrassed if the information was stolen, you shouldn't be sending it via email. Even if you set up the connection between your computer and your mail server to be encrypted, you have no control about the rest of the message's journey, such as from the recipient's mail server to the recipient's computer.

Following Best Practices for Safer Web Use

Web browser security features are a good start for keeping safe online, but nothing can replace good old common sense. Here are some tips for avoiding malware and sidestepping online criminals.

Watch out for phishing

A website that purports to be the official site of a trusted company but is actually an impostor is known as a *phishing* site. Phishing sites try to steal your login information for a legitimate site by presenting you with a fake username and password prompt, or by asking you to fill out a form containing personal information.

Your web browser may have a phishing filter as one of its security options; it's a good idea to leave that enabled. In Internet Explorer, the anti-phishing filter is known as the SmartScreen Filter. Phishing filters don't always catch every fraudulent site, however, so you still need to be wary.

When a website or email asks for sensitive information, such as your account number, Social Security number, or other information that you don't routinely give out, stop and think a minute and let your inner skeptic do his or her thing.

- **If the email or website says you need to update your information or your account will be disabled, it's almost always a phishing message. Real companies don't** shut down your accounts if you don't respond to an email.

- **Shouldn't this company already have my information?** If it's an organization that you already have a working relationship with, such as your bank or credit card company, it's a sure bet that they already know your account number, name, address, Social Security number, and so on. They wouldn't ask for it in an email.

- **If you get an email that says you have won a contest of any kind, it is probably a fake.** Real contests usually contact winners via telephone or postal mail.

- **If you get an email advertising any product or service and it's not a company you have done business with in the past and you haven't signed up for their mailing list, it's probably a rip-off.** Delete the email without clicking any of its links.

- **Why would this company be contacting me via email?** If there's an urgent issue with your account, a company would be telephoning you or sending you postal mail. Most companies use email only for marketing.

- **Does the email address me by my name?** Sending out a generic message without any user details is one clue that a message may be fraudulent.

- **Are there typos or layout issues in the email or on the website?** People trying to fake legitimate websites are often not native English speakers, and they tend to make grammar and spelling errors that give them away.

- **Does the address in the Address bar on the web page match the domain name expected for this company?** For example, a phishing site purporting to be Chase bank (their real URL is `www.chase.com`) might show a URL that begins with or includes "chase" somewhere in it but ends in a different domain, such as .biz.

- **In an email, when you point to a URL, does the ScreenTip that appears show a URL that matches what's in print?** The text for the URL might show the company's real website, but the link might point to somewhere totally different.

Enter financial information only on secure sites

A secure site is one that uses some type of encryption, such as Secure Sockets Layer (SSL), to encrypt the data as it travels between your computer and the web server. You can tell a site is secure because its URL begins with https:// rather than http:// and a padlock appears in the address bar.

Don't enter any sensitive information, such as financial accounts, credit card numbers, or information that could be used to steal your identity, at a non-secure site.

Pay attention to security certificates

How do you know if a secure website is what it purports to be? Many secure websites have purchased a *digital security certificate*, which is a code on the web page that automatically contacts an online agency called a *certificate authority* to independently verify the site's integrity. If the certificate is valid, your browser will show some indication, such as the address bar background turning green as in Figure 14-9. On the other hand, if the site fails the certificate check, a warning message may appear, and the address bar may have a yellow or red background.

Figure 14-9:
Trust me, the address bar background is green, indicating a secure site.

Shop at stores you know

It's better to shop at well-known online stores than small, fly-by-night ones. A well-known store is more likely to have the proper security measures in place to protect the data you provide when you place your order. If there's a bricks-and-mortar retail store you like, see if they have a website you can buy from.

If you need to do business with a company you have never heard of, check online reviews for that company at sites such as Epinions (`www.epinions.com`), BizRate (`www.bizrate.com`), and the Better Business Bureau (`www.bbb.org`).

Be careful with online payments

First and foremost, use credit cards when shopping online, not debit cards or ATM cards. The US Federal Trade Commission limits your liability for credit card purchases to $20 if your financial information is stolen. In most cases, there is no limit to your liability with debit or ATM cards, however. Having your debit card information stolen online can result in an empty bank account with little or no recourse.

When possible, use payment services such as PayPal that enable you to send payments directly to merchants and individuals without disclosing your actual credit card information to them. The fewer sites you enter your credit card number into, the lower your risk of having the number stolen. This tip is especially important when buying merchandise at person-to-person online sites like eBay or craigslist; don't give your credit card information to any seller you connect with at one of these sites.

Be stingy with the information you provide

Be skeptical when it comes to sites that ask for lots of information about you when you are making a purchase or signing up for a mailing list. A company doesn't need your Social Security number or a copy of your driver's license in order to sell you printer ink, for example. Any company that says they need to positively verify your identity like that is probably going to use that information for criminal purposes.

Stay away from "vice sites"

I'm not saying that you visit adult-oriented sites, and I'm not saying that you don't. What I *am* saying, though, is that these sites are likely to try to do bad things to your computer, such as download malware, change your browser settings, install unwanted software, or pop up endless ads for other adult sites. The same goes for other "vice" sites, including gateway sites for illegal gambling, illegal movie, music, and software downloads, and sources of various products and services that try to circumvent government or health regulations (such as sites that sell prescription drugs without a doctor's prescription).

If you absolutely *must* visit a site of questionable character, use your web browser's private browsing feature, so that the page is not allowed to modify your computer in any way. From Internet Explorer, click the Tools button, point to Safety, and click InPrivate Browsing. This opens up a new IE window in InPrivate mode. That window remains in InPrivate mode until you close it. InPrivate mode does not allow any websites to save any trace of themselves on your computer in any way, including in your browser's History list. You can tell you're in InPrivate mode because of the blue indicator on the Address bar, as shown in Figure 14-10.

Figure 14-10:
InPrivate browsing mode is turned on.

Chapter 15

Safeguarding Your Privacy

. . . .

In This Chapter

▶ Understanding online privacy threats

▶ Increasing your privacy on the Internet

▶ Learning how to protect children from online predators

▶ Finding out how to identify and avoid copyright violations

. . . .

Most people would be pretty shocked to realize how much information about them is available online. Anyone who is determined to collect information about a particular individual — such as a potential identity thief — can often find that information quickly and easily just by consulting publicly available information sources.

After information about you is online, it's hard to get rid of it; information online tends to persist indefinitely because the whole system is so decentralized; you can get it removed from one site, but 20 other sites have already copied that information. It's far better to be cautious from the get-go about putting your information out there.

In this chapter, I explain some of the major privacy threats online today and I teach you how to make it as difficult as possible for both advertisers and criminals to target you.

Understanding Why Personal Information Is Big Business

To get a feel for the scope of the online onslaught against you having any privacy, consider the financial model that drives the Internet. How do people make money online?

✔ They sell products and services.

✔ They sell advertising for products and services.

> ✔ They collect personal information about people and sell it to other people for the purposes of doing one or more of the previously mentioned things.

> ✔ They commit crimes using personal information that they either personally gather or buy from a company that collects it.

Yes, there's a multi-billion-dollar industry built around gathering as much personal information about as many people as possible and then selling it to whoever can pay for it. And those who sell that information aren't very picky about to whom they sell it, either; personal information of all types can end up in the hands of not only aggressive salespeople but also criminals.

Targeted Advertising

Information gatherers are getting smarter and more technologically sophisticated every day, and are now able to put together disparate facts from multiple sites to create more complete portraits of each consumer.

For example, the other day, I was shopping online for a certain kind of boots. A few hours later, when I was on Facebook playing a game, an ad popped up on the screen for the exact brand of boots I had been looking at earlier on a completely different website. It's unnerving how well advertisers can target people.

How advertisers target consumers

The data used to target you with ads is gathered in the following ways:

> ✔ **Clickstream data:** That means a record of web pages you've visited. This data comes from little text files called *cookies* that are saved on your hard disk when you visit certain sites. There are two types of cookies. *First-party cookies* are placed on your computer by the actual website you are visiting, and are usually a good thing. *Third-party cookies* are placed by advertisers on the website, and these are usually used to track your habits. In "Browser settings for increasing privacy" later in this chapter, you learn how to change cookie settings in Internet Explorer.

> ✔ **Purchase data:** Online stores (like Amazon.com, for example) keep track of what you buy, and when you return to that same online store (or a partner store), the items you see "on sale" are often in the same category as your previous purchases. If you log in to the site, your records are accessed that way, but even if you don't log in, cookies can still provide a history of what items you've browsed or bought. In Figure 15-1, for example, you can see that Amazon remembers that I love chocolate and that I recently bought toner for a Brother brand printer.

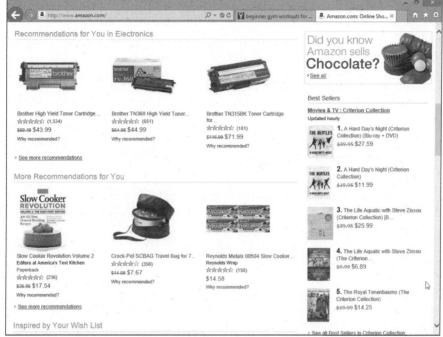

Figure 15-1:
Amazon
uses your
past pur-
chases
to market
to you.

✔ **Search data:** Every time you use a search engine like Google, Yahoo!, and
Bing, targeted ads appear along the margins based on your searches.
If you log into the website on which you are searching, even more data
may be saved about your searches.

✔ **Profile data:** If you create a profile on a site like Facebook or Myspace,
all that basic information about you gets "shared" with the companies
that advertise on that site. That's why, for example, I see ads for products of interest to people with my demographic (middle-aged, female,
college-educated, Midwestern) when I browse Facebook.

Minimizing the information advertisers gather

Your browser settings are your first line of defense in protecting yourself
from advertisers who want your information. Each browser's settings are different, but they're equivalent — that is, each browser has basically the same
privacy features, but they may be called by different names and set differently. Check your browser's Help system for details.

In Internet Explorer, the following features are available.

Tracking protection

This feature prevents sites from tracking your behavior across multiple sites. Click Tools (the cog in the upper right corner), point to Safety, and click Turn on Tracking Protection. See Figure 15-2. If instead you see a Turn off Tracking Protection command, the feature is already on; do nothing.

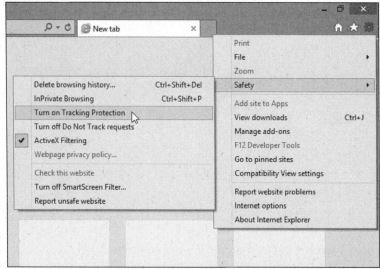

Figure 15-2:
Turning on
tracking
protection.

Tracking protection can be enhanced by installing a *tracking protection list (TPL)*. A TPL contains a list of known sites that try to track user habits; Internet Explorer blocks all the sites on the installed list from doing so. If a site is not on the list, but tracking protection is turned on, IE will send a Do Not Track message to any sites not on the list.

To install a TPL, follow these steps:

1. **Open Internet Explorer from the desktop and go to** www.iegallery. com/PinnedSites.

2. **Click Tracking Protection Lists.**

3. **Select one of the tracking protection lists and click Add.**

4. **A confirmation dialog box appears, as in Figure 15-3. Click Add List.**

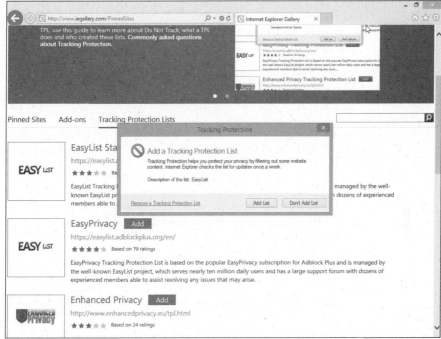

Figure 15-3:
Adding a tracking protection list.

Limiting third-party cookies

As you may have read earlier in this chapter, first-party cookies are the benign ones placed on your hard disk by the actual sites you are visiting. They store useful information that you might want that site to store on your behalf, like your user name and your country preference (so, for example, you don't have to tell the site each time you visit that you are in the United States so it can show prices in U.S., currency).

Third-party cookies, on the other hand, are the ones that invade your privacy. A third-party cookie is generated by an ad on a website, and the ad may be owned (and the cookie used) by some advertiser that has nothing to do with the site you are visiting.

Some websites have a *compact privacy policy*, which is a document that explains how they handle the data they collect. Having such a policy is no guarantee of your privacy — after all, the terms of the policy are probably extremely slanted in favor of advertisers — but the presence of such a policy shows a good faith effort on the part of the website.

In Internet Explorer, you can set an overall cookie handling policy by choosing a preset collection of settings that govern how and when first-party and third-party cookies will be accepted and how the presence of a compact privacy policy changes the rules. You can also completely allow or prohibit certain kinds of cookies, or ask IE to prompt you for a yes/no answer each time a page tries to write a cookie. (Warning: It can get exhausting responding to all those prompts.)

Cookies can be temporary (called *session cookies*) or permanent (called *persistent cookies*). In most cases, session cookies are useful and harmless. A session cookie is automatically deleted when you close the browser window, so it can't be used to store data about you over time. A session cookie might remind the browser that you have items in your shopping cart, for example. Most cookie-handling policies exclude session cookies from restrictions placed on other cookies.

Follow these steps to adjust the cookie handling policies in Internet Explorer:

1. **In Internet Explorer, click Tools (the cog in the upper-right corner) and click Internet Options.**

   The Internet Options dialog box opens.

2. **Click the Privacy tab.**

3. **Drag the slider up or down to change the overall cookie-handling policy. See Figure 15-4.**

4. **Click the Advanced button. The Advanced Privacy Settings dialog box opens. Here's where you can optionally apply a global policy for all first-party or third-party cookies by doing the following:**

   a. Select the Override automatic cookie handling check box.

   b. Under First-party Cookies, choose Accept, Block, or Prompt. See Figure 15-5.

   c. Under Third-party Cookies, choose Accept, Block, or Prompt.

   d. If desired, select the Always allow session cookies check box.

   e. Click OK.

5. **Click the Sites button. The Per Site Privacy Actions dialog box opens. Here's where you can optionally specify a different policy from the default for a certain site. To do that,**

   a. Enter a site in the Address of website text box.

   b. Click the Block button or the Allow button.

   c. Click OK.

6. **Click OK to close the Internet Options dialog box and apply the new cookie-handling rules.**

After changing the cookie-handling rules, you might want to visit some sites that have a lot of ads and see how things go. To see what Internet Explorer is blocking, choose Tools⇨Safety⇨Webpage privacy policy. The Privacy Report dialog box opens, listing what sites tried to create cookies on your computer and whether they were blocked from doing so by your current policy. Figure 15-6 shows an example.

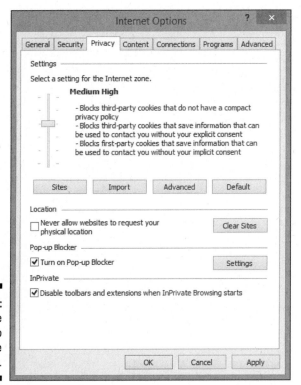

Figure 15-4: Adjust the slider to set cookie policy.

Figure 15-5: The Advanced Privacy Settings dialog box.

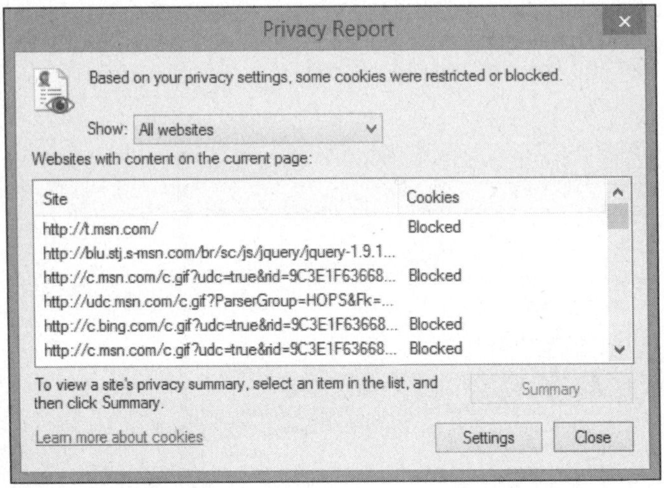

Figure 15-6:
The Privacy
Report
dialog box.

Identity Theft

As creepy as most targeted ads are, they don't mean you any real harm. They just want to "get to know you better" so that they can "serve you better." On the other hand, there are also people on the Internet who want to get to know you better for criminal purposes: so that they can open new credit cards in your name and stick you with the bill, for example

Identity theft is a growing problem online because of the increasing amount of information available about individuals there. You might give up a little bit of information about yourself at one site, and a few other facts at another site, but what you might not realize is that these sites are all in partnership with one another, and that data gets combined into a central base of knowledge about you, ripe for a thief's picking.

Identity thefts are categorized according to what the thief does with your data:

- **Financial identity theft:** Obtains credit, buys things with your credit cards, empties your bank accounts

- **Identity cloning:** Uses your information to assume your identity in daily life, such as using your Social Security number for employment

- **Medical identity theft:** Uses your identity, and your health insurance, to obtain medical care or prescription drugs

- **Criminal identity theft:** Uses your identity when apprehended for a crime, so that the conviction appears on your record

Having your identity stolen can be a terrifying experience, as well as financially draining. It can take years of persistent work to follow all the administrative steps needed to regain your good name and credit score.

The people who steal identities for a living don't have anything against you personally — they're just looking for the easiest targets, the way a hungry lion looks for the slowest antelope in the herd. Don't let that be you! Here are some tips for avoiding identity theft:

- **Never enter your full Social Security number online** except when securely logged into a site that has a legitimate need for it, such as when paying your taxes or filing for government assistance.

- **Don't use the same username and password at multiple sites.** When hackers break into the server at any of those sites and steal customer data, the first thing they do is to try all those account names and passwords at other sites, knowing that most consumers are careless and use the same data everywhere.

- **Monitor your credit report regularly** so you will notice if new credit is opened in your name. Each of the three major credit reporting bureaus provides one free report per year to each consumer. Stagger your requests throughout the year so you are getting a fresh credit report every four months.

- **Use strong passwords** on every online account you have. As you learned in Chapter 14, a strong password is one that's difficult to guess.

- **Limit the amount of information you provide about yourself online.** Every bit of information you provide online is more ammunition for an identity thief. For example, you might want to rethink including your home address and phone number on social networking sites (and that includes professional ones like LinkedIn too).

- **Don't participate in online offers** of free stuff or sweepstakes entries in exchange for providing information about yourself. There may be a 1 in 100,000 chance you'll win something, but there's a 1 in 1 chance that any information you provide here will be sold to online advertisers, and after you get in their databases, that information can be sold to anyone who has the money to buy it — including sophisticated identity theft networks.

- **Use only one credit card when you buy things online.** That way, you only have one card you have to closely monitor to make sure the number is not being used fraudulently. Don't use debit or ATM cards online because there is limited consumer protection available if the number is stolen and used fraudulently.

Social engineering

Social engineering is the practice of psychologically manipulating people into sharing confidential information inappropriately. One of the ways that identity thieves get enough information from their victims to commit their crimes is by lying to them in various ways, telling some story that is designed to make them want to give up information that should be kept private.

Such criminals prey most often on easy targets — naïve people who are new to the Internet and not well-schooled on its threats. This group often includes elderly people who have recently started using the Internet, as well as children who haven't been coached by their parents and teachers that telling strangers details can be dangerous.

Contact can come in many forms. A potential victim might get a phishing email, as described in Chapter 14, for example, asking him to log into a website to confirm account details or to claim a prize.

If the potential victim has provided a phone number and other personal details online, the criminal might even be so bold as to place a phone call, and to use an emotion-producing lie to put the person in an emotionally vulnerable state so that she is not thinking clearly. For example, a friend of mine got a phone call awhile back from someone who said she was a nurse at a hospital. She said that my friend's son had been in an accident, and she needed the son's insurance information so he could be treated. My friend immediately saw through the ruse because her son happened to be right there beside her. She later figured out that the criminal had found out her phone number and the fact that she had a son from Facebook.

Another common phone scam consists of someone calling to tell you that your credit card has been fraudulently used. The person asks you to confirm your credit card number, expiration date, and name on the card. But if you think about that one a minute, you would realize that if it were really your credit card company, they would already have that information.

To reduce the risk of being tricked in this way, here are some suggestions:

- ✔ Establish specific rules in your household about how and when information can be shared online, on the phone, and in person. Make sure everyone knows the rules, both children and adults.

- ✔ Be skeptical of anyone who calls or emails you with a story about a problem or crisis that can only be solved by you providing information or paying for something.

- ✔ Never respond to requests for personal information that come via email, and don't click links in such requests.

✔ If you receive a phone call from someone who says they are with your bank or credit card company, ask them to prove that they are who they say they are by telling you information about your account that only the real organization would know.

✔ Be more skeptical of phone callers who called you; if there's any doubt as to their identity, hang up and call the number you have on file for the company.

Oversharing on social media

Sometimes would-be criminals don't have to trick a person into providing information — that person just willingly puts the information out there in public for all to see on social media sites like Facebook.

Don't be that oversharing person who becomes a target for identity thieves by volunteering data that can be used against you. Here are some ways identity thieves use social media, and some ways to avoid becoming a target:

✔ Edit your privacy settings on the social media site so that only your friends can see information about you, including not only your profile information but also the posts you make. For example, Figure 15-7 shows the privacy settings in Facebook.

✔ Explore the security and privacy settings available for your social media account, and adjust those settings to very conservative levels where possible, so that people who are not your friends receive as little information about you as possible.

✔ Don't accept friend requests from people you don't know personally.

✔ If you play online games on your social media account that require you to have a lot of friends playing them also and you are tempted to accept friend requests from strangers, create a separate account on the social media site just for playing games and do not put any personally identifying information on its profile.

✔ Do not post your mailing address or telephone number on social media.

✔ Do not list your family relationships and link to your family members' accounts, especially children's accounts.

✔ Create a new email address to use on your social media account; do not associate it with the email address you use daily.

✔ Don't post messages to social media about when you are going on vacation or how long you will be gone. Combined with your street address, this is an open invitation for burglars to rob you.

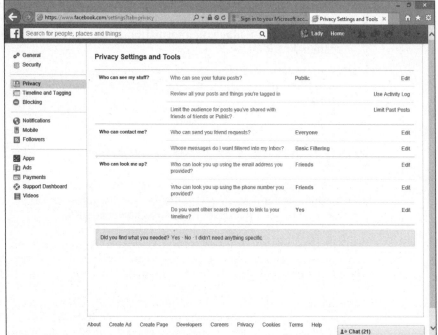

Figure 15-7:
Privacy
settings on
Facebook.

✔ If a friend who you thought was already on your Friends list suddenly has a new account and is sending you a friend request again, be skeptical. A favorite trick of identity thieves is to steal a picture from someone's profile and create a new account with it, and then to send friend requests to all of that person's friends. Alert your friend that this has happened so she can address it.

Increasing Your Privacy on the Web

Now that you know the basics of what you're up against privacy-wise, take a look at some settings in your web browser, instant messaging, and email applications that can make it more difficult for others to invade your information sanctum.

Browser settings for increasing privacy

You already saw earlier in the chapter how to adjust cookie settings and how to use a tracking protection list in Internet Explorer to make it harder for advertisers to track you. So what else can you do?

As I showed you in Chapter 14, one way to safeguard your privacy while browsing is to use InPrivate Browsing in Internet Explorer. (I talked about it there in the context of keeping malware at bay, but it's actually primarily a privacy tool.)

To start an InPrivate session, click the Tools button in Internet Explorer, point to Safety, and click InPrivate Browsing. In InPrivate mode, Internet Explorer does not save any record of the site visit, and does not allow any website to save anything on your computer in any way.

Because InPrivate browsing doesn't save cookies, you can't use it for sites where you have to log in.

By default, InPrivate browsing windows do not show toolbars and disable all browser extensions. You might run into a problem occasionally, in that a particular site won't work well without some of those browser extensions that are being disabled. Sure, you could just visit that site in regular mode, rather than InPrivate mode, but there's a workaround that may allow you to have the best of both worlds. Choose Tools, Internet Options to open the Internet Options dialog box, and on the Privacy tab, clear the Disable Toolbars and Extensions when InPrivate Browsing Starts check box. See Figure 15-8. Then click OK, and then start a new InPrivate browsing session to apply the new settings.

You can also prevent websites from discovering your physical location if you want. Some websites determine (approximately) where you are located by querying the ISP that you are going through for Internet service. They use this information to display helpful local information such as weather reports, but they may also use it to display local ads too. To turn this feature off, on the Privacy tab in the Internet Options dialog box (Figure 15-7), mark the Never Allow Websites to Request Your Physical Location check box. Then click the Clear Sites button next to the check box to erase the memories (that is, the cookies) of any existing location information that's been saved for certain sites.

Instant messaging privacy settings

Instant messaging programs such as Yahoo! Instant Messenger and AOL Instant Messenger (AIM) provide convenient ways of communicating with others, but they can also give others more information about your whereabouts and status than you might prefer. For example, people who you have added to your Friends list in these programs will be able to see when you are logged in, and depending on the program and its features, they may be able to see when your computer has been idle for a certain number of minutes too. They may be able to see what music you have listened to on a related music service, and on certain websites that are related to the application, users may be able to see whether you are online without even opening the IM program itself, and to send you messages from there.

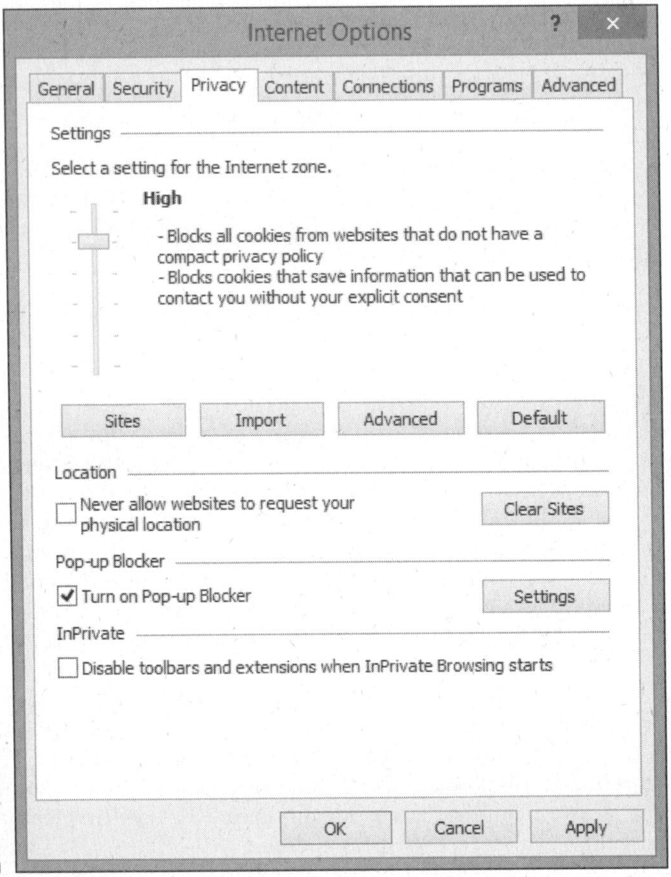

Figure 15-8:
The Privacy
tab.

Fortunately, IM applications that violate your privacy in these ways let you can opt out of having that information shown. For example, in Yahoo! Instant Messenger, you can use the Privacy tab in the Preferences dialog box to choose whether to sign in as invisible or not. That way, you have control over whether you become visible to others. You can also decline to allow the program to show you as idle or for how long, and decline to let others see what music or games you are enjoying. See Figure 15-9.

Email privacy settings

When it comes to email privacy, your main concerns are

- ✔ The email message might get intercepted on the Internet on the way to or from one of the mail servers.

✔ If you use a web-based email service, someone might steal your user-name and password, log in as you, and snoop your messages. The best defense against this is a strong password that you change often.

✔ Someone else who uses your computer might snoop your sent or received messages when you aren't looking.

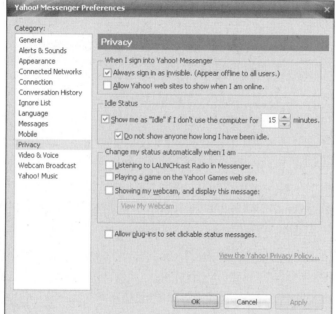

Figure 15-9:
Set your
Yahoo!
Messenger
preferences
here.

The first two of those were covered in Chapter 14 when talking about email security, but let's look at that last one now. There are two ways to prevent local snooping. One is to password-protect the email application or data file itself, and the other is to delete anything you don't want seen from your Inbox and from the Sent Items folder before you leave the computer.

In Outlook 2013, you can password-protect the data file in which you store messages by doing the following:

1. **Choose File⇨Account Settings⇨Account Settings.**

2. **Click the Data Files tab.**

3. **Select the data file, and then click Settings.**

4. **Click Change Password.**

   The Change Password dialog box opens.

5. **In the Old Password box, if you previously had a password on the file, enter it here; otherwise, leave this box blank.**

6. **Type the new password in the New Password box, and then in the Verify box.**

7. **Click OK.**

8. **Click OK.**

9. **Click Close.**

Then close and reopen Outlook. When you do, the data file that you password-protected appears collapsed in the navigation pane. When you click it to expand it, you are prompted for the password, as shown in Figure 15-10.

To remove the password, repeat the process, but in Step 6, leave the New Password and Verify Boxes empty.

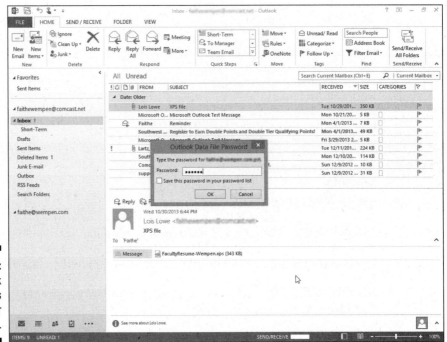

Figure 15-10:
Outlook prompts you for your password.

Protecting Children from Online Threats

Kids may understand computers better than you, but many of the risks online have nothing to do with technology and everything to do with human nature. It's important to monitor their computer usage, to make sure they understand how important it is to keep their personal information private, and to cultivate a sense of skepticism about the real identities of the people they meet online.

How online predators operate

Anyone can fall victim to an online predator, regardless of age. For every lonely person who wants to connect with another human being online, there are thousands of other lonely people who want the same thing, but there are also dozens of unscrupulous people who want to target these people to abuse them mentally, physically, and/or financially.

Children, however, are especially vulnerable to online predators because they lack the experience and skill to differentiate between people who "seem nice" and who actually are nice. Children tend to be less skeptical and take everyone at face value, and that can make them easy targets for predators who want to find out as much information about them as possible. An online predator's ultimate goal is typically to convince the child to interact with them online in sexual ways or meet with them in person. (If this happens, the child may be molested or abducted.)

According to the Microsoft Safety & Security Center article about online predators (`www.microsoft.com/security/family-safety/predators.aspx`), online predators do the following:

- ✔ Find kids through social networking, blogs, chat rooms, instant messaging, email, discussion boards, and other websites.

- ✔ Seduce their targets through attention, affection, kindness, and even gifts.

- ✔ Know the latest music and hobbies likely to interest kids.

- ✔ Listen to and sympathize with kids' problems.

- ✔ Try to ease young people's inhibitions by gradually introducing sexual content into their conversations or by showing them sexually explicit material.

- ✔ Evaluate the kids they meet online for future face-to-face contact.

If your child does become a target, such as being solicited sexually or being sent explicit photos, contact your local police. Save any documentation, along with email addresses, website addresses, and chat logs.

How children leak information

Children can inadvertently leak information to online predators because they don't understand how their information can potentially be used against them. For example, a child doesn't have the reasoning to think through why it's a bad idea to post to a social media site that their family is going out of town for two weeks, or to tell a new online friend their full name and what school they attend. It doesn't occur to a child that a new online friend may be lying to them, and may not even be a child at all. Some of the ways that children leak information are

- They use their full real names as user IDs.

- They will give away personal details about themselves and their families in exchange for the promise of some small prize or reward.

- They give out personal information to anyone who asks for it. If they think the person is another child, they might not see any threat in doing so. If they think the other person is an adult, they might think they are being bad to disobey an adult.

- They are susceptible to emotional manipulation and can be talked into giving out private information even if they have been coached not to by someone who convinces them that this is a special situation where it's okay to do so.

- They don't think through the consequences of posting an aggregation of information on social media that, when put together, can create a complete picture of their habits, their locations, and their friends.

Best practices for keeping children safe

Fortunately, kids have a basic sense of self-preservation most of the time. They don't want to be insulted, ripped off, or abused by a scammer, thief, or criminal. And when they realize their actions may place not only themselves, but their family members or friends, at risk, they become fairly interested in safety measures.

Discuss online safety positively with the children in your care — especially those who want to go online from your computer(s). Listen to what they want to do, and talk about what it takes to respect each other's safety needs. Figure out what works for your personal and family values. Treat each child and teen uniquely because there is no one-size-fits-all solution. Decide which activities they are ready for, and create a plan to help them get ready to take on new activities with the corresponding responsibilities that go with them.

Talk to them about sexual predators using age-appropriate language. Encourage the children in your care to be selective about who they interact with online and which sites they visit. Emphasize to them that there are many imposters online, including adult predators posing as children. Cultivate in them a healthy sense of skepticism. Set clear rules about sharing personal information online in web forums, chat rooms, instant message conversations, and email. Tell them never to respond to instant messages or emails from strangers.

Help children choose safe email addresses, IM names, chat nicknames, and other identifiers that do not give away too much personal information. Educate children about the dangers of opening attachments and following links in email messages.

Follow age limits on social networking sites. Most sites require that users be age 13 and over. Do not let children use sites that they don't qualify for.

Do not allow young children to use chat rooms at all. As they get older, direct them towards well-monitored kids' chat rooms such as `www.kidzworld.com` or `www.kidscom.com`. If a child does use chat rooms, make sure you know which ones they visit and who they talk with. Monitor the chat areas yourself to see what kind of conversations take place. Instruct kids never to "go private" in chat with anyone.

Don't give your child much privacy online. Make sure the computer is in a high-traffic area in your home, with the screen positioned so that everyone passing by can see it. Then pass by it frequently. You can also install family safety filtering or monitoring software (covered in the next section). If you do use such tools, be upfront about it and explain why it's there.

Using family safety applications

A family safety application (also called a parental controls application) is one that sets limits on the activities of one or more user accounts on that computer.

Windows includes a feature that allows an Administrator user to set limits on other user accounts' activities. This feature is called Family Safety in Windows 8, and Parental Controls in Windows 7. However, the activities it monitors are computer-based, not online-based. It lets you do the following:

- ✔ Set time limits so that certain user accounts can use the computer only during certain days of the week and certain times, or for a certain length of time. This can prevent a child from using the computer when no adults are available to supervise.

✔ Set game limits based on the Entertainment Software Ratings Board (ESRB) game ratings, so that a child can play only games that are rated for his age.

✔ Set application limits, so that the child can run only certain applications.

✔ Set web filtering, so that adult sites are blocked. You can also set the account to allow only websites designed for children, or to block social media sites.

You can set up Parental Controls from the Control Panel in Windows. In Windows 8, the Control Panel page redirects you to a website where you can configure the settings; in Windows 7, they're local to the PC.

If you find these tools to be inadequate, or want more control, consider a third-party service such as NetNanny (www.netnanny.com). Such programs implement aggressive family safety controls on the computer to block pornography, predators, cyberbullying, violent content, and content with adult language.

Avoiding Copyright Violations

Intellectual property refers to the ownership of original thoughts, ideas, and creations of individuals and companies. It can include books and articles, creative works like music and videos, and patterns and blueprints for creating items. They fall into three basic categories:

✔ **Copyrights** are for creative works. A copyright is automatic; you do not need to register with any government organization. If a person can prove that she was the first to develop that work, she has its copyright.

✔ **Patents** are issued for designs for products. Patents are granted by the United States Patent Office.

✔ **Trademarks** are issued for artwork and slogans that identify companies and products. A trademark can optionally be a registered trademark, making it more legally defensible.

Theft or misappropriation of intellectual property is generally considered a civil matter, rather than a criminal one. In other words, if someone has reprinted your copyrighted book without getting your permission, you can sue that person in civil court to recover monetary compensation, but you cannot bring criminal charges against them unless there are criminal aspects to the theft.

Plagiarism

Plagiarism is the practice of copying someone else's work and pretending that it is your own. Thanks to the Internet, it is all too easy to download a document from an obscure website and submit or republish it as yours.

Plagiarism comes in several forms:

✔ Copying work produced by someone else word for word and presenting it as your own

✔ Inserting portions of someone else's work into your own and claiming full credit

✔ Changing a few words and phrases of a piece of work so it looks different but is based on someone else's work

✔ Taking material from multiple sources and putting it all together as your own work

Plagiarism has become a big problem in colleges and universities. Often, when students receive assignments, they simply research on the Internet, copy large blocks of text from various sources, stitch them together into a single document, and pass the result off as their own work. Even worse, some students patronize any one of several Internet-based companies that write assignments for them.

It is not always wrong to use someone else's words or ideas. In many cases, you can quote or paraphrase someone else's work in your own piece — provided you include a reference to the source (in other words, to the author and name of the work). This is called a *citation*. Including a citation to give credit to the original author of a piece of work is the only way to avoid plagiarism.

Recent years have seen the development of a range of anti-plagiarism software products, such as Turnitin (`www.turnitin.com`). These programs compare a submitted document against a large database of quotes and texts. Mathematical processes check not only for actual word-for-word plagiarism, but also for paraphrased text where it can identify the original source. The results then highlight any suspect or copied areas in text and state where citations should be applied.

Using software like this, it takes only a few seconds to examine a document. Some educational institutions use this type of software as standard practice for all work handed in by students. Students can also use this type of software before turning in an assignment to ensure they have not inadvertently plagiarized.

Copyright violations

Besides plagiarism, there are many other types of copyright violations rampant on the Internet. Just a few examples are

✔ Posting of copyrighted music and videos on sharing sites such as YouTube

✔ Copying and forwarding images of copyrighted characters (for example, well-known cartoon characters) as jokes, inspirational quotes, and so on

✔ Making copyrighted music and video files available for public anonymous downloading without making payment to the copyright holder

✔ Publishing the text of copyrighted books on public websites

✔ Sharing music files with friends and family

Copyright holders have a very hard time combatting online violations because small violations are everywhere, the people violating the copyrights are usually individuals who are not worth suing because they don't have many assets, so even if you win a big judgment, they can't pay it, and the people violating the copyrights are usually not making any money on the violation that could be recovered. Therefore, copyright violation cases are mostly pursued by one big business against another big business, both of which have the funds and lawyers to make the whole prospect doable. (Remember, copyright violations are civil cases, not criminal.) If the copyright holder wins the lawsuit, the violator owes them a portion of the profit they made from the violation, plus any punitive damages awarded.

Even though it's mostly big businesses, some companies that have lost a lot from copyright violations, such as music companies, have occasionally gone after individual consumers who have been particularly flagrant in their violations, such as individuals who have actively and frequently participated in illegal file sharing sites. This action has been intended to make average consumers fearful of violating copyrights.

Keeping on the right side of the law

So what can you do, as an individual, to stay on the right side of the intellectual property law, and avoid the possibility of being dragged into court, receiving a failing grade in a class, or getting threatening letters from lawyers? Here are some tips:

✔ Don't make illegal copies of music and movie discs to give to friends and family.

✔ Download digital content (movies, music, and software) only from sites that pay the appropriate licensing fees for the content.

✔ Don't download from sites that promise copyrighted material for free. And especially don't allow these sites to use your computer to distribute material to other computers.

✔ Cite sources meticulously in your writing. Whenever you quote anybody or any work of writing, whether it's a web page or a company slogan, make sure you say where it came from.

✔ Don't publish anything including anyone else's copyrighted text or graphics without their written permission to include it.

✔ Don't "borrow" logos or images from websites to include on your own online sites (blog, social media, personal website, and so on).

Part V
Mobility and Multimedia

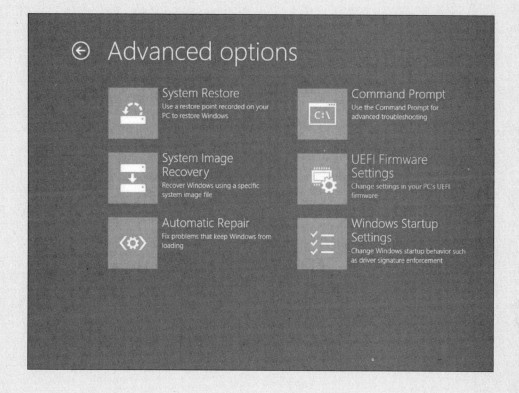

In this part . . .

- Learn how tablets and smartphones can extend and enhance your computing experience.

- Find out how to take pictures with a digital camera, organize your pictures, and share them with others.

- Discover how to play digital music and video clips on a computer and how to use speech-technology features to control your computer with your voice.

Chapter 16

Expanding Computing to Other Devices

. . . .

In This Chapter

▶ Selecting and using a tablet computer

▶ Choosing and using a smart phone

▶ Managing content between computers and TVs

. . . .

*O*ur digital world is not just computers anymore. (Well, not in the traditional sense of the word "computer" meaning a desktop or notebook.)

It might be more accurate to say that computers are not just what they used to be. A decade ago, most people's computer was a big boxy affair in the corner of the family room, with everyone clamoring for their turn on it. Nowadays, it's much more likely that each person in the family has his or her own notebook, tablet, or smart phone.

In this chapter, I look at several of these non-traditional computing devices in terms of features and functionality. You also discover how TVs and computers intersect and how you can make them work together.

Getting a Handle on Tablet Computer Basics

A *tablet computer* is like an electronic slate that you can write on with your finger or a *stylus* (which is basically a small stick that feels like a pen in your hand but doesn't have any ink in it). You touch, tap, and drag across the touch-sensitive screen of the tablet to interact with the operating system and applications. See Figure 16-1.

Figure 16-1:
A tablet
computer.

A tablet's main benefit is its extreme portability. A typical tablet weighs about one pound. You can take it with you almost anywhere: school, work, airplanes, restaurants, and so on.

Tablets are great for on-the-go email and web connectivity. Tablets have built-in Wi-Fi adapters, so anywhere there is an available Wi-Fi signal, you can be online. Some tablet models take that even a step further, including 3G/4G adapters for specific wireless phone companies, so you can use the Internet via your phone data plan wherever you are, even if there is no Wi-Fi.

A tablet can run simple applications designed for it, and there are hundreds of thousands of applications available for each of the major tablet operating systems. Tablet applications are usually narrowly focused on a particular activity that you might want to do when you are away from home, such as checking the weather report, getting driving directions, reading a magazine, or looking up movie times and reviews. A tablet comes with a few basic apps, and you can download more from the store for your operating system. For example, for iPads, you use the Apple Store app, and for Windows tablets, you use the Windows Store app. Some apps are free; others require a small payment (usually $5 or less).

Historically, there haven't been a lot of full-blown productivity apps for tablets. That's because it's generally assumed that your tablet is not your only computer, and that you have a larger computer for doing business-y stuff like spreadsheets, databases, and mail merges. Most tablets also lack the hardware needed to perform heavy-duty work: no real keyboard or mouse (and on most models, no way to attach external ones), limited printing support, and not enough processing power, memory, and storage space to work efficiently with large data files.

Microsoft has a line of tablets called Surface that blurs the line between a tablet and a notebook computer. They have a 12" screen and a detachable keyboard, and they run the full Windows 8.1 Pro operating system (not the more basic Windows RT version). There is enough memory and CPU power to run Microsoft Office and other desktop apps. Other companies may soon follow suit, and by the time you read this, tablets may be powerful enough to substitute in full for a desktop or notebook computer.

Tablet sizes

A standard tablet is about the same size as a sheet of notebook paper, with a screen that's about 10" diagonal. A mini tablet has a screen size of about 8" diagonal. The sizes vary somewhat depending on the brand and model. The two sizes of tablets run the same operating systems and have similar processing power and memory. Some tablets, such as the Microsoft Surface models, go up to 12" in screen diameter.

Tablet computer operating systems

There are three major operating systems for tablet computers: Apple iOS, Windows RT, and Android. These are all system-on-chip (SoC) operating systems that come preinstalled on the tablet, so by selecting a particular brand and model, you are also selecting the operating system you will use.

Apple tablets such as the iPad, iPad Air, and iPad mini all come with the iOS operating system, shown in Figure 16-2. The iOS operating system is great for people who use a Mac as their main computer because all the same apps are the default there. For example, the Safari web browser is used both in Mac OS X and in iOS, and there are other familiar apps like iTunes and FaceTime.

Android, developed by Google, is a popular operating system for low-cost tablets. It is based on Linux, it is an open-source, free operating system (although most devices that use it as an OS come with a mixture of free and commercial apps installed). Android provides an icon-based interface similar to that of iOS but at a lower cost. It is a very flexible operating system, with versions available not only for tablets but also for smart phones. There are over 1 million apps available for Android devices.

Most Windows tablets (except the larger models with their own keyboard, like the Surface models I mentioned earlier) use a special version of Windows 8.1 called Windows RT. It looks a lot like the Start screen on Windows 8.1; the main difference is that there is no desktop you can flip over to; it's all about the Start screen and its tablet-optimized apps. Figure 16-3 shows a Windows RT screen. Instead of icons, it uses resizable tiles for each application.

Navigating a tablet computer OS

Each tablet OS works a little differently, but they all have one big thing in common: touchscreen gestures. A gesture is a way of interacting with the screen with one or more fingers. For example, dragging in from the left or right side of the screen toward the center is called swiping, and touching an area of the screen (for example, to select an icon) is called tapping. Table 16-1 lists the touch gestures that any tablet user will need to know.

To start up the device, press its Power button. It's probably located somewhere around one of the edges. Press the Power button again to turn it off. You don't need to worry about losing your work when you turn off the device; tablets are different from desktops and notebooks in that way, and your computer's state doesn't reset when you turn off the power.

Figure 16-3:
The
Windows RT
interface.

Table 16-1	Touch Gestures
Gesture	*What It Does*
Tap	Tap the screen with your finger, pressing and quickly releasing on the same spot. You tap to make a selection or issue a command.
Pinch	Touch two fingers to the screen in different spots, and then drag the fingers together. You pinch to zoom out (and display a larger area).
Stretch	Touch two fingers to the screen in adjacent spots and then drag the fingers farther apart. You stretch to zoom in (and display a smaller area).
Drag (slide)	Touch one finger to the screen and then slide it along the surface. You drag to perform a variety of functions, depending on the software and context. For example, dragging can open menu bars, exit application, scroll the display, or move items around onscreen.
Swipe	To drag starting from the edge of the screen inward. For example, to swipe in from the left means to drag from the left edge of the screen to the center of the screen. Swiping often opens a menu or scrolls a display.
Rotate	Touch two fingers on the desired object or area and then drag in a circular motion.

To start an app, tap its icon on the main screen. On most tablets, there is a button you can press or tap to return to the main screen at any time.

The process for closing an app varies depending on the operating system and its version. For example, on the iPad, there is a hardware button adjacent to the display screen. You press it once to return to the main screen. If you press it twice, thumbnail images of all open applications appear, and you can drag one up to the top of the screen to close the app. Check the documentation for your operating system to find out how things work in your version.

Each operating system has a different way of adjusting settings. On the iPad, there is a Settings app that provides access to all the different settings in one place, such as network setup, screen brightness, battery life management, and so on. On Windows RT, you can access settings by swiping in from the right and then touching the Settings button. On an Android, choose Menu (tap the three dots on the top of the action bar) and then choose Settings.

Understanding Smart Phone Basics

A smart phone (shown in Figure 16-4) is a mobile phone that includes some characteristics of a tablet in it, such as the ability to connect to a Wi-Fi network, install and run apps, send and receive email, and surf the web. In some ways, a smart phone is like a tiny tablet; it has the same touchscreen, and the same gestures work on it (see Table 16-1).

A smart phone, though, has the addition of telephone service through whatever network you have signed up with. The settings for the phone part of the device are determined by its SIM card, which is a small plastic chip that's installed in the phone. Some phones are locked to a certain phone provider, such as AT&T or Sprint; others can be used with different phone providers with different SIM cards.

Types of smart phones

As with tablets, there are three basic operating systems for smart phones: iOS, Android, and Windows Phone. The first two, iOS and Android, operate much the same on phones and on tablets because they are essentially the same operating systems. On Windows devices, however, there are some differences because it's actually a different operating system on a Windows phone (the operating system is called Windows Phone) than on a Windows tablet. The Windows Phone operating system uses tiles, as Windows RT's Start screen does, but the functionality is more basic. See Figure 16-5.

Figure 16-4:
A smart
phone.

Selecting a smart phone

Before you commit to a particular smart phone, check out the operating systems in all the available models. The way a phone looks physically is ultimately less important than how the operating system feels to you when interacting with it; if you are annoyed with how your OS works, you won't enjoy the phone. (And you may be stuck with that phone for up to two years if you get a discount on it by signing up for a phone service contract.)

Another consideration when choosing a phone OS is the apps that it supports. There are many more apps for iOS and Android than there are for Windows Phone; some of the apps that you want or need may not be available if you choose Windows Phone. For example, some credit-card processing apps such as Square don't work with the Windows Phone OS.

Some OSes provide special apps unique to them. For example, Apple phones have Siri, a voice-activated digital assistant; Windows 8.1 phones have a similar assistant called Cortana.

Figure 16-5:
Windows
Phone.

After you have decided on the OS you want, find out which phone providers support phones that use that OS. Not all phone providers support all operating systems.

Some of the features that differentiate one smart phone from another (regardless of operating system) include

- ✔ **Amount of memory:** On a phone, memory and storage space are one and the same. A phone with 16GB of memory can hold a little less than 16GB of data because some of that memory is used to hold the OS itself.

- ✔ **Screen size and quality:** Some phones have larger screens than others. Larger isn't always better; some people prefer a more compact device that fits more easily into a pocket. Some screens have a higher resolution than others, or appear brighter or sharper.

- ✔ **Camera quality:** One measurement of camera quality is the resolution, measured in megapixels (millions of pixels). The higher the number, the finer the picture resolution.

   ✔ **Global Positioning System (GPS):** Most smart phones have GPS capability built into them, so you can use them to pinpoint your location and get driving directions using GPS software.

Navigating a smart phone interface

Navigating a smart phone is very similar to navigating a tablet. The same gestures apply. You start out on a main screen, or Start screen, and tap an icon or tile for an app you want to run. Because it's a phone, there are apps for placing phone calls and sending and receiving text messages in addition to the apps you would find on a tablet. There will also be an app for keeping track of people's contact info, and one for using the built-in camera (if the phone has one, and most do). You'll also find a Store or Shopping app, which is where you can go to download additional applications.

Just like on a tablet, there will be a button or command that returns you to the main screen. You don't have to close each application when you are done with it; it's okay to leave apps open in the background. There will be a way to close them if you want to, though; check your phone's documentation, because it's different in every operating system (and sometimes even different between versions of the same OS). On some systems, closing apps that you are not using can make the battery charge last longer.

The power button on your smart phone doesn't really turn it all the way off; it just makes the phone go to sleep so it uses less power. The phone will go to sleep all by itself after a certain period of inactivity too. If you need to completely power off the phone, you can do so by holding down the power button for a few seconds.

Grasping Digital TV and Movie Basics

Many TVs, DVD players, and cables boxes today are "smart," meaning that they have some computing capabilities to them. For example, many TVs have built-in networking adapters (wired or wireless) that enable the TV to connect to your home network, and from there to the Internet. Being connected to your local computers and to the Internet opens up an array of entertainment possibilities.

Signing up for online movie and TV services

With so much movie and TV series content available online, you technically don't even need a separate TV; you can watch all the programming you need directly on your computer, either through free services or through services where you pay a small amount per month. Some of the most popular online services include

✔ **Netflix** (www.netflix.com)**:** This service enables both digital stream-ing over the Internet and also DVD movie delivery to your home. It also offers original programming developed just for Netflix users. You can watch Netflix on any computing device that has a Netflix app for it: desktops, notebooks, smart TVs and DVD players, digital video record-ers, tablets, and even smart phones. You can set up a queue for each member of your household, and each person can then access their movie and TV show listing from any device. Figure 16-6 shows a sample queue of instant programming ready to be viewed.

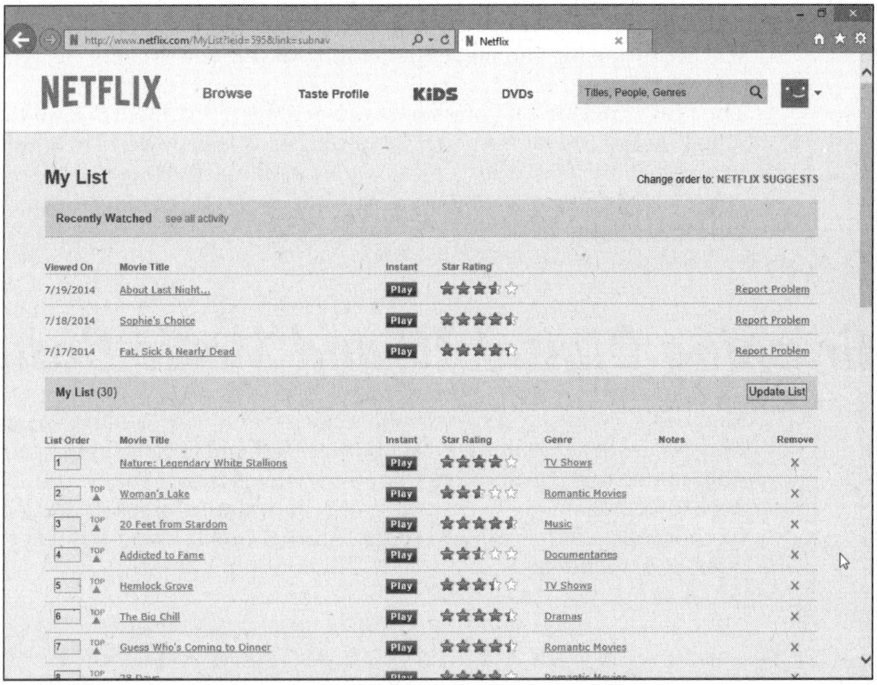

Figure 16-6:
A Netflix
queue.

✔ **Amazon** (www.amazon.com): Not only is Amazon a giant online retailer, but they also provide online movie rentals and sales. You can purchase individual rentals, or you can sign up for the Amazon Prime service to get free access to thousands of titles. You can watch on any device that has an Amazon app.

✔ **Hulu and Hulu Plus** (www.hulu.com): Hulu is a free service for watching TV shows and movies online; it is ad-supported and works only on computers. Hulu Plus is the for-pay version of the service, which has more shows available, no ads, and the ability to watch on TV and mobile devices.

Watching online content

Services like Netflix, Hulu Plus, and Amazon Prime enable you to stream movies and TV shows from the Internet to your computer. You can also stream to tablets and smart phones.

It's easiest to sign up for a new account on one of these services using a computer that has a real keyboard because of the amount of text entry required. After you have your account, though, you can easily pair any compatible device with your account. The exact steps vary depending on the device and the service; some services generate an access code that you then enter into the device, whereas others have you connect to the service via the same username and password you use to log into the website.

Watching TV on a computer

There are two ways to watch TV shows on a computer. You can either record them on a DVR and then stream them to the computer(s), or you can buy a TV tuner card for the computer, so that your home TV service treats the computer as if it were an additional TV in your home. Both of those solutions are hardware-dependent; they don't work with all makes and models of hardware, and the steps for setting them up and the software needed will vary greatly depending on the hardware.

Depending on the service, you might be able to stream movies from your cable box or digital video recorder (DVR) device to computers on your network. For example, if your cable box includes a DVR, you might be able to play back recorded shows on a tablet device on your network, or to transfer shows to a computer and then burn a DVD of them (subject to copyright limitations, of course). As for the specifics, it really depends on the devices you're working with. The Tivo Roamio DVR enables you to stream from the DVR to many different computing devices, for example. To find out what's available for the hardware you have, do a quick web search to see how others have managed it.

If you want to watch TV on a computer and you don't necessarily need it to originate from your home cable box, there is another option: You can get a TV tuner for the computer, so that the computer is treated like any other television in your home. A TV tuner can be an expansion board (for a desktop computer) or a USB device (for either a desktop or a notebook computer). You will also need some sort of TV software. Windows Media Center, which comes with some versions of Microsoft Windows, includes this capability. The TV tuner you purchase may also come with compatible software for this purpose. For more information, read `http://windows.microsoft.com/en-us/windows/understanding-tv-signals-tuners`.

Showing computer content on a TV screen

Today's digital TVs have a lot in common with computer monitors, and most of them can be used as a computer monitor simply by connecting the computer to the TV using an interface they both support. (Many TVs have a VGA port or DVI port, for example, which are the two most common port types for connecting a monitor to a computer.)

You can also use a smart TV's applications to access content from a computer on your network. For example, suppose you want to show your vacation pictures on the large screen of your TV, and they are stored on your computer's hard drive. If both the TV and the computer are connected to your local area network, you may be able to browse the computer's content with the TV's file management interface, find the pictures, and open them in the TV's photo viewing application.

If your TV isn't as smart as you'd like and doesn't have an appropriate application for viewing photos, your next-best bet is to go through a device that does do that, such as your DVD player (maybe), a Nintendo Wii, a PlayStation, an Xbox, or a Roku device. All of those devices have photo viewing and networking capabilities and can neatly feed the images to the TV (which gets to play dumb in that transaction and just show what it's told to show).

Chapter 17

Digital Cameras and Photography

. . . .

. . . .

Digital cameras put all the art and science of photography into your hands. Few things are as personal and instantly gratifying as a photograph. We freeze a moment in time to be marveled over for years to come.

You may already have a camera, either a standalone model or as part of your mobile phone. This chapter runs through the specs that differentiate one camera from another, so if you need to make a camera purchase, you'll know what you're doing.

With a computer and software, you can edit a digital photo in many ways, correcting annoying faults like red-eye and cropping images to get rid of extraneous background clutter. You can fix or improve the brightness of the photo too, rotate it, and even apply artistic effects to it.

Finally, you can enjoy your digital photos and share them in many ways, from digital picture frames to glossy printouts. In this chapter, I explain the various photo printing options, so you can pick the best one for your needs.

Digital imaging refers to taking photos with a *digital camera*. A digital camera is an electronic device that is able to digitally capture a visual representation of whatever it "sees" through its lens. Digital imaging has these advantages over film camera imaging:

- ✔ **Cost per photo:** After the initial camera purchase, it costs nothing to take as many pictures as you like. In contrast, with a film camera, you pay for the film and then you pay for the developing. Because you don't have to pay per photo, you can take hundreds of images and pick the best one; this results in better end results.

- ✔ **Editing capabilities:** You can edit digital photos using a variety of different applications, making corrections and improvements that are possible only during developing — or not at all — on film pictures.

- ✔ **Low-cost sharing:** With a film photo, you have to order extra copies of prints to share them with others. With a digital photo, you can email it to friends and family at no cost, or print a hard copy on your printer for only the cost of paper and ink.

Learning How Digital Imaging Works

Picture a picture. No, really. Think about what you see when you look through a camera's lens. You see a rectangular area with an image in it. Imagine a nice landscape scene, or a family pet.

Now, imagine that the image is divided into thousands of tiny squares called *pixels*, both vertically and horizontally. If you zoomed in on the image, you could see each one individually, as in Figure 17-1. Each of those squares can be only one color, so the more (and smaller) squares the image is broken up into, the higher its *resolution* and the finer the image's detail.

In a nutshell, that's what a digital camera does. It breaks up the image that the lens sees into thousands of tiny squares, and uses a light-detecting sensor to detect the amounts of red, green, and blue in each pixel. It assigns a numeric value to each square representing the amounts of each color.

How many binary digits (bits) are used to describe the color of each pixel? That depends on the image's *color depth*, also called *bit depth*. For example, with 4-bit color, there are only 16 possible colors. Why? Because there are 16 possible binary values when you have four binary digits: 0000 through 1111. (You can calculate that as 2 to the 4th power.) With 8-bit color, you get 256 color choices, and with 16-bit color, you get 65,536 color choices.

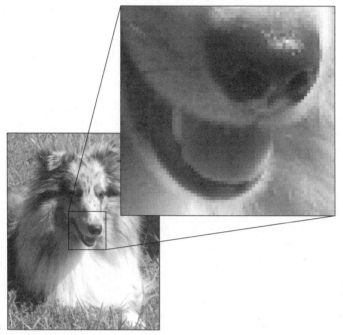

Figure 17-1:
Pixels make
up an image.

Most modern digital cameras capture images at 24-bit bit depth. That's more than enough for a realistic image because the human eye can't detect more than about a million colors, and 24-bit is more than 16 million colors.

Bit depth is described with separate values for red, green, and blue, with each of those three colors represented by an 8-bit value (between 0 and 255 because there are 256 possible combinations of an 8-digit binary number). When describing a color of a pixel, you provide its RGB numbers. For example, pure red would be R:255, G:0, B:0, and a purple is R:127, G:0, B:127. You don't need to know this for taking digital pictures, but when it comes to modifying them in a photo editing application, that information can come in handy.

Choosing a Digital Camera

Most people are pleasantly surprised at the high quality of digital images, even on a very inexpensive model. You don't need to spend a fortune to get a digital camera that will serve well for casual use. It's primarily the professional photographers who buy the expensive models. Nevertheless, it helps to know what you're getting for your money. Here are some of the main considerations when camera-shopping.

Body style

Some cameras are extremely compact, whereas others are larger and accept add-on lenses. The number of features available is determined by the type of camera:

✔ *Compact point-and-shoot cameras* are small and easy to use, as the name implies. You don't have to worry about having too many options or controls with most point-and-shoot cameras. This is a great camera type for casual photography and snapshots. Figure 17-2 shows an example.

Figure 17-2:
Point-
and-shoot
cameras.

✔ *Digital single-lens reflex (DSLR) cameras* are the choice of professionals and serious amateurs or hobbyists. Unlike a simple point-and-shoot camera, a DSLR has many features designed to give you control over every aspect of picture taking. DSLRs have a faster response time than other types of cameras, with almost no delay between the moment you click and when the photo is taken. (Non-DSLR cameras often have a fraction-of-a-second delay.) Canon and Nikon dominate the DSLR category. Figure 17-3 shows a Nikon model.

Figure 17-3:
A DSLR
camera.

There are also cameras that fall somewhere between those two, sometimes called bridge or *prosumer* (professional/consumer) cameras.

Price range

Digital camera prices start near $50. Anything cheaper than that may not really be a bargain — though it might make a good door stop. If you're look-ing for a DSLR model, expect to pay between $250 and $600 for it — but look out at the lower end to make sure you get a good lens. Professional-quality DSLR cameras with exchangeable lenses and lots of advanced settings start around $600 and go upward from there, into the thousands.

Cheaper cameras may need more time to turn on, store pictures, or ready the flash than more expensive models need. Response time matters if you plan on shooting photos in rapid succession, such as at a fast-paced event.

Features

Do you want a camera that fits in your pocket or purse to pull out for spontaneous photos? Do you want to get close to flowers or wildlife? Is photography your passion (or can you imagine it becoming that)? As you look at cameras, consider which features matter most to you. The following lists describe all the features and options you should consider before you purchase a digital camera.

Here are some factors to consider:

- **Ease of use:** If you want decent photos under most conditions without making many decisions, look at point-and-shoot models.

- **Image resolution:** As you learned earlier in the chapter, the width and height of a photo are measured in tiny dots called pixels, and the area of the photo is measured in millions of pixels (megapixels, or MP). Having more megapixels is especially important when you want to edit or print the photo. The megapixel total is less important if you don't plan to print or edit.

- **View options:** A *viewfinder* lets you hold the camera up to your eye to compose or frame your photo, just like a film camera. An *electronic viewfinder* (EVF) displays information about camera settings superimposed over the scene. Some cameras have a small display screen on the back that you can use instead of an electronic viewfinder, and that you can also use to review your photos. Look for a camera with both a viewfinder and a display screen for maximum flexibility.

- **Battery type:** All cameras use batteries to power every aspect of operation. A spare battery of a proprietary type could cost between $30 and $60, so you might want a camera that uses standard AA or AAA batteries.

- **Close-ups:** A macro setting allows you to put the camera extremely close to the subject, even less than an inch away. The result is an extreme close-up that reveals details that are often missed, such as the heart of a flower or the pattern on a butterfly's wings. Figure 17-4 shows a composite shot of an extreme close-up of a flower. The regular shot on the left is out of focus, whereas the macro shot on the right is in focus.

- **Zoom:** A zoom lens makes a distant subject appear closer. You can photograph an entire sports team or zoom in to photograph one player. If you plan to photograph birds and other wildlife, you want an extreme zoom — 10X or larger.

  A 3X zoom is adequate for most close-ups of people and pets. A 12X zoom will bring distant subjects much closer to you, as shown in Figure 17-5.

Regular focus

Macro shot

Figure 17-4:
A close-up.

1X   3X   5X   12X

Figure 17-5:
A comparison of different zooms.

TIP

Ignore references to *digital* zoom or *combined* zoom. *Optical* zoom is the measurement that means the most when you're comparing cameras.

✔ **Image storage:** In a digital camera, photos are stored as digital files in the camera. Although some cameras have built-in, non-removable memory for saving pictures, that is usually limited to a few photos. Most cameras use removable *memory cards* to enable you to save more photos. Consider buying more than one memory card if you plan to shoot more photos than one card can hold before you can delete photos or move them to a computer. Buy a large capacity memory card — at least 1 gigabyte (1GB) — that is the correct type for your camera. Read the camera specification on the box or in the manual to identify the correct card for your camera. The wrong type of card won't fit your camera. Figure 17-6 shows four types of memory cards.

Figure 17-6: Memory cards.

✔ **File format:** Photos are usually stored as JPEG files (JPEG stands for Joint Photographic Experts Group), which is an optimal file format for photos. Some bridge (prosumer) cameras or DSLRs store photos as RAW files, which may be a better file format for you if you plan to edit your photos extensively on your computer by using advanced software tools.

Choosing a Photo Organizer Program

Photo organizing software enables you to move photos from your camera to a computer. Further — as the name implies — such software helps you organize your photos, so that you can find specific photos when you want to. With photo organizing software, you can easily arrange your photos into folders or by name, date taken, location taken, and so forth. With the right software, you can also add titles, comments, and even ratings to your photos.

The following photo organizers are free or included with certain cameras or computers:

 ✔ **Your camera's software:** Some cameras include a disc with software for viewing, organizing, and editing your photos. If a disc came with your camera, you may want to install the included software. If you decide to use a different program, you do not need to install the disc that came with your camera or you can uninstall the included software if you switch to another program.

 ✔ **Windows Live Photo Gallery:** This software contains a number of useful features for both organizing and correcting photos. It is available for free as a download from Microsoft for Windows computers. I use it for many of the examples throughout this chapter.

 To get Windows Live Photo Gallery, point your browser to `http://windows.microsoft.com/en-us/windows-live/photo-gallery`. Click Download now and follow the prompts to download and install it on your computer.

 ✔ **iPhoto:** This program is included on Macs as part of the iLife suite of programs. iPhoto is not available for Windows users.

 ✔ **Windows 8's Photo App:** This app comes free with Windows 8 and is the default photo-handling app when you connect a camera to a Windows 8 PC. This is the app I use in some of the upcoming examples in this chapter.

Of course, there are other choices for photo organizers. A very popular program is Adobe Photoshop Elements, which is not free, but may come with some cameras. Photoshop Elements is a powerful photo editor with organizer features.

Transferring Photos from Camera to Computer

Uploading photos from a camera to your computer is a very simple process, but it helps to understand what's involved. (This is similar to the process you can use to upload movies from a camcorder — in both cases, check your manual for details.)

The first thing you need to do is make the physical connection between the camera and the computer. Usually this is done via a USB cable. You may need to power on the camera and press a button on it to put it in a special mode for transferring pictures. When the connection is made, the computer will see the camera as if it were an external drive, like a flash drive.

Transferring photos with File Explorer

One way to transfer photos to the computer is to browse the camera like any other drive. Select the photos, copy them (Ctrl+C is one way) to the Clipboard, navigate to the destination location, and paste them (Ctrl+V is one way). The advantage is that it's easy and quick. The disadvantage is it doesn't help you make any modifications, such as changing the file names or rotating the images, and it doesn't automatically create a folder for the incoming pictures.

Transferring photos with a photo organizer program

Each photo organizer program has its own method of helping you transfer photos from the camera to the computer. They may offer extra features beyond the simple copy-and-paste, such as creating new folders, renaming each file, and adding metatags to the photos. *Metatags* are informational tags placed in a file's properties that provide information about it, such as the date the photo was taken or the photographer's name.

Importing pictures with the Windows 8 Photos App

If you have Windows 8, the Photos app may open automatically when you connect a digital camera. This app is a Windows 8-style app, optimized for tablet and touchscreen use, but you can also use it with a mouse and keyboard if that's what you have.

Follow these steps to transfer photos with the Photos app:

1. **Connect the camera to your Windows 8 computer.**

   The Photos app opens automatically and displays the contents of the camera, as shown in Figure 17-7. All files are selected by default.

2. **If there are any photos you don't want to import, click the check mark in the upper-right corner of that file's tile to clear it.**

3. **Click the Import button on the command bar at the bottom of the screen.**

   The photos are imported into the Pictures library, in a folder that is named for today's date. The photos remain on the camera.

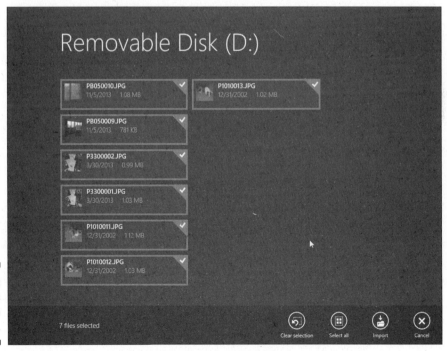

Figure 17-7:
The Photos
app in
Windows 8.

Importing pictures with the Windows Live Photo Gallery

After it's installed, you can run Windows Live Photo Gallery from the Start screen (Windows 8) or Start menu (earlier Windows versions). The first time you run it, you may see a dialog box regarding how to handle different picture file types (JPG, TIF, PNG, and others). Use this dialog box to determine which file types Photo Gallery can open. To get Windows Live Photo Gallery, point your browser to download.live.com/photogallery. Click Download now and follow the prompts to download and install it on your computer.

Figure 17-8 shows the Photo Gallery screen. At first glance, it looks a bit like File Explorer, complete with a Ribbon interface. In the main pane, thumbnail images of your photos appear. You'll have different photos, of course. The Pictures library (or My Pictures folder) is the default location displayed, but you can change locations in the navigation pane.

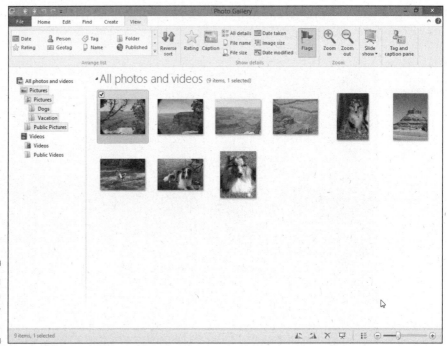

Figure 17-8:
The Photo
Gallery
screen.

Before you import pictures using Photo Gallery, you may want to adjust its settings. Choose File⇨Options, and in the dialog box that opens, click the Import tab. See Figure 17-9. These options control how your computer copies photos from the camera, including where the photos will be placed and how the photos will be named.

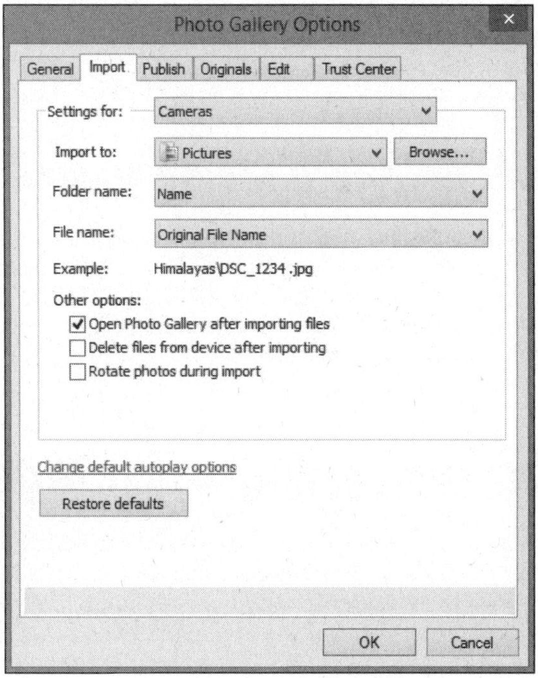

Figure 17-9:
The Import tab of the Photo Gallery dialog box.

When you import pictures, a new folder is created each time. The Import To setting determines where that new folder will be stored. The default is the Pictures library. The Folder Name setting enables you to choose a naming convention for the new folder, such as Name + Date Imported. The File Name setting lets you (optionally) rename each image file as it is imported.

To import photos with Windows Live Photo Gallery, follow these steps:

1. **Connect the camera to your Windows 8 computer. If some other app opens, close it.**

2. **Start Windows Live Photo Gallery.**

3. **Choose File⇨Import photos and videos.**

4. In the Import Photos and Videos dialog box, select the camera. It may appear generically, as a drive letter. Then click Import.

5. A message appears letting you know how many pictures were found. Choose Import all new items now.

6. In the text box, enter the name for the folder in which to place the pictures, and then click Import.

7. Wait for the pictures to be imported into Photo Gallery and copied to your hard drive in the folder you specified.

Copying photos from a memory card

If your camera stores photos on a memory card, you may be able to remove that memory card and insert it in a compatible card slot on your computer. The memory card appears as a removable drive, the same as the camera itself would. Copy the files as you would from a camera. Then eject the memory card and put it back in the camera.

Storing and Managing Digital Images

There's nothing special about picture files; you can manage and store them just as you would any other files. Most people keep their photos in the Pictures library or My Pictures folder for their user account, but that's just customary — it's not required. You can use any application you like to view and move photo files around, including Windows Live Photo Gallery, the Windows 8 Photos app, or even File Explorer. The following sections offer some tips for various things you might want to do with your stored photos.

Previewing and viewing photos

All of the photo organizing apps show thumbnail images of the pictures, and most of them enable you to change the size of the image thumbnails.

- ✔ **File Explorer:** Change the icon size on the View tab as you would when browsing any other files.

- ✔ **Windows 8 Photos app:** When browsing a list of photos, click the View button in the upper-right corner to switch between Details view and Thumbnails view.

- ✔ **Windows Live Photo Gallery:** Use the Zoom In button on the View tab to increase the thumbnail size, or the Zoom Out button to decrease it.

To view a single photo full-screen size:

- ✔ **File Explorer:** Double-click the photo to open it in Windows Photo Viewer. Close the Windows Photo Viewer window when finished.

- ✔ **Windows 8 Photos app:** Click the photo. Press Esc to return to the list.

- ✔ **Windows Live Photo Gallery:** Double-click the photo. To return to the list, choose Edit⇨Close File.

To show a full-screen slide show of the photos in a location, navigate to that location in the application you're working with, and then

- ✔ **File Explorer:** Double-click the first photo to open it in Windows Photo Viewer. See Figure 17-10. Then click the Play Slide Show button at the bottom of the window, or press F11 to start a slide show. Press any key to move to the next photo. Press Esc to end the slide show.

Figure 17-10:
Open an image in Photo Viewer.

- ✔ **Windows 8 Photos app:** Right-click to display the command bar and then click Slide show. Press Esc to end the slide show.

- ✔ **Windows Live Photo Gallery:** Click View⇨Slide Show. Or, for a special-effect slide show, open the Slide show button's drop-down list and choose some special effect, such as Pan and Zoom or Fade. Press Esc to end the slide show.

Moving and copying images

To move or copy images, the Clipboard works well in most photo organizing applications, as well as in File Explorer. Select the images to move or copy and then use Cut or Copy to place them on the Clipboard. Then use Paste to paste them into a new location, the same as you would any files in File Explorer.

In the Windows 8 Photos app, there are a few little quirks. One of them is that to select or deselect a file, you right-click it, rather than clicking it. (Clicking it opens it full-screen.) To access the Cut and Copy commands, right-click anywhere in the app screen to display the command bar.

Deleting images

To delete an image, select it and press the Delete key on the keyboard, or right-click it and choose Delete. This works in almost all apps, including File Explorer.

If you want to delete the images from the camera, your best bet is to use File Explorer to browse the camera's file system like a drive and delete the files as you would any files in File Explorer (selecting them and pressing the Delete key, for example).

Editing a Digital Image

There are many ways to edit a digital image, and your options depend largely on the application in which you open the image. Some photo organizer applications are also image editing applications, at either a basic or deluxe level, whereas others just show the files, and don't let you do much with them.

In the following sections, I'll show you how to make some basic edits using Windows Live Photo Gallery. If another app that we've talked about can also do the same thing, I'll point that out, but in most cases it can't. Windows Photo Viewer, File Explorer, and the Windows 8 Photos app are mostly just for looking at images, not making changes to them.

Rotating an image

When a photo is taken, the photographer might have tilted the camera 90 degrees to get a differently shaped photo. That's fine, except you might need to rotate the image on the computer so you can see it without tilting your head.

Rotating is one of the few edits that you can make in several different applications that we've worked with so far. Here's a quick summary:

✔ **File Explorer:** Right-click the photo and choose Rotate right or Rotate left on the shortcut menu.

✔ **Windows Photo Viewer:** Click the Rotate counterclockwise or Rotate clockwise button below the photo.

✔ **Windows Live Photo Gallery:** On the Home tab, in the Manage group, click the Rotate left or Rotate right button.

Color-correcting an image

There are lots of different color corrections you can make to a photo using Windows Live Photo Gallery. Select an image and then use the tools on the Edit tab to adjust the Color and Exposure settings. The Color setting changes the amount of red, green, or blue tint to the image; the Exposure setting makes the picture lighter or darker. You can also apply a color wash to the image from the Effects gallery, also on the Edit tab. See Figure 17-11.

Figure 17-11:
The Photo
Gallery.

If you aren't sure what to do to improve an image, try the Auto Adjust command. If you don't like what you end up with, click Revert to Original.

Cropping an image

To *crop* an image is to remove part of the image on one or more sides. To crop an image using Windows Live Photo Gallery, you have to double-click the image to open it first. Then the Edit tab on the Ribbon becomes available, with a Crop command.

Click the Crop command. A grid appears over the image, as shown in Figure 17-12. Drag the selection handles on the grid until the grid covers the area you want to keep. Then click the Crop button again to accept the crop area.

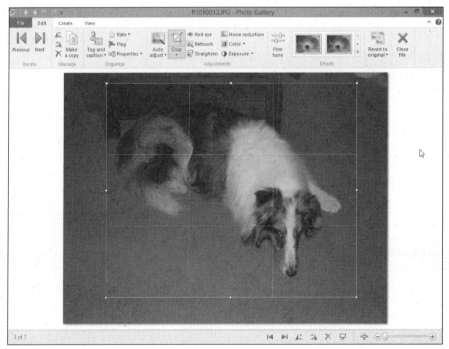

Figure 17-12:
Cropping an image.

Printing Digital Images

There are many options for printing your digital images:

✔ You can use your existing printer, which may or may not have decent photo capabilities.

✔ You can buy a printer designed specifically for photos.

✔ You can take your files to a store where they have a self-service photo printing kiosk. (Walmart's photo department has this, for example, and so do most drugstores.)

✔ You can use an online photo-printing service.

If you're going with one of the first two options, be prepared to spend some money on high-quality glossy photo paper. This paper supports the high-resolution printouts needed to make a photo look its best. It isn't cheap paper; expect to pay at least 20 cents a sheet, and that's if you buy in bulk and don't get the premium brands.

Depending on your printer, you may also need to outlay some money for special photo-printing ink. Most inkjet printers will print photos okay with their standard ink, but some models optionally accept special ink cartridges that make the photos look even better.

Checking out your printer's settings

Even if you didn't buy your existing printer to print photos, it still might be able to do a decent job on photos (with the right paper, of course) if it's an inkjet printer. Laser printers don't print well on glossy photo paper (the print technology is different, and doesn't lend itself to photo printing), so don't bother if that's what you have.

Check the printer's settings; it may have a Photo setting that prints on special glossy paper in a high resolution. To check a printer's settings, do the following in Windows 8:

1. **Right-click the Start button and choose Control Panel.**

2. **Under the Hardware and Sound heading, click View devices and printers.**

3. **Right-click the printer and choose Printing Preferences.**

   A dialog box appears with settings for the printer.

4. **Look for a setting where you can choose the type of paper and/or the resolution.**

   For example, the paper setting might be under Media.

5. **When you're done, click Cancel to close the dialog box.**

   You can always come back here later, now that you know what settings are available.

Selecting a photo printer

If you have decided to bite the bullet and buy a new printer specifically for photos, you have some trade-offs to make between price, maximum photo size, cost of paper and ink, and quality level:

- ✔ **Paper size:** Photo printers come in two basic types. The standard size uses regular letter-size paper and can print large photo images; it can also be used as a regular printer. The smaller size is a special-purpose printer only for photos; it takes smaller paper stock (such as 4" x 6").

- ✔ **Number of ink cartridges:** For a standard printer, four is the norm (cyan, magenta, yellow, and black). However, for a dedicated photo printer, it's typical to have five or more. For example, in addition to the standard four, a printer might have separate ink cartridges light versions of magenta and cyan, a special photo version of black (designed for glossy paper), and a couple of different shades of gray.

- ✔ **Printing technology:** Inkjet is the economy level of photo printing. It does a decent job, at a decent price. The higher-end technology is dye sublimation. These printers lay down mixed dyes on specially coated paper, producing a continuous-tone print. Then they add a clear protective layer over the dye, making the print less vulnerable to smearing.

- ✔ **Card reader:** Most photo printers have one or more memory card slots, in which you can insert a card from a camera directly. This enables you to bypass the computer altogether to print.

- ✔ **Display screen:** If a printer accepts images from memory cards, it's a nice feature if it also has a small display screen so you can preview the images before printing them. Otherwise, you have to rely on the filenames.

- ✔ **Networking**: The printer may have multiple ways it can connect to computers. In addition to a standard local USB interface, it may support Ethernet, Wi-Fi, or Bluetooth.

Printing from Windows Live Photo Gallery

After you've got an appropriate printer ready to go, the rest is easy. All photo organizing programs have a Print command that you can use to send photos directly to any printer that's available to the operating system. It may be on the File menu or on the Home tab. You can also try the Ctrl+P keyboard shortcut, which usually opens the print controls.

To print from Windows Live Photo Gallery, follow these steps:

1. **Select the photos to print, and then choose File⇨Print⇨Print.**

   The Print Pictures dialog box opens.

2. **Select the printer, paper size, quality, and paper type from the drop-down lists provided. See Figure 17-13.**

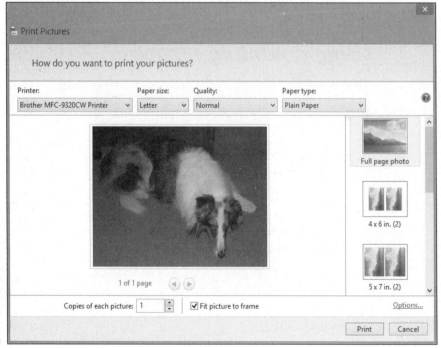

Figure 17-13: Printing pictures.

3. **In the bar along the right side, select a layout that represents the desired the image size.**

   If you choose an image size where more than one copy fits on a page, it will print multiple pictures per page, as will fit.

4. **In the Copies of each picture box, make sure the appropriate number is selected.**

5. **Mark or clear the Fit Picture to Frame check box.**

   When this option is selected, the picture will stretch itself in one dimension or the other to fit inside the area that the layout allots for it. This can distort the image. When you mark or clear the check box, the preview of the image changes, so you can see what you're getting.

   If you're using expensive paper, be cognizant of the number of copies and the number of photos you are printing to avoid wasting print area. For example, if you are printing using the Wallet layout, which prints nine pictures per page, and you choose to print three copies of each of three pictures, it will take exactly one sheet of photo paper. However, if you have four pictures and you print three sheets of them using the Wallet layout, you'll have one full page and one page where there are only three little images, wasting more than half of the (expensive) paper.

5. **Click Print to print the picture(s).**

Using a printing service

If you don't print photos often, it may be more economical in the long run for you to use a printing service when you need photo prints. Many stores have do-it-yourself printing kiosk computers. You can also order prints online.

To prepare for printing, you may want to crop the images so that they have a standard aspect ratio that matches the size of the photo paper, such as 4 x 6 or 5 x 7. Doing so will help you avoid having blank areas on the sides of the prints.

Most online photo printing services make it easy for you to upload multiple pages via their web interface. You can fine-tune the options for each photo's printout on the website, sometimes including color corrections and special effects.

If you want to do it yourself, put your photos on a flash drive or a CD and take them to a photo printing kiosk at a local store. The kiosk has its own software interface, but they're usually pretty self-explanatory and easy to follow.

Sharing Digital Images

There are many ways to share photos with others in a digital way (that is, using computers and/or electronics). For example, you can:

✔ **Email them.** Send photos as email attachments, or embed the photos in the email messages themselves.

✔ **Use a photo-sharing service such as Flickr.** You can share for public viewing, password-protect your photo storage, or send individual invitations to others via email to view your stored photos.

✔ **Create a PowerPoint presentation that contains your photos.** PowerPoint 2013 even has a special type of presentation called a Photo Album that is designed for distributing photos; see the Help system in PowerPoint for details.

✔ **Create a movie that contains a slide show of your pictures.** You can do this by converting your PowerPoint presentation to video format, or by using an application such as Windows Movie Maker to assemble images with a soundtrack and captions.

Choose a photo sharing service

Use a web-based photo sharing service to share your photos with friends, family, or the world. Photo sharing services enable you to easily upload photos, to categorize your photos with tags, and to organize your photos into online albums or galleries. Choose from one of these popular services, each of which has free accounts:

✔ **Flickr:** Flickr has a large and active community worldwide. Flickr sets the standard against which other services are judged. It is a good choice for most people. See `www.flickr.com`.

✔ **Google+ Photos:** This is part of Google's online suite of services, including search and email. See `https://plus.google.com/photos`.

✔ **Microsoft OneDrive:** As you learned in Chapter 8, OneDrive is a free cloud storage service; you can use it to share pictures or any other content. See `www.onedrive.com`.

✔ **Facebook, Myspace, and others:** Many people have accounts with social networking websites. Most of these sites have places for photos. Such sites can be great for staying current with the daily activities of family and friends around the world.

Many photo printing services enable you to share your photos online. This may be an especially attractive option if you want to allow others to order prints and pay for their own prints from your photos.

Resizing a photo for sharing

When sharing photos with others, be aware of the file size. The photos you take with your digital camera are probably very high-resolution, and that means a large file size. When you share the photos with others, however, they aren't going to be interested in owning a high-resolution copy; they just want to see the picture.

It's considerate to reduce the file size of each picture before you share it with others. That way, the file will take less time to download and take up less space on the recipient's hard disk. You can include a note along with the picture that a higher-resolution version is available for the asking, but most people are not going to take you up on that.

Any photo-editing application will resize a picture, but since I've been working with Windows Live Photo Gallery in this chapter, I'll continue that.

To resize a picture in Windows Live Photo Gallery, follow these steps:

1. **Right-click the photo to resize and choose Resize.**

   The Resize dialog box opens.

2. **Select a size from the Select a Size drop-down list. See Figure 17-14.**

   The default setting of Medium: 1024 is a good size for photos to be shared: not too big and not too small.

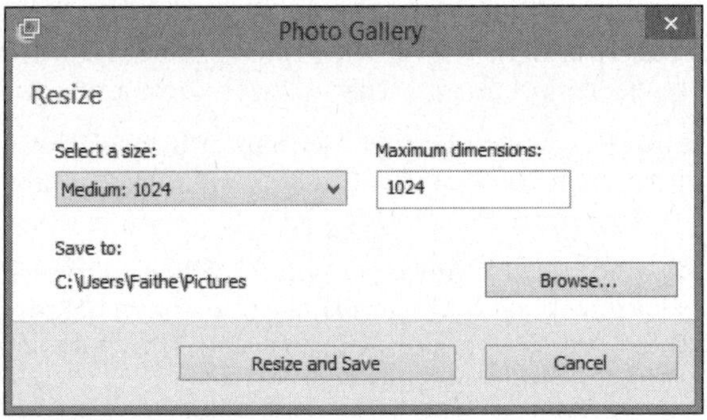

Figure 17-14: Select a size.

3. **(Optional but recommended.) To save the resized version in a separate location, click Browse, select the new location, and click OK.**

4. **Click Resize and Save.**

   The file is resized and saved to the location you chose.

Chapter 18

Working with Music and Video

Among their many other benefits, computers are also great for creating, storing, and playing back audio and video files. You can enjoy music and movies that other people have made, and you can create your own too.

In this chapter, you learn how digital audio and video work: how the files are recorded, stored, converted, and distributed. You learn how to use Windows Media Player to organize, play, rip, and burn music. You find out about the technologies behind DVDs and web videos, and you learn how to create your own videos with simple, free applications.

Understanding Digital Audio

Digital audio is audio that is encoded in a digital format — that is, a format in which the audio can be completely represented with binary digits and stored on a computer.

There are two forms of digital audio:

  ✓ **Waveform**: Audio that was recorded from an analog (non-computer) source, such as a recording of someone speaking or singing into a microphone or a digital copy made of an analog recording on an LP or cassette.

  ✓ **MIDI**: Audio that was created digitally from scratch with a digital instrument, such as a digital keyboard.

MIDI (pronounced *middy*) stands for Multi Instrument Digital Interface. It's the name of both a file format (.mid extension) and a hardware interface that used to be very popular for connecting digital instruments such as keyboards to computers in the years before USB was available.

Most of the audio that you'll deal with on a computer will be the waveform kind. Music that you get from CDs or music download sites is all waveform, as is any narration or music you record yourself with your computer's microphone.

What you need for digital audio

To play back any kind of audio, your computer needs a *sound card* (also known as a sound adapter or audio adapter). It may be built into your motherboard, or it may be a separate circuit board installed in a desktop PC. The sound card converts between the digital representations of sound stored on a computer and the analog representations of sound that a human can hear through speakers, or that you record through a microphone. If you have external speakers or an external microphone, they plug into the sound card's ports.

Nearly all computers come with sound support of some type, so whether you have a sound card isn't an issue these days. Some sound cards are better than others, however, in terms of accurate sound recording and playback, speaker support, and support for various input and output types.

How digital audio is recorded

So, what happens when you record a sound? Here's the basic process:

1. Sound input comes in through the computer's microphone, or through an input port on the sound card.

2. The sound card *samples* the sound using its *analog-to-digital converter*. In other words, it takes an audio snapshot of what it hears at a precise moment in time. Then it uses computer bits to describe what it hears, in terms of pitch, tone, and volume. It may use 8, 16, or 32 bits of data to store a sample, depending on the settings.

3. The sound card continues to sample the sound, a certain number of times per second, for as long as the recording continues. It stores all the samples of the sound in a single file. The *sampling rate* varies, but 44,100 Hz (that is, 44,100 samples per second) is typical.

Why 44,100? Because the sampling rate should be at least twice the highest frequency you want to represent. Humans can't hear frequencies higher than 22,000, so doubling that and adding 100 for good measure results in the smallest sampling rate needed for full human appreciation of the recording. Many people can't hear any difference in quality between the full 44,100 and lower sampling rates, like 96,000 or 192,000.

Audio file formats

From what you learned in the previous section, you can see why sound recordings take up so much disk space. A typical 16-bit recording uses 10MB or more per minute of recording. Because the raw file size can be so huge, most audio file formats employ some type of *file compression*, similar to the compression used in graphics files. File compression shrinks a file by representing numbers more compactly. For example, suppose there was a part of the file that had 200 zeroes in a row. In the raw form, that's 200 bits. But with compression applied, you could write that as 200 x 0. Violà! You've just shrunk the 200 bits by about 4,000 percent.

You can save audio recordings in various file formats, and each format has its own special type of encoding and compression formulas. Some file formats have much higher compression rates than others. Some compression is *lossless*, meaning you don't lose any quality when the audio is compressed; others are *lossy*, meaning you do lose some quality (although not usually enough for an average person's ears to notice).

Different audio playback and recording applications support different file formats. If an application supports a certain format, it has a *codec* for it. Codec stands for coder/decoder. The codec is the translation utility that deciphers the coding that the file format uses to store the sound.

Some audio file formats support *Digital Rights Management (DRM),* a security coding system that prevents music piracy (that is, unauthorized sharing or copying of music) by locking a particular downloaded copy to a certain computer or restricting the activities that can be performed on that copy.

For example, you might not be able to copy a DRM-protected file to another computer. Music companies and artists may consider DRM a feature, but most consumers consider it an annoyance, and many people choose to acquire audio in a DRM-free format to avoid any possibility of being limited in how they can use the files.

Table 18-1 lists some of the most common audio file formats and some notes about them.

Table 18-1	Common Audio File Formats		
Format	*Compression*	*DRM?*	*Notes*
Advanced Audio Coding (.aac)	Lossy	No	Default format for non-DRM music for many applications and platforms, including YouTube, iPod, iPad, iTunes, Nintendo DSi, Nintendo 3DS, and PlayStation, as well as many brands of mobile phones.
.m4p	Lossy	Yes	DRM-enabled version of .aac.
.mp3	Lossy	No	Digital music on computers (including ripped from audio CDs). The most popular format for digital music distribution today. Its quality is not the best, but most people can't tell the difference, and it is DRM-free.
Windows (.wav) Mac (.aiff)	None	No	Files recorded using the computer's microphone. Very large files because they are uncompressed. This format is commonly used for short-duration sound files in video games, such as sound effects.
CD Audio (.cda)	None	No	Format used on commercially produced music CDs, as well as home-burned audio CDs.
Windows Media Audio (.wma)	Lossless	Yes	Digital music on computers (especially using Microsoft Windows Media Player).

Organizing and Playing Digital Music

Now that some of the tech stuff is out of the way, get down to the good stuff: enjoying digital music.

Applications for playing digital music

If you have a Windows computer, you'll find that Windows Media Player can play music you've downloaded and any music CDs you insert. It will also play some video clips and movies. (See Figure 18-1.) As an alternative to Windows Media Player, you might use iTunes (Figure 18-2), which is a free download from Apple's website. iTunes can play music, videos, podcasts, audio books, and more.

There are many other digital music applications available. For example, you can play music online through a variety of online services like Pandora and Spotify. (These services require that you be connected to the Internet whenever you listen to music.) Amazon Prime also has a music-playing component.

Figure 18-1:
Windows
Media
Player.

Organizing digital media on your computer

The default location for music files in Windows is the logged-in user's Music (or My Music) folder. If you use the Libraries feature in Windows, that folder is part of the Music library.

The customary way to organize a music library is to create a folder for each artist, and within that folder, create a subfolder for each album. The individual track clips are then placed within the album folders. When you *rip* (copy) music from a CD to your computer, Windows Media Player automatically creates folders for the copied tracks automatically.

If you already have music files stored somewhere else on your hard disk, one way to make them available to your music applications is to copy them into an existing folder in your Music library (such as My Music). To avoid duplication, though, while still making the files accessible to Windows Media Player and other music-playing apps, you may want to add the folder where they already reside to your Music library.

In Windows 8.1, the Libraries feature is not enabled by default. To enable it, open File Explorer. Then right-click in the navigation pane on the left and choose Show Libraries. When the Libraries feature is enabled, File Explorer opens to the list of libraries by default, rather than to the This PC window.

To add a folder to the Music library in Windows 8.1, follow these steps:

1. **In File Explorer, click Libraries to display icons for each of the default libraries.**

2. **Right-click the Music icon and choose Properties.**

   The Music Properties dialog box opens.

   The folders currently being included in the library appear on the Library Locations list. See Figure 18-3.

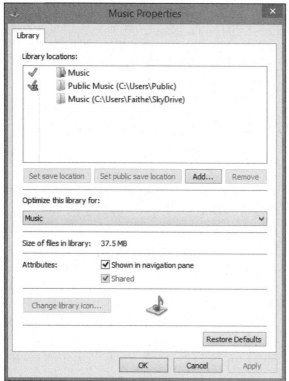

Figure 18-3:
The folders
included in
your Music
library.

3. **Click Add. In the Include Folder in Music dialog box that appears, select the desired folder and click Include Folder.**

4. **Click OK.**

The organizational system you set up in the Music library folders stays the same no matter what application you use to play the music. In each application, you can choose to sort the music files in different ways, to suit different purposes, without changing the file organization in the folders themselves.

Using Windows Media Player

Because Windows Media Player (WMP) comes free with Windows, it's the application I focus on in this chapter. Depending on your version of Windows, you may have a different version of WMP than shown here; however, the principles are the same, and the commands are mostly the same too.

Start Windows Media Player like any other application: from the Start screen (Windows 8) or from the Start menu (earlier Windows versions). Look back at Figure 18-1 for a full-screen look at the application.

WMP has a menu system, but it isn't enabled by default. I'll be referring to it in this chapter, though, so you might as well turn it on now. To do so, press the Alt key to make a pop-up menu appears near the top left corner of the window. On that menu, click Show Menu Bar. (Alternatively, you can press Ctrl+M to toggle the menu bar on or off.)

Playing stored music tracks

In the navigation pane on the left, click Music if it isn't already selected. All the music tracks from your Music library appear. Double-click the track you want to play, and it begins playing. Use the playback controls at the bottom of the window to control the playback, as shown in Figure 18-4.

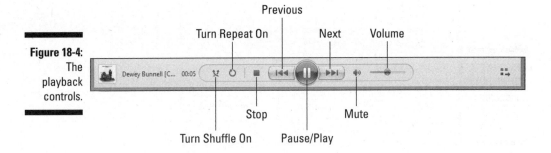

Figure 18-4: The playback controls.

What happens after that track is done playing? The next track plays. "Next" is defined as the track listed below the current one on whatever list is displaying at the moment. You can sort the track list in various ways, and you can create subsets of the full list called *playlists* (more on that in a minute).

From left to right, here are the buttons in the playback controls:

✔ **Turn Shuffle On:** When this option is enabled, the tracks in the current list will play in random order.

✔ **Turn Repeat On:** When this option is enabled, when all the tracks in the current list have played, they will play again.

✔ **Stop:** Stops the playback.

✔ **Previous:** Returns to the beginning of the previous track. (If you want to return to the beginning of the currently playing track, double-click the file name in the listing.)

✔ **Pause/Play:** This big round button in the center functions as a Pause button when a track is playing or a Play button when pause is enabled.

✔ **Next:** Jumps to the next track on the list when clicked. You can also click and hold on this button to fast-forward within the current track.

✔ **Mute:** Turns the sound off/on for this application only; does not affect overall Windows sound.

✔ **Volume:** Adjusts the volume of the playback for this application only.

Creating a playlist

You can create playlists in Windows Media Player so that you can quickly recall and replay certain combinations of tracks. For example, you might have a playlist called The 70s that includes all your favorite tracks from the 1970s. A playlist can contain any number of tracks, in any order.

You can create an impromptu playlist to play just for now — you don't have to save it. To pick tracks to play right now, do the following:

1. **Click the Play tab in the upper right corner of the window. If tracks already appear on the list that appears, click Clear List.**

2. **Drag-and-drop tracks from the center pane into the Play tab's pane.**

   You can select multiple tracks to drag-and-drop at once, just like you do when working with files in File Explorer. (Hold down Shift for a contiguous group or Ctrl for a non-contiguous group.) Figure 18-5 shows several contiguous tracks dragged to the Play tab.

3. **(Optional.) If you want to save the list as a permanent playlist, click the Save List button. Type a name for the playlist and then press Enter.**

You can also create a new playlist *before* you pick the tracks for it. To do that, choose File➪Create Playlist or press Ctrl+N. A new playlist appears on the Playlists section of the navigation pane, with the generic name (Untitled playlist) selected; type a new name and press Enter. You can then drag tracks to that playlist in the navigation pane.

Selected tracks   Play is selected

Figure 18-5:
Several
tracks
dragged to
the Play tab.

Drag selection to Play tab

Buying Digital Music Online

There are many online services where you can buy music to download to
your computer or other device. Some of the most popular services include
iTunes and Amazon. Some services allow you to pay a small fee per song and
have access to the track indefinitely; other services have you pay a fee per
month for unlimited access to their music library for as long as you are a
member.

When purchasing digital music online, be aware that there may be DRM
restrictions on the tracks you buy. For example, you might be able to burn a
purchased track to a CD only a certain number of times, or to transfer it to
only certain types of portable players.

If the track is in MP3 format, it doesn't have DRM restrictions on it. When
buying music online, look for sites that allow you to download in MP3 format.

Ripping a CD

As Table 18-1 noted earlier in this chapter, audio CDs store files in a format called CDA, which stands, as you might guess, for CD Audio. All audio systems can read this format, including home stereos, car stereos, and so on. The main problem with this format is that the files take up a lot of space. (It's an uncompressed format.) That's why the average CD has fewer than 20 tracks on it.

Ripping an audio CD means converting and storing its files on a computer-readable disk, such as your hard drive. When you rip a CD, you copy its tracks to a computer disk and convert them to a much more compact digital audio format, such as WMA or MP3. Ripping also makes the tracks available to you whenever you want them; you don't have to have the CD disc.

Windows Media Player includes a utility that very handily rips CDs and stores their contents in your Music library, in folders named for the artist and album.

Follow these steps to rip a CD in Windows Media Player:

1. **Insert an audio CD in your computer's CD or DVD drive.**

   The disc may start playing automatically.

   The disc's name and track list should appear automatically, but if it doesn't, right-click the disc's icon (next to Unknown album) and select Find Album Info from the menu that appears. Then search for the album in the database provided, selecting it if it appears there.

2. **(Optional.) If there are any tracks you don't want to rip, deselect their check boxes.**

3. **(Optional.) If you want to use a different file format than Windows Media Audio (WMA), click Rip Settings in the main menu bar, point to Format, and then choose a different format.**

   For example, you might choose MP3. I'm not going to evangelize one format over another in this lesson because the differences aren't that significant for the casual user; MP3 and WMA are both good general-purpose formats. MP3 is more popular. The various sub-types of WMA are significant mostly to audiophiles; if you have an opinion about what format you want — great.

   For some formats, you can also adjust the audio quality. Click Rip Settings, point to Audio Quality, and then choose the quality you prefer. The higher the quality, the larger the resulting file will be. On most computer audio systems, however, you won't be able to tell much difference between the default quality level and a higher one.

4. **Click the Rip CD button.**

   Windows Media Player begins converting and saving the tracks, one by one. The Rip Status column on the list lets you know the progress, as shown in Figure 18-6.

5. **Wait for the selected tracks to be ripped. When the process is complete, all tracks will show Ripped to Library in the Rip Status column.**

Tracks yet to be ripped show as Pending

Figure 18-6:
Ripping
tracks from
a CD.

Track currently being ripped

Copying music from another computer

You can transfer music from one computer to another via any portable drive or network interface, just like you would transfer any other files. Store the music in the Music library so that Windows Media Player can find them.

Where it gets a little sticky, though, is when you want to copy clips that have some sort of DRM attached to them. When you buy music from an online store, the files you get may have certain restrictions on them, and one of those restrictions may be that you can't copy them to other computers. Well, technically, you can copy them, but they won't play once they get there. You can sometimes circumvent the problem by burning a CD containing the protected track(s) — as you will learn in the next section — and then ripping that CD onto the other computer. However, that's time-consuming and it wastes blank CDs, so it's not a very good solution.

A better solution is to log into the online store where you bought the music and see if it allows you to enable more than one computer to access the purchased music. Most services do. You may also be able to stream music from one PC to another, as explained in "Streaming music to other people" later in this lesson.

Burning a CD with Windows Media Player

To *burn* a CD means to copy files to a writeable CD disc. There are two ways to burn (copy) music to a writeable disc.

- ✓ **Burn a data disc.** This can hold hundreds of files, but you're limited to playing it only in devices that support the file format you used (probably WMA or MP3).
- ✓ **Burn an audio disc.** This holds only about 20 files, but you can play it in any audio CD player.

Burning music to a data CD

If you know you'll play back the music on a device that supports digital audio formats like WMA and MP3, you can burn the CD as a data disc and take advantage of the much smaller file formats of digital audio. You don't need Windows Media Player to do this kind of burning; you can do it from Windows.

To burn music to a data CD, follow these steps:

1. **Insert a blank, writeable CD in your CD or DVD drive. Then open File Explorer, click This PC, and double-click the CD or DVD drive's icon.**

   The Burn a Disc dialog box opens, as shown in Figure 18-7.

2. **(Optional) Type a title for your CD in the Disc Title box.**

   The default title is today's date.

3. **Select the With a CD/DVD player radio button and click Next.**

   The dialog box closes.

4. **In File Explorer, navigate to the Music library and select the file(s) or entire folder(s) you want to include on the CD.**

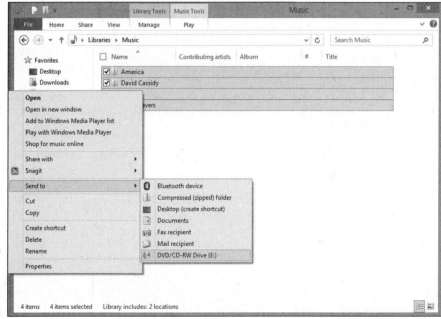

Figure 18-7:
The Burn a
Disc dialog
box.

5. **Right-click the selected group, point to Send To (as shown in Figure 18-8), and click the CD/DVD drive.**

A File Explorer window opens showing the CD's planned contents. Each icon for each file and folder has a small blue down-pointing arrow on it, indicating that it's a shortcut for a file to be written to the disc.

Figure 18-8:
Sending a
file to a CD.

6. **On the Drive Tools Manage tab, click Finish Burning.**

   The Burn to Disc dialog box opens.

   If you don't see the Drive tools Manage tab, close File Explorer and reopen it and then navigate back to the CD.

7. **(Optional.) Type a title for the disc.**

   The default title is today's date. Leave the Recording speed set at the default.

8. **Click Next. A prompt appears asking whether you want to Make an Audio CD or Make a Data CD. In this case we're going with Make a Data CD, so select that and click Next.**

9. **Wait for the burn process to complete and the disc to eject.**

10. **Click Finish.**

Burning music to an audio CD

If you aren't sure on what type of player you'll eventually play the CD, it's safest to burn it as an audio CD. That way, older CD players are more likely to be able to read it, as well as home stereo CD players that don't support digital formats like MP3.

You can use Windows to burn to an audio CD. Just follow the same steps as in the previous section, but in Step 8, choose Make an Audio CD instead.

You can also use Windows Media Player to burn an audio CD. First you create a playlist on the Burn tab, and then you insert a blank disc and issue the Burn command. It's pretty much automated after that point; you just sit back and wait for your disc to pop out, ready to use.

Follow these steps in Windows Media Player to burn a CD:

1. **Click the Burn tab. The Burn list opens in the main window.**

   Note that there is nothing on the Burn list by default.

2. **Drag the tracks from the file list to the Burn tab's pane.**

3. **Insert a blank writeable CD into your CD or DVD drive, and then click the Start Burn button.**

4. **Wait for the burn process to complete.**

   It will take several minutes. You can monitor the progress onscreen. When it's finished, the disc ejects automatically.

Synchronizing a portable device

Windows Media Player doesn't work with iPods, but it does work with a wide variety of other digital music players, both old and new. You can easily copy your favorite music to your portable device and take your tunes with you wherever you go. To sync files, connect your portable music player to the computer. Then drag music files to the Sync tab, just like you did with the Burn tab in the previous section. Then click Start Sync, and off you go.

Streaming music to other people

Even though Windows Media Player isn't required to stream music to other PCs, it does have some streaming controls built into it. Click the Stream button, as shown in Figure 18-9, and select a streaming option from the sub-menu that appears. Each option opens a different configuration dialog box.

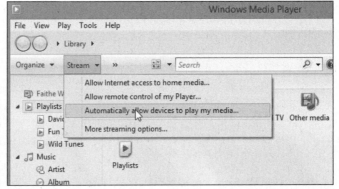

Figure 18-9:
This menu contains streaming options.

Some of these options can come in very handy. For example, with Internet Home Media Access, you can listen to music that's saved on your home computer while you're travelling — provided, of course, that your home computer remains turned on and connected to the Internet while you're gone. The Allow Remote Control feature enables other computers and devices to push (copy) music, pictures, and videos to Windows Media Player on your PC.

Understanding Speech Technologies

Windows supports some very basic speech technologies, but if you use the features frequently, you will probably want some third-party software to make the process more reliable and customizable.

When we talk about speech technologies, I'm basically talking about three features:

- ✓ **Reading text out loud (text to speech):** The computer reads text out loud to you. If you want the text in a document read to you, open the document in an application that supports speech, like Microsoft Word, and then use the application's speech feature. (In Office applications it's called Speak.)

- ✓ **Dictating text into a microphone (speech to text):** You speak into a microphone and the computer types what you say into the application and data file you have open. This feature is part of the Windows Speech Recognition application that comes with Windows; you can also use third-party applications such as Dragon Naturally Speaking.

- ✓ **Controlling Windows using a microphone:** You speak into the microphone and the computer follows your instructions. This feature is also part of the Windows Speech Recognition application.

If you want everything onscreen read to you (file names, dialog box messages, and so on), check out Narrator, one of Windows' Ease of Access tools. People who are visually impaired often use Narrator to interpret the Windows desktop for them verbally.

Reading written text aloud

To have Windows read dialog boxes to you (useful if you're blind, for example), turn on Narrator. From the start screen, type Narrator, and then in the search results, click Narrator. To turn the Narrator off, close its dialog box.

To have Word or some other Office application read data files to you, enable the Speak feature. The easiest way to make it available is to add it to the Quick Access toolbar (QAT). To do so, follow these steps:

1. **At the far right end of the QAT, click the down arrow button (Customize Quick Access toolbar) and then click More Commands.**

2. **In the Choose commands from list, select All Commands.**

3. **Scroll down to the Speak command, select it, and click Add. See Figure 18-10.**

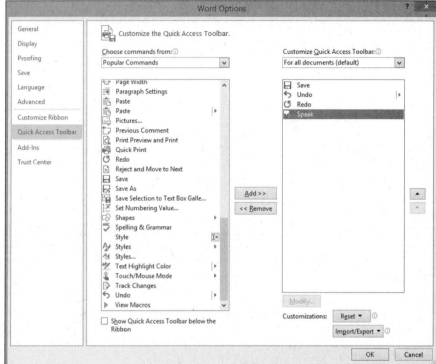

Figure 18-10:
Customizing
the Quick
Access
toolbar for
the Speak
command.

4. Click OK.

Then, whenever you want to use the Speak command, click its icon on the QAT.

Now, to practice, type some text in Word (or whatever application you are working with), select the text (Ctrl+A is one way), and then click the Speak button on the QAT. The application reads the text to you.

Setting up a microphone

Before you start doing anything that involves speaking into a microphone, you should go through Windows' microphone setup process. From Windows 8, display the Start screen, and then type *microphone*. In the search results that appear, click Set Up a Microphone. Then follow the prompts to complete the setup.

Dictating text using a microphone

To dictate text into an application, you must have an application that supports voice input, or you must use voice input software that works in multiple applications.

There are two kinds of voice input software: voice recognition and speech recognition. *Voice recognition software* recognizes spoken words that match words in its database. It does not pay attention to the tone or inflection of the speaker's voice. People who speak with a heavy accent may have difficulty with such software. Voice recognition is included with Microsoft Windows and Microsoft Office. *Speech recognition software* is teachable software that learns an individual's pronunciation and vocal inflection. Each user trains the software by reading long passages of text into the microphone; the software records what each word sounds like when that person pronounces it, and can also learn new words.

To set up Speech Recognition in Windows 8.1, from the Start screen, type Speech and then click Windows Speech Recognition and follow the prompts.

After you set up Speech Recognition, you can use it as-is. (It may make some mistakes, but you can correct them using the keyboard.) When the Speech Recognition application is running, a small toolbar floats at the top of the Windows desktop. You can click the big round microphone button to signal that you are ready to dictate a command, or you can say *start listening*. See Figure 18-11.

Figure 18-11: Click the round microphone button.

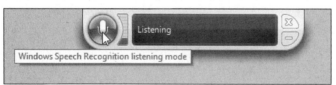

To train the application to understand you better, right-click anywhere in its toolbar and choose Configuration➪Improve Voice Recognition. The Speech Recognition Voice Training wizard runs. Follow the prompts to train Windows in your voice pattern. As you can see in Figure 18-12, the wizard puts text up onscreen for you to read into the microphone, and it notes how you pronounce certain words. If you do enough of this training, it can learn to recognize the way you talk even if you have a heavy or unusual accent.

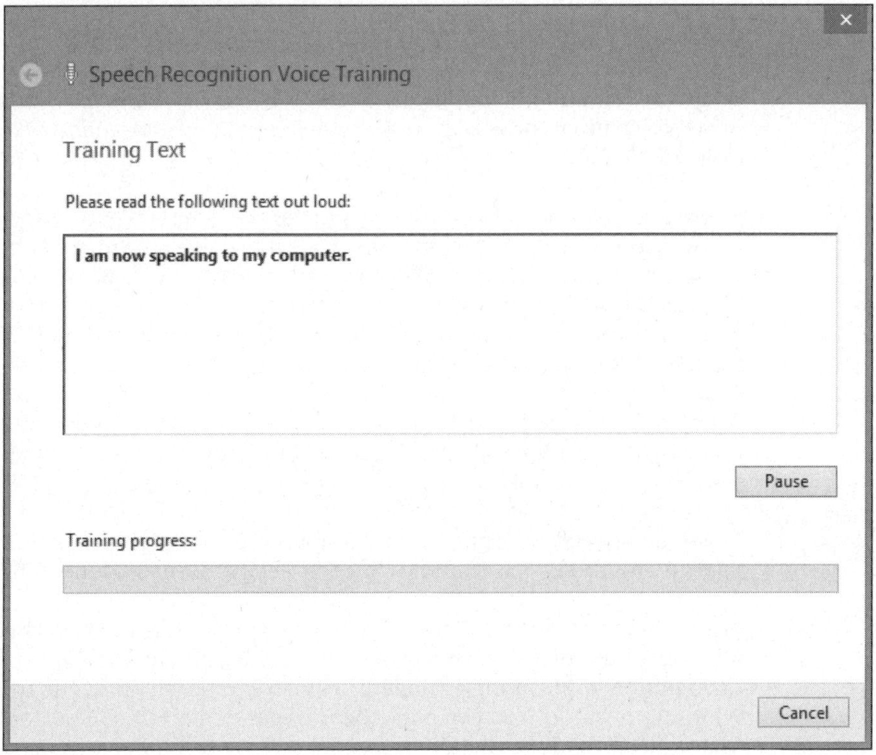

Figure 18-12:
Speech
Recognition
Voice
Training.

Controlling Windows using a microphone

Windows Speech Recognition recognizes many short, simple commands.
To get a list of them, you can say *what can I say?* into the microphone when
Windows Speech Recognition is enabled. You can also look up a list of them
in the Help and Support tool.

Understanding Digital Video

Next, take a look at digital video. Conceptually, digital video takes the basic
idea of a digital still image, like the ones you learned about in Chapter 17, and
combines them with the idea of sampling that you learned about earlier in this
chapter. Rather than sampling audio, it samples images. Then it plays back
the still images in rapid succession, giving the appearance of motion video.

Video formats

A digital video clip may seem like just one file, but it is actually a container file that holds both audio and video data. There are lots of different specifications, not only for the container files but for the audio and video data inside them, and I'm not going to get into the details of all of the possible combinations of those here. (You're welcome.) The main things you need to know are

- At a very basic compatibility level, you need a playback application that can read the file format of the container file (like .mov or .avi, for example).

- Because each video file is a container, one may have differently formatted audio and video contents inside it than another. That's why an application supporting a certain file extension is no guarantee that it will be able to play *all* files with that extension.

- Whether an application supports a particular video file depends on the codecs used. Remember codecs from earlier in the chapter? A *codec* is a coder/decoder. For an application to be able to play a certain video file, it must have the correct codecs that match up with the ones used to encode the file's content.

Table 18-2 lists some of the most popular digital video formats.

Table 18-2	Common Digital Video Formats	
Format	*Extension*	*Notes*
Adobe Flash Video	.flv	The streaming format used by YouTube.
AVI	.avi	A very popular file format for video clips on computers.
Flash media (Shockwave)	.swf	Common for creating animated and sometimes interactive demos and games.
GIF	.gif	Very simple animation, no audio. Commonly used for web banner ads.
M4V	.m4v	Developed by Apple and used on iTunes. Similar to MPEG-4 but may have DRM.
MPEG-1	.mpg, .mp2, .mpeg, .mpg, .mpe, .mpv	An older format, but there's still a lot of content out there in this format
MPEG-4	.mp4, .m4p, .m4v	A high-quality format used for many full-length digital movies.

(continued)

Table 18-2 *(continued)*

Format	Extension	Notes
QuickTime	.mov or .qt	Originally developed by Apple.
RealMedia	.rm, .rmvb	Made for the RealPlayer application.
Windows Media Video	.wmv	A Microsoft format, widely supported for content from home video cameras.

A couple of the formats in Table 18-2 deserve special mention because they're different from the others: Adobe Flash Media and GIF.

Adobe Flash Media

Flash media (.swf) is a very versatile format for creating animated, and sometimes interactive, demos and games. Other names for this format are Shockwave and Macromedia Flash. (Macromedia was the company that developed Flash; it was acquired by Adobe.)

Flash media is commonly used in education because of its interactivity. It's a video clip, but it's also a mini application in some ways. Not only can a Flash clip show movement through a process, but it can accept mouse clicks from a viewer. So, for example, after illustrating a process, the clip can offer a multiple-choice quiz for review, with the viewer clicking the answers.

Animated GIF

Animated GIFs are not really videos in the traditional sense. An animated GIF is a special type of graphic that stores multiple versions of itself in a single file and flips through them in sequence, like an animation created by flipping the corners of a book. When the file is displayed — on a presentation slide, a web page, or some other place — it cycles through the still graphics at a certain speed, making a very rudimentary animation. You cannot control the animation of an animated GIF, nor can you set it up to repeat a certain number of times and then stop. That information is contained within the GIF file itself. The application or file that plays it back (for example, a web page) simply reads that information and plays the GIF accordingly. They are more like animated clip art than real videos.

Applications for playing videos and movies

When you double-click a video clip, it plays using whatever application is set up to be the default for that file extension. If you haven't installed another video playback application, videos will probably open in Windows Media Player on your Windows PC. Figure 18-13 shows Window Media Player playing a high-resolution video. It adjusts the window size to match the video's resolution. Notice that the controls at the bottom of the screen are the same when playing a movie as when playing audio.

Figure 18-13: Windows Media Player playing a high-resolution video.

DVD movies are a different story from single-file video clips. When you pop a DVD disc into your computer, the application designated to play DVD movies runs (if you have one). Your computer may come with a DVD movie player application, or you might choose to buy one such as RealPlayer Plus, WinX, or CyberLink PowerDVD. This software provides an interface you can use to watch movies on DVD and Blu-ray discs (provided, of course, you have an appropriate disc drive).

On some versions of Windows, Windows Media Player plays DVD movies just fine, and on others it doesn't. If Windows Media Player won't play DVDs, you are missing the codec needed for them.

If you have Windows 7 Home Premium, Ultimate, or Enterprise, you should have the DVD codec for WMP already. If you have some other Windows 7 version, you don't.

In Windows 8 and 8.1, neither the regular nor the Pro version contains the DVD codec, but you can get it in the Windows Store. (Look for the DVD Player add-on.) For earlier Windows versions, go to `http://windows.microsoft.com/en-us/windows/windows-media-player-plug-ins`.

Before you put down the money for the WMP DVD codec, though, see whether there is some other application installed on your PC that will play DVD movies. Most PCs that come with a DVD drive also come with such software.

How DVDs store movies

The video portion of a typical movie is sampled at 24 frames per second (fps), so if you'll picture 24x the number of seconds in the movie, multiplied by the number of pixels in each frame, multiplied by the number of bits used to describe each pixel, you get some idea of how much space we're talking about here. (And don't forget to add in the audio soundtrack that goes along with the video portion too.)

So, to fit a whole two-hour movie on a single DVD disc, that movie has to be compressed quite a bit. Fortunately, DVD movies are encoded in the MPEG-2 format, which is a format that compresses digital content very efficiently. A DVD player in a home theater system contains an MPEG-2 decoder, which decodes and decompresses the data on-the-fly as it plays the movie. DVD player software in your computer does the same thing, using a software codec that decodes the MPEG-2 format.

If you explore a DVD disc using File Explorer, you'll see that there are two folders on it: AUDIO_TS and VIDEO_TS. AUDIO_TS is empty; that's normal. The entire movie, both audio and video, is in the VIDEO_TS folder. The main files have a .vob extension; all the other files in the folder are smaller helper files.

Most commercially produced DVDs include some type of encryption to prevent unauthorized copying. The encryption code is different for various countries and regions; in the United States, Region 1 encoding is used. Your DVD player includes a decoder for the encryption, so you don't even notice it's there.

Streaming audio and video on the web

Some websites enable you to download audio and video files just like the ones you work with on your local PC. However, it is more common for a website to provide streaming audio and video instead of downloads.

Streaming video is stored on a file server on the Internet somewhere, and delivered on-demand to computers that request it via a web interface. *Streaming audio* is the same thing except it's just an audio track. When you play streaming audio or video, the data is transferred to your computer just long enough to play it, and then deleted; the clip isn't stored on your computer.

Why streaming audio and video? Here are some reasons:

- ✔ **To prevent people from keeping it**. Say you're a musician. You might let people stream your music for free, but if they want to download it for keeps, they should have to pay.

- ✔ **To prevent people from redistributing it.** Same deal here. If you have a musical product to sell, you don't want people to give it away or sell it without you getting a cut of that.

- ✔ **Because people don't want to own it forever.** Some videos are fun to watch once, but you don't want them clogging up your hard disk indefinitely.

YouTube is the largest streaming video site on the Internet, with millions of video clips. Most of these are uploaded by individuals and companies, who use the YouTube site as free hosting space for their content. Figure 18-14 shows the YouTube website after a search for *cute kittens*. Because that's really what we need to see more videos of, right? You could click on any of the search results to watch the movie on the web page. You don't need a separate viewer application.

To play YouTube videos, you need the Adobe Flash Player plug-in to be installed in your web browser. Most web browsers come with that plug-in, and the ones that don't can easily get it for free the first time it is called for. YouTube accepts uploads in many different formats, but it then makes them all available the same way, in Adobe Flash Video format, so the people who log in to view them don't have to have all those different codecs; all they need is the Adobe Flash Player.

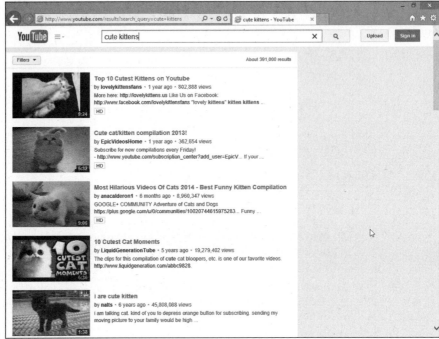

Figure 18-14:
Cat videos
on YouTube.

Although YouTube is the most popular streaming web site, it is far from the only one. For example, sites like Pandora stream audio files.

Several different audio and video player applications also accept streaming input, including

- QuickTime, which streams .mov files
- RealMedia, which streams .rm files
- Windows Media Player, which streams .wma, .wmv, and .asf files
- Adobe Flash player, which streams .flv and .swf files

Some streaming sites enable you to pause and restart a streaming clip; others, like Internet radio services, simply send whatever is being currently broadcast, like regular broadcast radio and TV, and you can't pause it.

Creating and Editing Audio and Video

Digital video cameras are inexpensive these days, and most smart phones can record audio and video, so almost everybody is a potential videographer. You can easily transfer footage from your smart phone or a digital video camera to your computer for editing.

Audio editing applications

Many applications are available for editing audio tracks. For example, the freeware program Audacity (`audacity.sourceforge.net`) lets you import multiple audio tracks, trim out the parts you don't require, and then splice everything together. Mac users can record and mix digital piano, guitar, and drum tracks in the excellent GarageBand application. You can also buy more full-featured products such as Adobe Audition. Figure 18-15 shows Audacity. The squiggles are visual representations of the sounds.

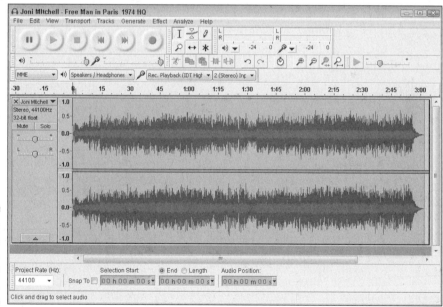

Figure 18-15: Audacity is an audio-editing application.

Video editing applications

Microsoft has a free Windows Movie Maker program that you can use to trim and combine video clips and photos and to add a sound track or commentary. On a Mac, iMovie offers slick tools to quickly create your own mini movie. Neither of these programs will tax your computer's processor, but if you want to create professional-looking movies, you need to use a dedicated video-editing program such as Sony Vegas Pro or Adobe Director. As with the animation and 3D graphics programs described earlier, you need a powerful computer; a quad-core or eight-core processor and powerful graphics card are essential for professional video editing.

Editing a digital video with Windows Movie Maker

When you shoot video with a video camera, it's just raw footage. You will probably want to edit it to make something more artistic. Some of the things you can do include

- ✔ Trimming the video clip to remove sections of it

- ✔ Adding a voice-over narration

- ✔ Adding a music clip as a soundtrack

- ✔ Adding text that appears over the video image

- ✔ Adding still images and applying transition effects between them (like a slide show)

There are many professional-quality video editing programs, but for casual use, Windows Movie Maker works just fine. It can do everything on that list and more. To get a free copy, go to `http://windows.microsoft.com/en-US/Windows-Live/movie-maker` and click Download Now.

You'll need to shift your thinking about editing when using Windows Movie Maker. In programs like Word, when you edit a file, you work directly on that file, and save your changes to it. But Windows Movie Maker doesn't work like that. You don't open and edit videos directly. Instead, you create a movie project file, and you import your video into it. The video footage is just one element out of many in the project. Other elements may include voice-over narration, text superimposed text over video, and still images.

Suppose you have some video footage that you've shot with your digital video camera or smart phone. Here's how to start a movie project with it in Windows Movie Maker:

1. **Start Windows Movie Maker, and on the Home tab, click Add Videos and Photos.**

2. **Select the video that you want to include and click Open. Wait for the file to be imported. The complete movie appears in the right pane. A preview pane appears on the left.**

3. **Click the Play/Pause button under the preview pane to see the video as it is to start with. See Figure 18-16.**

Vertical line shows what part of the clip is playing in the Preview pane

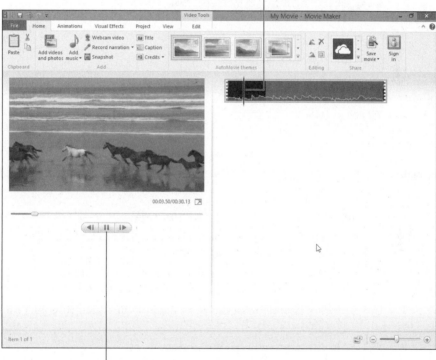

Figure 18-16:
Click Play to
watch the
video.

Play/Pause

4. **Click the Animations tab and point to one of the transitions.**

    The video previews its opening with that transition applied.

5. **Click the Visual Effects tab, and then point at one of the effects.**

    The view previews with that effect applied.

6. **On the Home tab, click Title.**

    A title slide appears before the video clip with the generic text My Movie on it. See Figure 18-17.

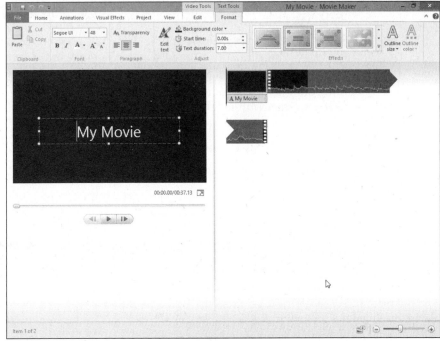

Figure 18-17:
A title
slide with
a generic
caption.

7. **Edit the text to show the title you want to assign to the movie.**

8. **On the Text Tools Format tab, open the Background Color button's gallery and choose a different color.**

9. **On the Text Tools Format tab, point at several of the thumbnails in the Effects group to see what they do, and then click one you like.**

10. **On the right side of the screen, click the video (the part after the title you just added).**

11. **On the Home tab, click Caption.**

    A text appears in the preview area, with the generic text *Enter text here.*

12. **Replace the generic text with text of your choice.**

13. **Click the Play button to see your video.**

14. **Choose File⇨Save Project to save your video project. The project is saved in .wlmp format.**

This is not a movie yet; it's still just a project. To learn how to make it an actual movie, see the next section.

Outputting your digital video project

When you are ready to output your project to a movie, you have a variety of
options. You can

✔ **Publish the movie directly to a variety of online sites.** To do this, use the
File➪Publish Movie command. You can publish to OneDrive, Facebook,
YouTube, Vimeo, Flickr, or Microsoft Groups. See Figure 18-18.

Figure 18-18:
Publish your
video to an
online site.

✔ **Save the movie to your hard drive, in a variety of resolution choices.**
To do this, use the File➪Save Movie command. You can save for high-
definition display (large size), for a regular computer (medium size),
or for email (small size). You can also save for various types of smart
phones and various websites (such as Blip.TV, DailyMotion, Facebook,
or Flickr). See Figure 18-19.

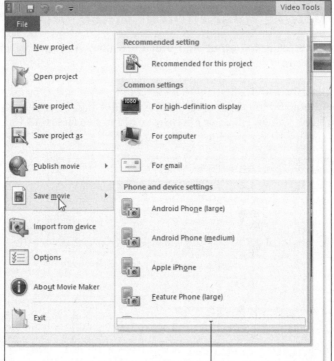

Figure 18-19:
Save your
movie to
your hard
drive.

Move mouse pointer here to scroll for more choices

Part VI
The Part of Tens

Check out www.dummies.com/extras/digitalliteracy for a list of ten websites you ought to know about.

In this part . . .

- ✔ Get ideas for troubleshooting common computer problems.

- ✔ Learn tips for working productively with Windows 8.1.

Chapter 19

Ten Computer Problems (and How to Solve Them)

In This Chapter

▶ Understanding why your computer won't start up

▶ Figuring out why your Internet connection is down

▶ Understanding why Windows is acting weird or running slowly

▶ Discovering why your favorite game won't run right

So, when you went to bed last night, your computer was fine, but when you turned it on this morning, something's wrong. *Wrong* could be anything from "it doesn't work at all" to "it seems a little slower."

The annoying part about computer problems is that the computer can't usually tell you where it hurts — well, not directly anyway. Your computer can't say to you, "Ya know, that new driver you installed for your mouse, it just isn't setting well with me" or "I think that last email attachment you opened gave me a virus."

Although computers aren't very communicative about their problems, they are at least pretty consistent. The same bad things happen to a lot of computers. In this chapter, I run down ten things that I've seen a lot of in my years of work with computers, and tell you what to do about them.

Your Computer Has No Power, No Nothing

You press the power button, but nothing happens. Not a great way to start the day. Don't panic, though. This is actually one of the easier problems to troubleshoot because there are only a limited number of possible causes.

First, check the power outlet. Is there perhaps a light switch in your home that controls that outlet that someone has flipped? If the computer plugs into a surge protecting power strip, does it have an on/off rocker switch on it that may have gotten flipped? You'd be surprised how often these types of power issues turn out to be the culprit. Plug something else into the same outlet, like a lamp, to make sure there is power.

If you're sure the outlet is not to blame, start working from the computer's power cord inward. Check the power cord: Are there any chew marks on it from your pets? Is it securely plugged into the computer? On a notebook power cord, there are usually two segments, and they join together at the big boxy block (the transformer). Even if the cord is plugged into the wall and into the computer, you might still have a loose connection where the cord plugs into the transformer.

It's possible that the problem isn't hardware-related at all, but caused by software. Windows enables you to put it into Sleep mode, where it appears to be off but it's actually in a low-power state. Sometimes a computer isn't able to wake up from Sleep, and will appear to be dead. Luckily, there's an easy fix for that. Press and hold the computer's power button for 10 seconds, and then release it. Doing so will clear away any low-power state that the computer might be in. Then press the power button again to see if the computer will start up.

With all that out of the way, assume that it really is the computer at fault. On a desktop computer, the power supply (the big silver box where the power cord plugs in) is a likely candidate. When you turn the computer on, its fan should spin up. If it doesn't, the power supply may be kaput. Don't assume that it's the power supply, though, and run out to buy a new one. There are several components that, if they're blown, will cause the computer to seem dead. One is the motherboard, for example. At this point, it's time to take the computer to a repair shop.

Windows Won't Start Up Normally

When you power on your computer, Windows is supposed to load and the desktop or Start screen is supposed to appear. If the computer gets hung up sometime during that process, something may be wrong with Windows, or with one of the programs that is trying to load itself at startup.

First off, make a note of the error message that appears, and go look it up on the Internet (on a different computer, of course, because yours isn't working). There are many good online reference sources that can interpret an error message for you.

With Windows 8, if your computer fails to start up, an Advanced Startup Options menu appears, offering you some choices, as in Figure 19-1. Depending on your computer, you may not have the UEFI Firmware Settings item.

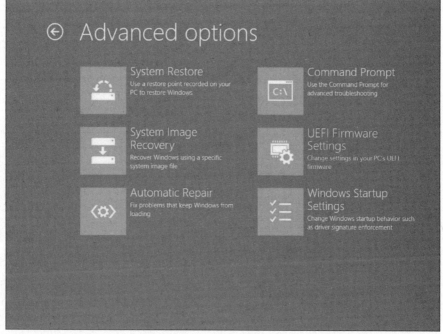

Figure 19-1:
The
Windows 8
Advanced
Startup
Options
menu.

From this screen, you have the following choices:

- ✔ **System Restore:** This is a good first start. If Windows isn't starting right because of a recent change to system settings, System Restore can help you by going back to an earlier system state. You'd be amazed how often this fixes the problem.

- ✔ **System Image Recovery:** This option enables you to return your computer to a previous state using a disk image file. (Unless you happen to have a backup that is stored as a disk image — and most people don't— this option isn't going to do you any good.)

- ✔ **Startup Repair:** Here's a good place to go if System Restore doesn't solve the problem. You'll be prompted to choose your user account and enter your password. Then Windows starts a diagnostic routine that examines your account, including the drivers and applications you have set to load at startup, and helps you fix the problem. This is a great option for someone without a lot of techie knowledge, as it doesn't require many decisions on your part.

- ✔ **Command Prompt:** If you're a power-user with knowledge of command-line commands, you will appreciate this option, which lets you type commands directly to the computer. Most people don't have the knowledge to do that, though.

✔ **Startup Settings:** Choose this option to reboot to a Startup Settings menu, which is similar to the startup menu that you could access in previous Windows versions by pressing F8 as the computer was booting. See Figure 19-2. From here you can start up in Safe Mode, which disables all non-essential drivers and services, so you can troubleshoot problems with devices or applications that may be preventing Windows from starting normally.

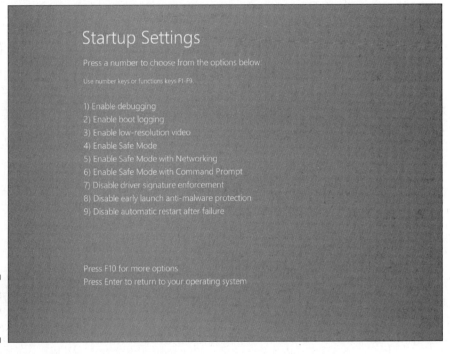

Figure 19-2: Startup Settings.

Startup Settings

Press a number to choose from the options below:

Use number keys or functions keys F1-F9.

1) Enable debugging
2) Enable boot logging
3) Enable low-resolution video
4) Enable Safe Mode
5) Enable Safe Mode with Networking
6) Enable Safe Mode with Command Prompt
7) Disable driver signature enforcement
8) Disable early launch anti-malware protection
9) Disable automatic restart after failure

Press F10 for more options
Press Enter to return to your operating system

Everything's Running Slower than Normal

If Windows starts up but appears sluggish, there could be a variety of causes. There may be a malware infection, or it may not like a recent Windows Update that was installed or a recent driver update.

First of all, though, have you tried rebooting? I mean really rebooting, not just putting your computer into Sleep and waking it up again. To do a full reboot, go to the Start screen, click the Power button, and click Restart.

System Restore

After rebooting, System Restore is a good first thing to try. As you learned in the previous section, System Restore returns your system files to an earlier version (where, presumably, your computer worked better). You can get to System Restore while Windows is running by doing the following:

1. **In the Control Panel, choose System and Security, and then choose System.**

2. **In the navigation bar on the left, choose System Protection.**

   The System Properties dialog box opens with the System protection tab displayed.

3. **Click the System Restore button. The System Restore utility runs. Click Next.**

4. **Choose a restore point. Choose one that was saved right before you started having the problem (if you remember when that was).**

   See Figure 19-3. If you aren't sure what programs may be affected by going back to that point, click Scan for Affected Programs. The results that appear will tell you what you might need to do after the system restore to re-update the things that will be un-updated. Click Close to close the report window. Then click Next to continue.

5. Click Finish. Then wait for the system restore operation to complete.

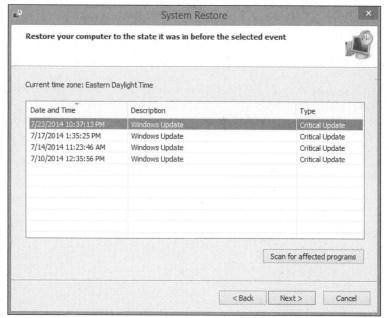

Figure 19-3:
The System
Restore
dialog box.

Refreshing Windows

Problem solved? Great. Problem not solved? You might try refreshing your system files. This isn't a complete reinstall of Windows, and it doesn't affect your data. It just makes sure nothing is amiss in your Windows installation.

Follow these steps to refresh Windows 8.1:

1. **On the Charms bar, click the Settings icon, and then click Change PC Settings.**

2. **Click Update and recovery, and then click Recovery.**

3. **Under the Refresh Your PC Without Affecting Your Files heading, click Get Started.**

4. **Follow the prompts to refresh Windows.**

   You may be asked to insert your Windows installation disc. (If Windows came preinstalled, you might need to dig out the disc from the materials that came with the computer.)

If you don't have a Windows disc, your system probably came with a utility for making a set of recovery discs using your DVD drive and blank DVDs. You did do this when prompted when you first got your computer, right? If you didn't, you might still be able to. Check your system documentation to find out how.

You Have No Internet Access

You don't know what you've got till it's gone. And you don't truly appreciate your Internet connection until it goes away. But when it does — oh, the pain.

The first question to ask: Are other computers in my home (or office) able to use the Internet? If no, start at the Internet connection. If yes, start trouble-shooting with your own PC.

Check your Internet connection

Check the cable modem, DSL modem, or whatever other box delivers Internet to your home. Are most of the lights on, with only one or two flashing inter-mittently? That's normal. Are only a couple of lights on, with perhaps one of them flashing in a steady pattern? That means there's a problem.

Unplug the modem from the wall outlet, or power it off (if it has a power button) and leave it unpowered for at least 20 seconds. Then turn it back on and give it a few minutes to restart itself. Sometimes this is enough to solve the problem.

Check with your Internet provider to find out if there are any known issues in your area with service being down. Sometimes service goes out for an hour or so, and you just have to wait it out. If you can't get the modem to provide service, you're stuck until it does.

Check your router

If the Internet itself is working but you can't get it on a specific computer, perhaps the router — the device that's sharing the Internet connection among all the PCs — is having a problem. On some modems, the router is built into the modem; if your modem doesn't include a router, you have a separate router box that connects to the modem, and all the computers connect to the router (either with cables or wirelessly).

If you aren't sure whether the problem is the modem or the router, connect a PC directly to the modem using a cable. If the Internet works, you know the problem is with the router.

Power the router off for 20 seconds and then back on again; this sometimes corrects a problem by forcing the router to reset.

Check your computer

Look in the notification area in Windows for a network icon. (Point to the icon to see its name.) With a cable connection, if you don't have a network icon, you don't have network connectivity. With a wireless connection, if you are connected to the router (or modem) you see a series of stairstep bars. If you see a star on the stairsteps, wireless networks are available but you aren't connected to them. If you see a red X on the stairsteps, your wireless network adapter is disabled or there aren't any networks available.

Right-click the network icon and choose Troubleshoot Problems. Then use the troubleshooting wizard that appears to step through a troubleshooting process that may include resetting your wireless adapter.

Some notebook computers have a button that toggles the wireless network adapter on/off. If you accidentally press that button, your wireless adapter won't work until you press it again. An easy fix, but also easy to overlook.

You Can't Get Email

If you can access web pages just fine but your email application gives you an error when you try to send or receive mail, it's probably not your fault (and not your computer's fault either). Unless you have recently changed your mail settings, your mail server is probably temporarily unavailable, through no fault of your own. If you wait an hour or so, it will probably be back up again. You can also try restarting the computer.

One of the mistakes that beginners make is to try to mess with their mail settings when the mail server is temporarily unavailable. Mail settings don't just magically become wrong. If they worked before, they should work still, unless you have changed providers or changed your email password. Experimenting with mail settings without understanding them can cause more problems than it solves.

An Application Stops Responding

When an application crashes in Windows, it stops responding to commands. Here are some clues that an application has crashed:

- ✔ The menus and toolbars no longer respond.
- ✔ A white haze appears over the entire application window.
- ✔ A [Not Responding] indicator appears in the title bar.
- ✔ The mouse pointer does not appear when it is over that window.
- ✔ The window can't be moved, resized, or minimized.
- ✔ An error message box appears letting you know the program has stopped responding, asking whether you want to close the program or wait.

Sometimes you can wait out a crash, because it is not really a crash, but merely a temporary bog-down. Over time, you will learn which applications tend to bog down and say they have stopped responding, only to bounce back to life a minute later.

Assuming that waiting doesn't solve the problem, you can terminate the application. If you get the error message offering to close the program, choosing to close it that way is an easy path. You can also right-click the unresponsive program on the taskbar and choose Close, and this will usually cause that error message box to appear with the offer to close it.

If you don't get any prompt that offers to help you close the program, and it won't close normally (for example, by clicking its Close button in its window), you can shut it down via Task Manager. To display Task Manager, right-click the taskbar and choose Task Manager. Click the Processes tab, as shown in Figure 19-4. (If you don't see any tabs, click More details.) Click the non-responsive program under the Apps heading, and click End task.

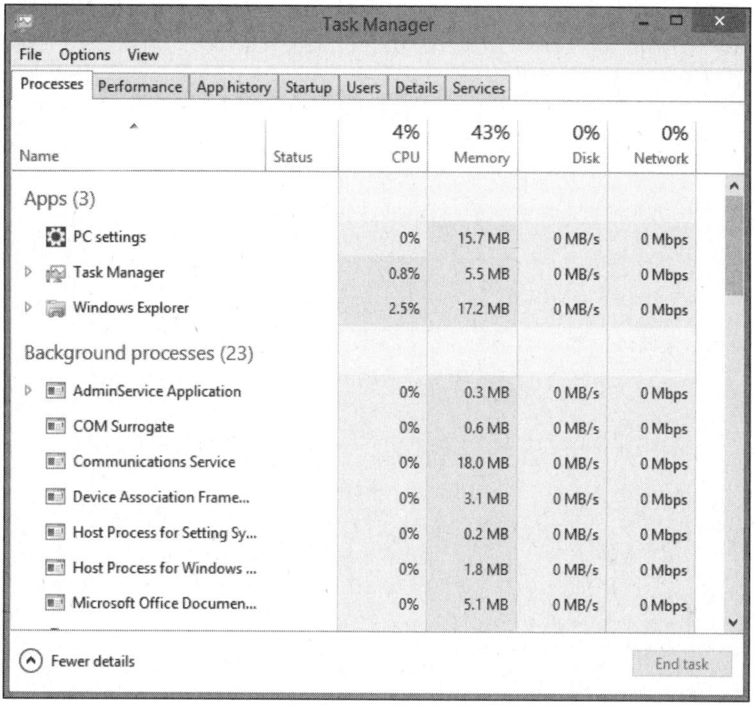

Figure 19-4: The Task Manager dialog box.

The larger question, after you get the program shut down, is *why did it crash in the first place?* Try restarting your computer. If the problem reoccurs with the same application, check for updates for the application that might solve the problem. If the crashing is repeated, try uninstalling and reinstalling the application.

You Get the Blue Screen of Death

Ah, the dreaded Blue Screen of Death (BSOD). It's been around for many Windows versions now, and it always spells doom. A BSOD is a serious error message that appears on a bright blue screen, letting you know that a problem has occurred that is so severe that Windows had to stop. After you read the error message (and probably can't make heads or tails of it), your only recourse is to press the computer's power button to shut it off, and then turn it back on again and hope the problem doesn't reoccur.

As of Windows 8, the error messages on the BSOD are somewhat less cryptic than they used to be. Figure 19-5 shows one from Windows 8 that even has a smiley face on it (sort of).

If you get one BSOD message, you can just ignore it. However, if you get the same message over and over (several times a week, for example), you should investigate the cause of it. BSOD message are often hardware-related; have you installed new hardware lately? Have you updated a device driver? Follow the advice in the error message (Figure 19-5 for example) and look up the error code online.

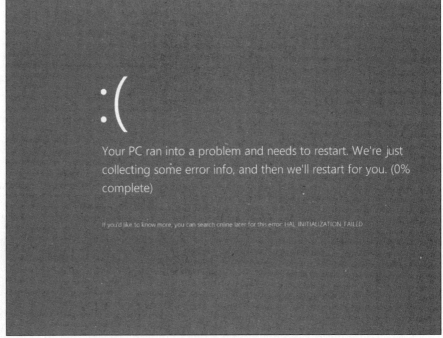

Figure 19-5:
A
Windows 8
error
message.

You See Frequent Pop-Up Ads on the Web

If you suddenly start getting a lot of pop-up ads while you are using the web, especially when the ads don't relate to the page you are looking at, your computer is probably infected with adware.

First, remove the adware. Look through your list of installed programs in the Control Panel and see if there's anything you don't recognize, like a special toolbar application; these are often adware-related. Run an anti-malware utility to find and remove any additional malware your system may have acquired. There are many free online scanning tools, including

- ✔ **TrendMicro HouseCall:** `http://housecall.trendmicro.com/`
- ✔ **Bitdefender QuickScan:** `www.bitdefender.com/scanner/online/free.html`
- ✔ **Microsoft Safety Scanner:** `www.microsoft.com/security/scanner/en-us/default.aspx`

The next question is *How did this adware get through your existing security software?* (I'm assuming you have security software. You should.) Maybe your security software needs an update, or maybe it has somehow gotten disabled. Perhaps you clicked Yes instead of No when a website asked if it could install a helpful toolbar, or perhaps you visited a website that downloaded malware to your computer that for some reason your security software didn't notice. Maybe your web browser's security settings are set too low. Take this opportunity to do a thorough security evaluation of your computer and see if you can't patch some of those weaknesses with more robust and up-to-date security measures.

Your System Has No Sound

If you aren't hearing any sound, but you've had sound in the past on your computer, you've probably accidentally muted the sound. There are a variety of ways to do so.

Look in the notification area and see if there is a red circle and diagonal line on the speaker icon. That means the sound is muted. Click the speaker icon and then click the Mute button at the bottom of the slider to toggle the sound back on again, or drag the volume slider up.

Now, figure out how you might have turned the sound off, so you can avoid doing it again. Some keyboards have a button that mutes the sound; you may have pressed it accidentally. Learn the positions of the keyboard shortcuts for adjusting the sound volume. For example, on my notebook computer, I can adjust the sound by pressing the Fn key along with the F7, F8, and F9 keys, to mute, decrease, and increase the volume, respectively.

If the sound icon isn't present in the notification area at all, or if it's unavailable (gray and unresponsive), there may be a problem with your sound card (audio adapter). In the Control Panel, use Device Manager to check the status of your sound card. To do so, right-click the Start button (Windows 8.1) and choose Device Manager. Then expand the Sound, Video, and Game Controllers category and double-click the entry for your sound card. In Figure 19-6, it's called an Audio Device, and it appears to be working normally.

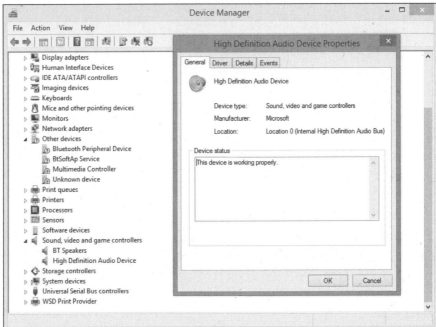

Figure 19-6:
A dialog box
in Device
Manager.

The Video in a Game Is Messed Up

Picture this: You buy the latest and greatest game, and you install it on your PC. It seems to install okay, but a half hour or so into the game, you start seeing weird white patches on the landscape of the background. When your character jumps off buildings, sometimes it seems like he sinks knee-deep into what should be solid rock. It's just weird, the different video quirks you run into.

You've probably got some sort of incompatibility going between your current display adapter's driver and the game. Many games are extremely picky about which display adapters they will work with, and there may be a list of known issues with certain brands and models of display adapters on the game's support site.

What are your options? Here are some ideas:

- ✔ Update the driver for your display adapter. Get the updated driver from your PC's manufacturer or from the manufacturer of the display adapter.

- ✔ Replace your display adapter with one that the game supports better. (This is an option only on a desktop PC.)

- ✔ Check the game's support website to read about workarounds and expected release dates for bug fixes that may solve the problem.

- ✔ Play the game on a different computer.

Chapter 20

Ten Tips for Working with Windows 8.1

*W*indows 8.1: Some people love it, and some people hate it. But whatever your opinion, it's here to stay — at least until the next version of Windows is released.

Windows 8.1 is a hybrid. It's both a desktop operating system and a tablet, touchscreen-enabled operating system. If you install it on a touchscreen notebook computer, you can tap and drag your way through it just like on a tablet. If you install it on a desktop, you can navigate it with a mouse and keyboard.

No matter how you use Windows 8.1, there are some ways to make it easier and more efficient to use. In this chapter, I outline some of my favorite tips for getting the most out of Windows 8.1.

A lot of what is said here applies to Windows 8.0 also, but not everything. You will rarely run into Windows 8.0, however, because Microsoft offers a free update from Windows 8.0 to Windows 8.1, and that update is automatically installed by default through Windows Update.

Use Search to Start Applications

When you click the down arrow button at the bottom of the Start screen, you see the Apps list, which contains a list of all the apps installed on your computer. There's an alphabetical list, on the left side, and if you scroll to the right, you'll see other lists broken down by categories such as Windows Accessories and Windows System.

However, there's no need to browse the Apps list to find a particular program, and no need to remember what category it's in. To start an application, display the Start screen (pressing the Windows key is one way) and then type the first few letters of the application's name. In the search results that appear, click the application. See Figure 20-1.

Figure 20-1:
The
Windows 8.1
Start screen.

Reorganize the Start Screen

The Start screen contains tiles for many applications, mainly the ones that come free with Windows. These shortcuts are merely suggestions, though; you aren't bound to any of them. Removing a tile from the Start screen doesn't uninstall the application, and you can still access that application from the Apps list any time you want it.

In short, don't be afraid to remove tiles from the Start screen and replace them with tiles for the applications that you actually use on a regular basis. You can always re-pin any applications there that you end up using more than you thought.

To remove a tile, right-click the tile and choose Unpin from Start. See Figure 20-2. Notice that you're not deleting the application. You are just releasing it from being represented on the Start screen.

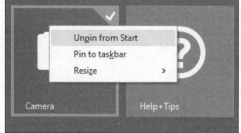

Figure 20-2: Unpin a tile from Start.

If you want to reduce the prominence of a certain tile but you don't want to get rid of it altogether, you can make it smaller. You can change the size of a tile by right-clicking it and choosing Resize. The choices of size will be different depending on the application; Small, Medium, Wide, and Large. Figure 20-3 shows examples of each size.

You can also rearrange the tiles on the Start screen by dragging them. This gets a little tricky because clicking a tile starts its application. You have to click and hold the mouse button down on the tile for a second or two, and then start dragging.

The Start screen's tiles can be arranged in groups. The first group (that is, the leftmost one) is called Main, and it's shown in Figure 20-3. You might have other groups, like Microsoft Office, and you can create your own groups too.

Figure 20-3:
The different
size icons in
Windows 8.1.

To edit the group names on the Start screen, right-click an empty area of the Start screen and choose Name groups. The group names become editable; for example, you could change Main to something else. Scroll to the right to see and work with other groups. When you're done, click an empty area to turn off the name editing mode.

To create a new group, drag-and-drop tiles into the empty area to the right of all other groups. This creates a new group. It doesn't have a name by default. You can name it as described previously.

When your Start screen is all lean and mean, with only essentials on it, you might consider pinning other applications there that you use regularly. To pin an application, do the following:

1. **Click the down arrow button at the bottom of the Start screen to display the Apps list.**

2. **Right-click an app on the list and choose Pin to Start. See Figure 20-4.**

3. **On the Start screen, move and resize the tile as desired.**

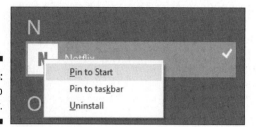

Figure 20-4:
Pin an app
to Start.

Pin Shortcuts to the Taskbar

In that last section, you saw how to pin applications to the Start screen, but a lot of people don't like to use the Start screen; they prefer to work primarily from the desktop.

If you're one of those people, you might appreciate that Windows lets you pin shortcuts to the desktop's taskbar. You could pin all your favorite apps there, and avoid the Start screen altogether 90 percent of the time. Pinned shortcuts on the taskbar appear on the left side, just to the right of the Start button. By default, the taskbar has two pinned shortcuts: Internet Explorer and File Explorer.

Notice in Figure 20-4 that there's a Pin to Taskbar command on the right-click menu for an app. You can use that to pin any application to the Start screen. You can even pin Windows 8-style applications that don't run on the desktop; when you run one of those, Windows switches to full-screen view for that application.

To unpin a shortcut from the taskbar, right-click the icon there and choose Unpin This Program from Taskbar. (I don't recommend unpinning File Explorer, though, because it's an important part of the desktop, and you'll want quick access to it to manage files.)

Make Icons and Text Larger

An LCD screen looks best at its highest resolution (its native resolution), but with today's high-res screens, the highest resolution is pretty darned high. That means that the text and icons on the screen may be very tiny. Unless you have great vision, and just happen to *like* everything being small, that can be a problem. For example, in Figure 20-5, this screen is in 1920 x 1080 resolution and uses the default size for text and icons (Smaller). So tiny! In contrast, Figure 20-6 shows the same screen with text and icons set to the Larger setting.

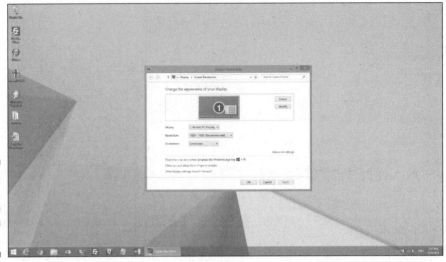

Figure 20-5:
A screen with 1920 x 1080 resolution.

Figure 20-6:
A screen at the Larger resolution setting.

To change the icon and text size without changing the resolution, follow these steps:

1. **Right-click the desktop and choose Screen Resolution.**

2. **Click the Make Text and Other Items Larger or Smaller hyperlink near the bottom of the window. See Figure 20-6.**

3. **In the Change the Size of All Items area, choose the desired size: Smaller, Medium, or Larger. See Figure 20-7.**

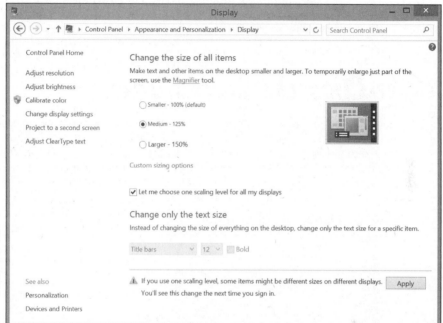

Figure 20-7:
Change
the size of
onscreen
items.

4. **Click Apply. A prompt tells you that you must sign out to apply the changes.**

5. **Click Sign Out Now, and then sign back in to Windows.**

Switch Between Programs Quickly

When you are running multiple applications, there are lots of different ways to switch among them. Try each of these methods out for yourself to see which ones work best:

✔ Hold down the Alt key and press and release the Tab key. Each time you do so, a different application becomes active on the bar that appears in the center of the screen. When the item you want is highlighted, release the Alt key to make that window or application active.

✔ If you're viewing the desktop, click the application's icon on the taskbar.

✔ To switch among Windows 8 style apps, point the mouse pointer to the top left corner of the screen. A thumbnail of the last-used Windows 8 app appears. Click it to switch to it, or move the mouse downward to see a bar containing thumbnails of all open Windows 8 apps, and then click the one you want. If nothing happens when you point at the upper-right corner of the screen, no Windows 8 apps are open.

Right-Click the Start Button

This is my absolute favorite Windows 8.1 trick. From the desktop, right-click the Start button, and a shortcut menu appears. On this shortcut menu are links to almost every utility program you might ever want to access in Windows, including Control Panel, Device Manager, Computer Management, File Explorer, Search, Run, and Power Options. It's all right here. See Figure 20-8.

Figure 20-8:
Find links on the right-click short-cut menu.

Programs and Features
Mobility Center
Power Options
Event Viewer
System
Device Manager
Network Connections
Disk Management
Computer Management
Command Prompt
Command Prompt (Admin)

Task Manager
Control Panel
File Explorer
Search
Run

Shut down or sign out ▶
Desktop

Use Libraries (Or Not)

To review: A *library* is a logical location that combines the contents of multiple folders in a single view. A library enables you to browse files from multiple locations without having to know which of the locations a particular file is actually stored in. Windows has four default libraries: Documents, Music,

Pictures, and Videos. You can also create your own libraries. The Documents library, for example, monitors two folders: the Documents folder (or My Documents folder) for the current Windows user and also the Documents folder (or My Documents) in the Public User folder.

Windows 7 introduced the concept of libraries, and everyone has been slowly getting used to them since then. Conceptually, libraries are a bit difficult to visualize, but by the time Windows 8 came out, most people all pretty comfortable with the idea. However, in Windows 8.1, libraries are disabled by default. Well, not exactly disabled, but not so obviously available anymore. I guess Microsoft gave up on people catching on.

The long and short of it is by default, when you open File Explorer in Windows 8.1, there's no shortcut for Libraries in the navigation bar, and File Explorer opens to the This PC location. See Figure 20-9. Each of those folders in the Folders section of the listing represent system folders for the currently signed-in user. Let me repeat that: They represent the system folders for that user, *not* the libraries (which would also potentially include other monitored locations).

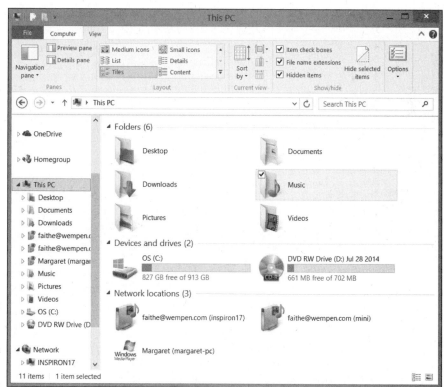

Figure 20-9:
The contents of This PC.

If you want to go back to Windows 8.0 and an earlier way of handling libraries, it's an easy fix. In the navigation pane in File Explorer, right-click and
choose Show Libraries. When you do that, the default location shown when
File Explorer opens is the Libraries list, showing the four default library locations, as in Figure 20-10. The Libraries shortcuts also appear in the navigation
pane.

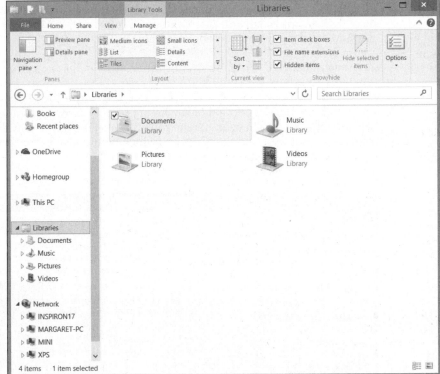

Figure 20-10:
The four
default
library
locations.

Save Location Favorites in File Explorer

If there are certain locations you use a lot, you can choose to place shortcuts
for them in the Favorites list in File Explorer. The Favorites list appears at the
top of the navigation pane.

To place a shortcut to a folder there, just drag-and-drop that folder from the
main pane into the Favorites list. In Figure 20-11, you can see that I've placed
a Books shortcut there. Books is a folder I created myself to hold all my book-
length project manuscripts.

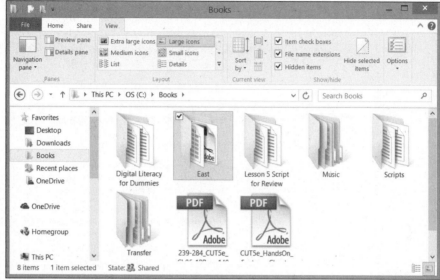

Figure 20-11:
Saving a
favorite
folder.

To remove a shortcut from the Favorites list, right-click the shortcut and choose Remove.

Uninstall Unwanted Applications

Most consumer PCs come with a lot of software that most people don't need or want. IT geeks often derisively refer to this as *bloatware*. Software companies pay big money to computer manufacturers to place their software on the hard drives of new computers, and we as consumers suffer for it. (Of course, the software companies will claim that they are doing you a favor by providing you all this free software — or at least trial versions for free.)

Removing unwanted software can free up hard disk space. On a computer that has an almost-full hard disk, doing so can actually improve system performance. Removing software can also make a PC run more cleanly and efficiently if the application being removed loaded a part of itself into memory when the computer started up. (A lot of applications do that.)

To see what software is installed, and potentially remove some of it, do the following:

1. **Open the Control Panel. (Remember my trick from earlier? Right-click the Start button and choose Control Panel.)**

2. **Under Programs, click Uninstall a program.**

3. **Click an unwanted program. See Figure 20-12.**

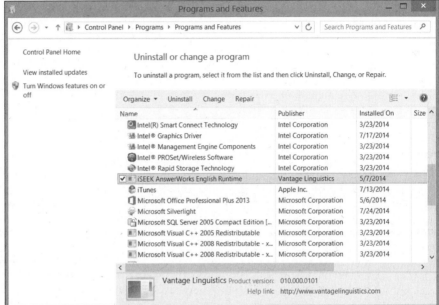

Figure 20-12:
Uninstall
a program
here.

4. **Click Uninstall.**

5. **Follow the prompts to complete the uninstall.**

These steps apply only to desktop applications, not Windows 8 apps. To uninstall a Windows 8 app, right-click its shortcut, either on the Start screen or on the Apps list, and choose Uninstall. No prompts or options — it just removes itself quietly.

Prevent Programs from Loading at Startup

As I mentioned in the previous section, a lot of apps load a piece of themselves at startup. They say it is for your convenience, and that the software that loads doesn't take up much memory, but the cumulative effect of dozens of programs all doing this starts to eat into your available memory to a substantial degree.

Some apps, of course, you *want* to load at startup and remain loaded, like your anti-virus software. But other pieces, like an updater that lets you know when a new version of iTunes is available for download, you might be better off without.

In previous Windows versions, there was a special app called System Configuration Utility (msconfig.exe) that users could employ to disable certain startup programs. In Windows 8, however, this functionality is handled in the Task Manager.

To see what programs currently load at startup, right-click the taskbar and choose Task Manager. If you don't see multiple tabs across the top of the window, click More details.

Click the Startup tab, and a list of startup programs appears. The Status column shows whether or not the program is currently set to load at startup, and the Startup Impact column shows how much of an impact on startup time and memory usage this program causes. Figure 20-13 shows an example; your programs will be different. To disable a program, click it and then click the Disable button.

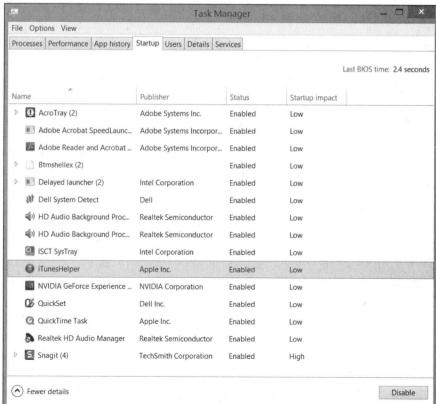

Figure 20-13: Use Task Manager to control what programs load at startup.

Appendix

Making a Living in Digital Technology

Computers are everywhere, especially in the workplace. By becoming a digitally literate person, as this book has prepared you to be, you greatly increase your career marketability.

In this appendix, I tell you about some careers that you might find interesting, all of which require some sort of computer literacy background. Some of them are simple administrative jobs in which you work with Windows and Office; others are more specialized and require years of advanced education.

The Changing Workplace

Remember the days when people used to go into an office in the morning, stay there and work all day, and leave in the evening? That model still works for some people and some companies, but it is no longer the only model out there. The great connectivity that the Internet and wireless networking has brought our society has led to some dramatic shifts in the way people work.

Now that our phones go with us everywhere we go, salespeople don't have to stay in their offices to communicate with clients on the phone, for example. A salesperson can take a call from an airport, a limousine, or his own back porch with equal ease. When someone works in his own home, or in some private location away from the office, it's known as *telecommuting*. The "tele" part comes from the olden days when remote employees communicated with the central office via telephone, but today this communication generally occurs via the Internet.

Computers used to be such bulky, expensive devices that a typical worker had access to only one of them, and it was usually inside an office building. Workers had to go to an office every day because that's where the computer was. Even if a worker had a computer at home, there was no fast and efficient way to connect it to the central office without running expensive dedicated lines. Nowadays, though, workers can work anywhere that there is computer and Internet access. They can work from their own homes, from coffee shops, from libraries, and even from their tablets and smartphones while on public transportation.

Many job descriptions are also evolving. In the days before computing (and the automation that comes with computing), work consisted of taking input, doing something well-defined and routine to it, and delivering output. For example, an administrative assistant would take hand-written notes and produce typed transcripts of them. Nowadays, however, most businesspeople do their own typing, and an administrative assistant's job is more likely to involve generating original content (like making a PowerPoint presentation based on an annual report) or scheduling in-person, telephone, or online meetings.

Careers for a Computer-Literate Person

Just for discussion's sake, consider a computer-literate person as someone who knows the basic information that's covered in this book. If you have a basic familiarity with computer hardware and software, Windows, Office, networking, the Internet, and the other topics I covered in this book, you're ready to take a job that involves using a computer for at least part of the workday.

In the following sections, I describe some careers that a computer-literate person might apply for.

Administrative assistant

An administrative assistant provides office and document support to a manager or executive, freeing up that person's schedule by handling many of the everyday administrative tasks. An assistant might answer phones, plan meetings, and send email. An assistant may have access to his boss's calendar and scheduling in Outlook. Although an administrative assistant might not spend all day on a computer, he is expected to know how to use one whenever a computer is the best tool to complete an assignment.

Supervisor

The primary job of a supervisor is to monitor and support workers as they do their jobs. That isn't computer-related necessarily, but there is very often paperwork involved — and that paperwork is very often filled out on a computer. It is assumed in most companies that a supervisor will be able to use a Windows-based computer with minimal training, and to enter basic data into a variety of applications. A supervisor may use Excel to enter or verify hours worked, Word to write performance appraisals and document safety violations, and Outlook to exchange email with supervisors in other departments and on other shifts.

Project manager

Project managers make things happen. They keep all the workers, equipment, locations, and materials on track for a building project, an event, a manufacturing process, or any other rollout that requires advance planning. Project managers need training in a variety of fields, including accounting, logistics, people management, and, of course, office productivity software. Excel is the go-to tool for project managers because it has so many different uses. A project manager can store financial data in Excel to calculate a project's budget, lists of items and their prices and availability, and scheduling constraints for multiple departments.

Accounting assistant

In large companies, the accounting department is much more than just a bunch of accountants. There may be dozens of clerical workers who handle the bulk of the everyday data management tasks, such as opening mail, tracking invoices and purchase orders, and printing and mailing checks. An accounting assistant might use a computer to key the data from received invoices into the company's accounting system, to print checks, and to run reports that summarize the day's activities.

Customer service representative

Most companies have telephone customer service available so that people who have questions about products or billing can call in and get them answered. The person who answers the phone calls must not only have good people skills, but must also be proficient with the software used to document the calls. She must be able to multitask, to type notes into a computer program or look up customer information, and at the same time project a professional and friendly image verbally to a customer.

Some customer service representatives work using text chat programs rather than telephone calls. A user on a website can click a Customer Service button to be connected with a representative who can communicate in a proprietary instant messaging program.

Careers for Information Workers

An *information worker* is someone who works with computerized information extensively on an everyday basis. Information workers typically have a high school diploma and perhaps a two-year associates degree as well. The term *information worker* refers to the fact that people in these jobs work mostly with information, rather than handling physical objects.

An information worker is a proficient end-user of computers. This person should be very familiar with Windows, Office, and the Internet, and may have specialized training in other applications as well, such as financial/accounting software or a proprietary business management program that's specific to the company.

Word-processing specialist

Although anyone can learn the basics of word processing, some people take that extra step to become really proficient in all aspects of the software. A word processing specialist is able to create consistent, professional-looking documents, including memos, forms, legal reports, letters, and technical articles, in a variety of formats. Word-processing specialist may be a full-time career in itself, or the duties may be combined with those of a general administrative assistant or receptionist. To prepare for this career, you should have specialized word-processing training. Microsoft Office Specialist certification in Microsoft Word at the Expert level is recommended.

Microsoft Office Specialist (MOS) is a certification you can earn by taking a series of computerized tests at a testing center. There are three levels of certification. You can earn a Microsoft Office Specialist certification in each application. For Expert-level certification, you must pass the Expert-level exams for Word and Excel. For Master level, you must pass the Expert-level exams for Word and Excel plus the basic level exam for PowerPoint and one other basic level exam of your choice (Outlook, Access, or SharePoint). See `www.microsoft.com/ learning/en-us/mos-certification.aspx` to learn about the certification program.

Social media marketer

A social media marketer specializes in helping companies promote themselves using social networking tools such as blogs, social networks, and microblogs, including Twitter. Their purpose is to increase public awareness of the company and its products. The role requires marketing expertise and a thorough understanding of how search tools work and how to call attention to the client companies. Using this knowledge, the social media marketing person adds keywords and hashtags to the content they create. This helps the client company's web pages appear more prominently and frequently in search results and rank higher in page rank indexes. The process of writing content in this way is known as *search engine optimization (SEO)*. Marketing and business skills and professional courses in SEO marketing are expected for such a role. A successful social media marketer will demonstrate her expertise by maintaining her own use of social networks.

Researcher/fact-checker

Newspapers, magazines, and non-fiction book publishers sometimes employ researchers or fact checkers to make sure that what they are about to publish is accurate. A researcher spends all day on the web and in computerized reference books, looking for whatever information is needed at the moment. She is an expert at using web searches to pinpoint information, evaluating the reliability of sources, and pointing out where sources may disagree.

Careers for IT Professionals

An IT (information technology) professional is someone with a two-year or four-year college degree in an information technology discipline such as Computer Information Technology, Computer Science, or Computer Graphic Design. IT professional jobs require formal education. A well-rounded IT professional should know at least a couple of programming languages, should be able to set up and troubleshoot networks, should be an expert-level Windows user, and should know her way around at least one other operating system besides Windows.

Information systems manager

An information systems (IS) manager is like a project manager but for computer systems. She looks at the "big picture" of a company's computer systems. An information system consists of people, procedures, software, hardware, and data. The IS manager is the person who brings them all together to get results. An IS manager might oversee an initiative to satisfy an information need, such as for production managers to receive daily reports. This initiative might include assembling a team of programmers, identifying the required hardware and software, developing procedures for handling the information request, and delivering the data to the managers in an easy-to-use format.

Health IT specialist

In many countries, governments have recently enacted laws that require health-care providers to computerize certain parts of their practices. For example, patient health records, medical billing, supply and drug inventories, and medical equipment maintenance records will soon need to be in electronic form if they are not already. This requirement opens up many job opportunities for health IT specialists. A health IT specialist plans and sets up healthcare recordkeeping systems that meet all government requirements, and keep such systems up to date and in good repair.

Network installer

Technicians who install networks have an active work environment. Rather than sitting at a desk all day, as most IT professionals do, installers are out crawling around in the ceilings and basements of buildings, running cables and mounting satellite dishes. They set up closets with stacks of switches and routers in them, configure network security settings, and make sure all network hardware is installed correctly and functioning well. To install networks, you should have at least a high school diploma, plus a technical certification such as

CompTIA Network+. To learn more about Network+ certification, see `http://` `certification.comptia.org/getCertified/certifications/` `network.aspx`.

Bench repair technician

A bench repair technician is like a mechanic for computers. As the word *bench* implies, this technician works primarily at a workbench in a repair shop, although mobile repair technician positions are also available. Bench repair technicians can diagnose system problems with computers that customers bring in for repairs, including both hardware problems like defective parts and software problems like virus infections. It is a good job for someone who prefers working mostly with the computers themselves rather than with their users.

Database administrator

Businesses store large amounts of data, and that data is often much more valuable than the hardware on which it is stored. Information about customers, orders, product inventory, suppliers, and market trends must be readily and reliably available for the business to thrive. A database administrator is an expert in managing, summarizing, and safeguarding large amounts of data. Database administrators also plan and create well-organized database systems for storing new and existing data.

Help desk technician

If you enjoy working with Microsoft Windows settings, as you learn how to do in this chapter, you might like a career as a help desk technician. In this career, you assist end users in making system changes, troubleshooting problems with Windows, managing a database of authorized users, and helping decide on appropriate policies for the company's computers that will allow users to do their work in safety and privacy.

Security specialist

Computer security is among the biggest growth areas in IT. With this comes a growing demand for engineers who have the skills to protect computers and networks. Security specialists are responsible for ensuring that all the security devices in a company are correctly configured. These specialists must also be able to spot different types of attacks and know how to respond to each one.

Careers for Developers

A developer is an IT professional who specializes in computer programming and/or web design. Many developer jobs are now going overseas, especially to India because foreign programmers will work for less money. However, there are still plenty of U.S.-based development positions for those who choose to specialize in that area.

Programmer

A programmer writes the instructions that become computer programs. Whether it's an operating system, a utility, or a game, a programmer takes a general concept like "open a dialog box with user controls for adjusting the graphics quality" and makes it a reality by writing the exact instructions needed, line by line. The programmer then compiles those instructions into a usable program or combines them with the instructions written by another programmer or group of programmers to make a larger program. More experienced programmers may also participate in developing the requirements for a program.

Web designer

A web designer creates websites for businesses, schools, organizations, and individuals. Web designers not only have a strong background in programming tools like HTML, Java, and ASP, but also an eye for what makes a page not only functional but attractive and easy to use. If you are interested in being a web designer, you will want to study computer technology, programming, user interface design, and computer graphics.

Instructional designer

An instructional designer uses a variety of computer development tools to create computerized education and training, both for academic courses and for worker training. Instructional designers create interactive content that teaches new concepts and then quizzes the students on those concepts, creating a full learning package. Although an instructional designer is not a programmer, he may use some high-level development tools to accomplish certain phases of a project.

Index

• G •

About the Author

Faithe Wempen, M.A., is an associate instructor of computer technology at Purdue University and an A+ certified PC technician. She is the author of more than 150 books on computer technology, including *Microsoft Office 2013 For Dummies eLearning Kit* and *PowerPoint 2013 Bible*, and has developed online computer literacy training courses that have educated over a quarter of a million students.

Dedication

For Margaret

Author's Acknowledgments

A book is truly a team effort. Thanks to my editorial team at Wiley for making the process as smooth as possible, including Katie Mohr, Linda Morris, and Sharon Mealka. Thanks also to the production department and proofreaders, whose hard work too often goes unacknowledged.

Publisher's Acknowledgments

Senior Acquisitions Editor: Katie Mohr

Project Editor: Linda Morris

Copy Editor: Linda Morris

Technical Editor: Sharon Mealka

Editorial Assistant: Claire Johnson

Sr. Editorial Assistant: Cherie Case

Project Coordinator: Emily Benford

Cover Image: © iStockphoto.com / Wavebreak